Literary Representations of the Irish Country House

Literary Representations of the Irish Country House

Civilisation and Savagery under the Union

Malcolm Kelsall
Professor of English
Cardiff University

First published 2003 by
PALGRAVE MACMILLAN
Houndmills, Basingstoke, Hampshire RG21 6XS and
175 Fifth Avenue, New York, N.Y. 10010
Companies and representatives throughout the world

PALGRAVE MACMILLAN is the global academic imprint of the Palgrave
Macmillan division of St. Martin's Press, LLC and of Palgrave Macmillan Ltd.
Macmillan® is a registered trademark in the United States, United Kingdom
and other countries. Palgrave is a registered trademark in the European
Union and other countries.

ISBN 0–333–77936–3

This book is printed on paper suitable for recycling and made from fully
managed and sustained forest sources.

A catalogue record for this book is available from the British Library.

Library of Congress Cataloging-in-Publication Data
Kelsall, M. M. (Malcolm Miles), 1938–
    Literary representations of the Irish country house : civilisation and
    savagery / Malcolm Kelsall.
        p.   cm.
    Includes bibliographical references and index.
    ISBN 0–333–77936–3
    1. English fiction—Irish authors—History and criticism.   2. Country
    homes in literature.   3. Literature and society—Ireland—History.
    4. Social classes in literature.   5. Civilization in literature.
    6. Landowners in literature.   7. Culture in literature.   I. Title.
    PR8807.C68 K45 2002
    823.009'9417—dc21   2002026754

10   9   8   7   6   5   4   3   2   1
12 11 10 09 08 07 06 05 04 03

Printed and bound in Great Britain by
Antony Rowe Ltd, Chippenham and Eastbourne

Contents

List of Plates   vi

Acknowledgements   vii

1   Introduction   1

2   Edgeworthstown 'Rebuilding'   29

3   Edgeworth's Heir: Charles Lever   79

4   Trollope as Mr Kurtz   113

5   Only Connect: Violet Martin and Edith Somerville   130

6   'The Duchess Too is Dead': Bowen and Gregory   166

Notes   189

Bibliography   195

Index   205

List of Plates

1. Ormond's 'brave mansion' (from a picturesque engraving, n.d., author's own collection)
2. The massacre at Scullabogue (from Maxwell's *History of the Irish Rebellion in 1798* (1887))
3. A No-Popery dance (from Charles Dickens' *Barnaby Rudge* (1841))
4. Edgeworthstown (from Mrs Hall's *Ireland* (1842))
5. 'Never opened a cabin-door without a blessing' (from Lever's *The Martins of Cro'Martin* (1856))
6. 'Savage' Connemara (from a painting by Peter Knuttel, author's own collection)
7. The demesne of 'Ballinahinch'
8. Tyrone House: the original of 'the big house' of Inver
9. Marriage stones at Ross House
10. Drishane
11. Ross House
12. The lake at Ross
13. The signature tree at Coole Park
14. The bust of Maecenas in the garden at Coole

(Plates 7–14: photographs were taken by the author)

Acknowledgements

I am grateful to Howard Weinbrot of the University of Wisconsin at Madison, and to the staff and postgraduates who attended my classes there during my residence in 1996. The present book was partly written in preparation for my seminars on 'The Country House and the Empire for Liberty; England, the United States, Ireland'. I had expected that my subsequent study of Jefferson's Monticello would close my work on Augustan tradition that began with Addison's *Cato* some forty years ago. The fall of the Roman Republic and its rise again in the new world formed a unifying theme. I reckoned without the generosity of the Arts and Humanities Research Board in the UK, the British Academy and the University of Wales in Cardiff, which supported me with time and money to add Ireland as a coda to the classical theme.

In some ways 'Ireland' is as much a 'new world' as the nascent United States for English writers, and in crossing that frontier I am immensely indebted to those writers of Irish nationalism and identity who are 'mere' marginalia in this book. This debt is acknowledged here because my concern with classicism and the transhistorical unity of European culture, of necessity, ignores national issues, but without that the self-hood of this enquiry could not be.

It is 'self-evident' (to use a Jeffersonism) that an approach to Ireland that begins with the Mosaic conquest of the Promised Land and then proceeds from the idea of Hellas to Romanitas will have a different context for words such as *colonus* and *imperium* than that of the post-colonialist theorist of Irish liberation and national identity. (In my view the problems in present-day Afghanistan might appear familiar to a Tudor statesman.) Yet, interfused with foundational European histori-ography, I acknowledge the influence of Edward Said's arguments on the textuality of power in culture, Homi Bhabha's idea of the frontiers of 'hybridity', and I was once introduced (to my surprise) at Charles University, Prague, as a Foucauldian iconologist. But the foundational historicism of all my writing, the location of my culture, is in Tacitus, Machiavelli, Gibbon, Hume and (the neglected) Adam Ferguson. For them irony is the essential rhetorical mode for dealing with the complexity of history. (Without slaves there would have been no Monticello.) I acknowledge these masters, yet this last incursion into symbolic history ('narrative as socially symbolic act', in Jameson's words) is a return to other sources: Auerbach on mimesis, Gombrich on illusion and (always) Panofsky.

This study accordingly withdraws as far as it is able from consideration of the historical interpellation of the literary text to a concern with the rhetoric of fiction. Ultimately it returns to the original theory of Platonism (albeit Plato filtered through Edmund Spenser). This strategy is determined by the nature of the subject, for (arguably) all nineteenth-century constructions of Ireland are mirages (images cast by an absent subject), and in particular the Irish country house (a vanished social phenomenon) exists only by virtue of a rhetorical memorial. One might defend this strategy theoretically by appeal to that postmodernist position which subverts all truth-telling claims. Some defence is necessary for the essays in this book might be attacked as an apologia for landlordism. They are not. The underlying subject (of which the architectural form is an iconographic expression) is the same as that in the fourth book of *Gulliver's Travels* (the ultimate historical text to be acknowledged here). The ironic conjunction of civilisation and savagery in that text is the profoundest critique I know of that state of mind called (in English) 'Ireland', yet the fourth book is never concerned with Ireland itself.

It is a pleasure to record four personal debts: to the present restorers of Ross House (and their generous hospitality); to Anthony Mandal for help beyond the call of duty; to Claire Connolly, 'exiled' in Wales; and (again) to Joan Byrne, at home in one of the fairest of European cities.

Malcolm Kelsall

'The fusion of all the inhabitants of these islands into one, homogeneous, English-speaking whole, the breaking down of barriers between us, the swallowing up of separate provincial nationalities, is a consummation to which the natural course of things irresistibly tends; it is a necessity of what is called modern civilisation, and modern civilisation is a real, legitimate force; the change must come, and its accomplishment is a mere affair of time.' (Matthew Arnold, *The Study of Celtic Literature*)

'There is no document of civilisation which is not at the same time a document of barbarism.' (Walter Benjamin, *Theses on the Philosophy of History*)

1
Introduction

This enquiry is concerned with the dichotomy between civilisation and savagery. That dichotomy is linked by a conjunction: *and*. The key words are cultural constructs, not things. The symbolic place where civilisation and savagery are related in this enquiry is the country house. It is a place (which will be called a *locus*, to distinguish it from a mere place) invested with meanings because of the symbolic role of the country house in European culture as a site of 'the good life' (in the moral and material senses of the word 'good'). The locus is read both iconographically, as a sign invested with written meaning, and iconologically, as a sign of an entire culture. The territory of the enquiry is Ireland, and the period is that of the Union (1800/1–1921/2). Ireland is chosen because it is an acute case. European civilisation has been (and is) critically tested there.

In this book the term 'European civilisation' is only vaguely defined. So too are the other key words in this enquiry. The imprecision is strategic. Yet the dichotomy between civilisation and savagery has been fundamental in European cultural history. As Joep Leerssen has written, it is 'a fundamental European myth', and one that is 'universalist and timeless as well as infinitely adaptable to the particular needs of a given time and place'.[1] The original story is that of *Genesis*. The earth was 'without form, and void; and darkness was upon the face of the deep'. A divine spirit spoke and the word (the *logos*) brought 'light' to the darkness and divided the twain. This is an imperial myth, and the word *imperium* is positive. Order is made by the imposition of an absolute and hegemonic power upon chaos. In the Pentateuch the imperial establishment descends from God to Moses. The law, divinely sanctioned, is imposed *vi et armis* upon 'lesser breeds' (to adopt Kipling's late imperial, and ironic, expression). The conquest and civilisation of the North American

1

wilderness by Thomas Jefferson's 'chosen people of God'[2] is exemplary of the later, self-aware, application of the Mosaic imperative. John Locke's well-known analogy extends the direct link with *Genesis*: 'In the beginning all the world was America.'[3] In the United States the civic humanism of the founding fathers united the legalism of *Romanitas* to Biblical authority. The law is both divine and human. In its human form it is embodied in the secular/sacred text of the constitution. It is this text that establishes the *civis* within civilisation. Obvious architectural icons of this ideology are the Capitol, Jefferson's villa in his Virginian estate, Monticello, and the cloning of both in the campus of the University of Virginia.[4]

This is a 'frontier' myth in which the light endlessly advances upon darkness. Its alternative, more pessimistic but equally fundamental formulation is that in which the savage remains ineluctably alien to the process of civilisation and represents an irreducible external threat. This is a Greek ideology in which Hellas is divided from barbarism, but the threat of the barbarian (who does not have the *logos* and hence does not speak our tongue) is so great that the frontier does not progressively advance but is a line of (sometimes desperate) defence. Hence the legend of Marathon and the signification of the (burnt and partially destroyed) Acropolis as the representative locus of Hellenic culture. In later history there is the Augustan decision, *ne plus ultra*, after the loss of the legions of Varus in the Vietnamesque forests of Germania; or in Irish history, the function of the Statute of Kilkenny, which divided those who were within from those who were without what was later called 'the pale'.

But it is the savage within civilisation that has perplexed the original European myth most profoundly. 'This thing of darkness I acknowledge mine', Prospero said of the enslaved but resistant Caliban (V, 1, 275–6). The presence of Caliban is intrinsic, the id in relation to the super ego, the heart of darkness (to use Conrad's phrase), which is present here and now, not alien and at some other time. This self-realisation unsettles the *logos*. God had no need to explain his *fiat lux* to Job: 'Where wast thou when I laid the foundations of the earth?' (38, 4). At that place and time, might was right. But unsettle that unity by questioning or ironising the relation between might and right, and all hell is let loose. Walter Benjamin's famous historical thesis that there is no civilisation without savagery is merely a late commentary on Thucydides and Tacitus, Euripedes and Virgil, or Virgil's heir and poet of the Irish epic, Spenser in *The Faerie Queene*. The Tacitean *Ubi solitudinem faciunt, pacem appellant* (*Agricola*, 30) is a reversal of the myth of *Genesis* in a history of genocide. Might is uncreatively wrong. What calls itself civilisation is savagery empowered, the Yahoo become master. The strategy of the ironic mode (which is pervasive in the liberal conscience in European literature) is one of reversal. One looks for civilisation outside the frontier, in Tacitean Germania or in the noble savage of the Enlightenment, whose barbarism may even (Edward Gibbon believed) revitalise decadent civilisation. Hence the centring of marginal cultures by contemporary postcolonial history. What is the relation of Ireland to these fundamental European myths of civilisation and savagery? The island (and no more is meant by the word Ireland) represents an 'acute case' because there especially the myth has been contested both in the *logos* and *vi et armis*. It is, as it were, a contested frontier, at one time the *ultima Thule* of Europe ('here be monsters'), but subsequently a frontier within an expanding *imperium* and a consolidating Union. But this is a commonplace of Irish cultural studies. Accordingly, there is, no need to do more than sketch the outlines of an already familiar story, and to remind rather than inform.

One may begin with Giraldus (so-called 'of Wales'); that is, with the period when Anglo-Norman/English feudalism first became implicated with Irish interclan conflict (the beginning of the notorious seven hundred years of those 'wrongs' which a nationalist ideologue in Ulster would now extend by another century). Later writers often appear little more than commentators on Giraldus. The warlike Irish, so it was claimed, are a 'barbarous' people because they lived like beasts upon their beasts, and unlike advanced cultures had not progressed 'from the forest to the field, from the field to the town, and to the social conditions of citizens'. (This was stadial history long before Enlightenment social and economic theory.) The *Expugnatio Hibernicae* accordingly argued that this land, as yet 'rude and uncivilised', had to be 'subjugated' by military conquest if it were to be 'reduced to order'.[5] Much the same view was put by Stanyhurst in the sixteenth century. The idealised purpose of war in Ireland was to remove 'barbarous savageness' so that 'civilitie' might be 'ingraffed, good laws established, loyaltie observed, rebellion suppressed'.[6] Likewise, for John Milton in the seventeenth century the 'lords and politicians' of Ireland, 'indocile, and averse from all civility' had to be improved 'by a civilizing conquest'.[7] Some, such as Edmund Spenser and Sir John Davies, at least showed knowledge, not always unsympathetic, of the system of Gaelic clanship; others, such as Oliver Cromwell, had no patience for antiquarian interest in the anti-Christ. 'All the world knows their barbarism', Cromwell told the Privy Council,[8] and all Ireland knows that he treated the barbarians in a manner fitted to their brutish understanding. It would be redundant to trace the dichotomy onward to Froude (and Lecky's response) in the nineteenth century.

So firmly was the historical dichotomy established discursively and theoretically that a prime endeavour of Irish nationalist cultural history from Geoffrey Keating to Douglas Hyde was to redefine the meaning of civilisation itself as it were from without rather than within the pale. The classic essay on this (anthologised by the Field Day project) was D. P. Moran's 'The Battle of the Two Civilisations' in *The Philosophy of Irish Ireland* (1905). The contrary cultural argument was that the invasive imperialists were the barbarians in Ireland (the blood-embued Teutons of Renan's *The Poetry of the Celtic Races*). It was they who brought about the destruction of the rich, ancient and uncontaminated 'civilisation and culture'[9] that the so-called 'Gael' had preserved (in racial and linguistic *Reinheit*) from prehistory to the present. The authentic Ireland of Keating and Hyde was the unified kingdom of the High King of Tara, where Cormac mac Art shone with gold among the thousand loyal thanes who constituted the patriot militia of the Fianna. (Even the imperialist Ordnance Survey confirmed, by archaeology, the reality of this.) This Ireland was governed by a triennial Feis, the achievement of its rulers celebrated by a glittering array of bards and historians (whose eloquence even Spenser admired), the laws periodically reviewed and restored. After the coming of Christianity the well-supported episcopal hierarchy (upon which Keating insisted) made Ireland, never conquered by Rome, a land of saints and scholars, 'a kingdom unique to itself like a little world' (in Keating's formulation)[10] and, in its civilising function, not unlike the Doric states of classical Greece (as Standish O'Grady saw it). Accordingly Ireland emerged as a kind of Christian Hellas, protected, like Hellas, by the sea, and originally uninvolved with the rest of a darkening and disturbed Europe. Thus, who are the civilised people, and who are the savages? Or in the words of another philosophical historian of civilisation in Ireland, Matthew Arnold, 'what is "culture" and what is "anarchy"?'[11]

It is a commonplace of postcolonial theory that nationalism is in reactive and symbolic relationship with imperialism (the provocative of nationalism). The reversal of the civilisation/savagery dichotomy in Ireland is a classic instance of the process (if one accepts the presuppositions of a far from self-evident theory). The reversal is belated and derivative. As a nineteenth-century phenomenon it was, in some respects, a mirror image of what in English nationalism has been called 'the return to Camelot',[12] and aesthetically it was closely involved with the post-Keatsian, pre-Raphaelite movement (witness the early poetry of W. B. Yeats). For the purposes of this enquiry one need do no more than note that the imperialist and nationalist readings of Irish history both employ the same vocabulary and a similar conceptual framework (*episteme* if one will). The dichotomous terms are semantically linked, as if one could not be had without the other, just as white implies black or west implies east.

In what way was the country house crucial to this attempt to define, impose or recreate civilisation in Ireland, and what was its relation to the concomitant other, savagery? Since that is the subject of this enquiry an answer cannot be presumed. The only *a priori* postulate is the existence of a European myth and its application in Ireland. But at least the significance of the country house is self-evident historically. Self-evident because it is a material fact that the country houses of Ireland were instruments of government, and because republican insurgents, post-1916, burnt some three hundred of them. The proportion of burnt houses was comparatively small, but the symbolic signification was not, and it is with the symbolism rather than the material fact that this enquiry is concerned. The burning is called symbolic because the tactical or strategic importance of the buildings was marginal or non-existent at that juncture. Some, such as Tyrone House (the original of Somerville and Ross's *The Big House of Inver*) had already been abandoned and were lapsing into decay. In many, the families who had already sold their land were resident only in genteel semipoverty. Powerful ideological imperatives were therefore at work, and were directed at the material frame of the building (and its contents) far more often than at the terrorised, but escapee, owners. In the absence of any definitive evidence of motivation it would be rash to invent too specific a cause for some three hundred separate acts. But the houses signified, and what they signified had to be destroyed. The student of Irish cultural history will be aware that the ghost of the country house has continued to haunt postnationalist fiction, a case, perhaps, of the return of the repressed, although this subject is beyond the historical parameters of this enquiry. Suffice it to suggest that burning houses (like burning books) is a sign of a hatred (and perhaps a fear) of something empowered or empowering; or in the original sense of the word, an ascendancy. The iconic concern of the present enquiry, however, is not with the nature of the thing (not the so-called 'ascendancy' as a 'class'), but with the meanings of icons, the houses themselves as embodied in writing.

To come closer to the subject we shall consider two dialectically opposed texts. One was written on the threshold of the Union and written from the point of view of the owners of property; the other is a clear marker of the post-Union nationalist position.

On 7 October 1777 Arthur Young,[13] now in the second year of his tour of Ireland, left Castle Lloyd, the home of the Reverend Mr Lloyd in County Limerick, and 'took the road by Galbally to Mitchel's Town' and the 'vast property' of Lord Kingsborough. The estate stretched 'from Kildorrery to Clogheen, beyond Ballyporeen, a line of more than 16 Irish miles, and it spreads in breadth from five to ten miles'. As was usual, Young enquired extensively about the nature of the soil, the price of produce, labour, rents, and improvements, and the condition of the poor. The famous cave at Skeheenrinky and the 'wild magnificence' of nature in the 'stupendous chain' of the Galtee mountains also led him to expatiate on the extraordinary 'prospects' that delighted the eye of the picturesque tourist. But perhaps most remarkable of all was the role of the 'liberal' Lord Kingsborough, who, although a young man, had left 'the various gaiety of Italy, Paris, and London' to devote himself to the improvement of 'a region so wild as Mitchelstown' and to construct a great mansion for himself and farmhouses for his major tenants. This led Young into an enlightened exposition of the role of the country house in Ireland:

> In a country changing from licentious barbarity into civilized order, building is an object of perhaps greater consequence than may at first be apparent. In a wild, or but half cultivated tract, with no better edifice than a mud cabin, what are the objects that can impress a love of order on the mind of man? He must be wild as the roaming herds; savage as his rocky mountains; confusion, disorder, riot, have nothing better than himself to damage or destroy: but when edifices of a different solidity and character arise; when great sums are expended, and numbers employed to rear more expressive monuments of industry and order, it is impossible but new ideas must arise, even in the uncultivated mind; it must feel something, first to respect, and afterwards to love; gradually seeing that in proportion as the country becomes more decorated and valuable, licentiousness will be less profitable, and more odious. Mitchelstown, till his Lordship made it the place of his residence, was a den of vagabonds, thieves, rioters, and Whiteboys; but I can witness to its being now as orderly and peaceable as any other Irish town, much owing to this circumstance of building, and thereby employing such numbers of the people.[14]

This is a classic Whig and enlightened statement of the civilising influence of architecture upon society. It is expressive of what was meant by the provocative words used above in relation to an original ascendancy: Mitchelstown house was 'empowered' and 'empowering'. A great building created a love of order even in a wilderness; from the combination of industry and order required to construct a great edifice even the uncultivated mind had to 'feel something, first to respect, and afterwards to love'. Or, within the dichotomy of this enquiry, the country house brought civilisation to the savage. That was Young's position. It was an 'imperial' formulation of the foundational European myth: *fiat lux*. In the United States, Jefferson's villa at Monticello directly paralleled Young's Mitchelstown. The Georgian architects of Ireland also gave the island its 'Capitol' (in the parliament building) and university (Trinity College).

Young's formulation of the myth was to acquire almost classic status. Writing almost two centuries later, in the darkest days of the Second World War, Elizabeth Bowen cited this passage from Young in the elegiac *Bowen's Court* (1942), her lament for her lost ancestral home. Here was the 'ideal' of the 'old order', she wrote, which, 'consciously or unconsciously', her aristocratic forebears had used to 'mould' themselves. It was on the terrace of Mitchelstown that she set a remarkable scene in which the old order gathered for the last time at the outbreak of the war of 1914–18, which for her marked the definitive moment of the destruction of her civilisation. The roots of that ideal require further exposition, and its provocative presence within the Union in Ireland is a later subject of the present enquiry.[15]

But compare an opposite ideology in the description of *baile misteala* (Mitchelstown) in the official guide of the Bord Fáilte Éireann (1967 edition), written according to a post-Pearse/de Valera nationalist agenda:

This town at the south-western corner of the Galtee Mountains near the Tipperary border, is the busy centre of a great agricultural district. Mitchelstown Creamery, the town's major industry, is noted for its large-scale production of butter and cheese.

In College Square stands a monument to the patriot John Manderville (d. 1888) which also commemorates the three men – Casey, Lonergan and Shinnick, shot by the police at a Land League meeting here in 1887. Three crosses are carved on the pavement at the southern end of the Square, where they fell.

In the former demesne of the Earls of Kingston, beside the town, are the ruins of the ancient *Brigown Church* (*Bri Gabhann*: Hill of the Smith). There are some remains of an ancient church and a castle at *Kilbeheny* village (County Limerick), at the foot of Galtymore, 4 miles to the northeast. John O'Mahony, Young Irelander and co-founder (with James Stephens) of the Fenian movement, was born at Kilbeheny. He died in New York in 1877 and was buried at Glasnevin, Dublin.

Whereas Young's discourse is that of classic and Whig enlightenment, Bord Fáilte Éireann writes the language of republican, nationalist history. Both accounts of the town, however, emphasise the importance of works of architecture as embodying culture. The nationalist visitor is directed primarily to a monument that recalls the murderous brutality of the members of the Royal Irish Constabulary who, in the defence of an evil empire, shot down innocent Irishmen who were merely demanding the restoration of their native land. Such brutality, one presumes, justified the decision by John O'Mahony, another local hero, to join with the famous James Stephens in founding the Fenian movement to free Ireland from the imperialist oppressor. (There is no memorial to those killed by the Fenians, nor to those Irishmen who died overseas in the interests of the United Kingdom in the war of 1914–18.) Like millions of Irishmen before him, O'Mahony left his native land for exile in that bastion of anti-imperialist liberty, the United States of America, but his body was brought home to rest in the nationalist shrine of Glasnevin cemetery. There is a direct line, as it were, from the square of this tiny market town to the pantheon of the nation's martyred dead.

There are also architectural memorials of the history of the oppressed people in the ruins of the ancient Brigown Church, the only monument worth mentioning in 'the former demesne of the Earls of Kingston' (Young's centre of civilisation against savagery) and in the church and castle at Kilbeheny. But for Bord Fáilte Éireann (as it was for Young) the land itself remains the fundamental source of employment and wealth. The great Whig mansion Young saw is now the town's creamery. Under a national government, Eire is a cooperative land flowing with milk and money. The factory is now the centre of 'industry and order' for the community.

This short and unremarkable passage on a small market town ('Pop. 2,655. E. C. Day Wed. C[oras] I[ompair] E[ireann] [omni]bus') is ostensibly a mere record of fact, but actually it is ideologically determined. Just as Young's discourse was shaped by the classic Whig Enlightenment (and his position as a land agent), so too is the guidebook the product of romantic nationalist iconography (and is conditioned by its status as a government-sponsored publication). Any historian writing on Young will take note of the significance of the date when he began his travels (1776), and (arguably) the 1960s marked an equally important watershed in Irish history. Ideologically the guidebook stands at the end of romantic nationalist ascendancy in Ireland, and at the threshold of the development of so-called 'revisionist' history, with the consequent demystification of the ideology of old-style republicanism. In the 1960s Eire was at a political and economic turning point at which the state again resolved to incorporate itself into a union, this time the EEC, thus rejoining the mainstream of European civilisation. The official account of Mitchelstown (now Gaelicised, at least by a form of linguistic tokenism) therefore has no claim to ascendancy in relation to Young as if it speaks definitive history. The guidebook is merely part of the Heraclitean flux of things.

What the guidebook omits from history is as significant iconographically as what it chooses to incorporate. In fact (if one might appeal to what the eye can see rather than what is controlled by language) Mitchelstown is arguably one of the most important examples of small town planning in Ireland.[16] Among its most remarkable features is Kingston College, begun by the fourth Baron Kingston (1693–1761) with an endowment of £25 000. The college buildings were erected for use by decayed Protestant gentlefolk and form half a square, later completed with private houses belonging to members of the town's professional classes. This square is at the junction of two major roads, one leading westwards to the gate of the former Mitchelstown Castle, the other leading southwards to the Protestant (CIE) church. But equally important is the Roman Catholic church, the superb location of which, facing the market square, is indicative of the confident triumph of postemancipation revivalism. Nothing is said by Bord Fáilte Éireann about the principles of liberal and enlightened tolerance that were intended, under the Union, to end sectarian division and religious and class conflict. The tourist is sent by the guidebook merely to look for crosses on the pavement, and is instructed in Fenian history.

At least 'the former demesne of the Earls of Kingston' merits a mention. Given the ideology of the tourist board one might suspect that a certain degree of pleasure is derived from the word 'former'. This is where the imperialist used to be and is no more (and the very name Kingston is resonant with overtones of Hanoverianism). There is a certain justification for saying no more, for little more is to be seen. Mitchelstown Castle was burnt in the civil war of 1922 when abandoned by the occupying IRA. The Free State government compensated the owners, who reinvested in real estate in Dublin. The ashlar was subsequently bought by the monks of Mount Melleray for their new church. The use of the ashlar of an old country house to build a new monastery historically reversed the process by which many English country houses first came into being: Henry VIII's dissolution of the monasteries. The significance of these terminal events is so symbolically apt that they might suggest the ideal order of fiction rather than the rough hurly burly of historical complexity.

Young's *Travels* and the guidebook mark the before and after of this enquiry – pre-Union and post-Union. Neither has authority, although both read authoritatively. Accordingly one cannot read the first in the light of the ideology of the second, nor with the implied superiority of hindsight, although in Irish cultural studies this is a not unfamiliar strategy: witness the canonical use of Edgeworth's *Castle Rackrent* as a text supposedly confessional of familial guilt and proleptically visionary of Ascendancy ruin (on to *The Last September* as the other end of the canon). But if one takes Young's *Travels* as a canonical text (as it was for Edgeworth), one of the most striking elements in the passage on Mitchelstown is its self-confidence. Young had no doubt about the (general) progress of history from savagery to civilisation. Why should he? The period in which he wrote was the (mythical) golden age of Grattan's ascendancy, when the land-owning aristocracy (*aristoi*: the best) of (Protestant) Ireland emulated the enlightened *aristoi* of Mount Vernon, Monticello and Montpelier in the institution of (so-called) independent government, and – at least in the early days of the subsequent revolution in France (and before 1798 in Ireland) – believed that Anglo-American Whig principles and propertied leadership would at last extinguish tyranny and superstition progressively throughout Europe and thence the world. As far as the iconic form of architecture was concerned, the buildings of eighteenth-century Ireland were not expressive of guilt, nor were their builders gifted with proleptic hindsight of their own imminent ruin.

But why is it that, iconographically, the advent of civilisation and the building of a country house were so self-evidently concomitant for Young? This is well-explored territory, although not in Irish cultural studies. But as James Ackerman has claimed, 'villa culture' (to employ his classical terminology) is historically one of the most widely diffused of original European ideologies.[17] No more than a summary history of this ideology will be offered here, and merely in order to recontextualise the literature of the country house in Ireland (and Young) by removing that literature from the introversion of nationalist history (that of Bord

Fáilte Éireann) and re-establishing a European dimension. This is of course an idealistic history, and hence an account of a fictional order. Writers were well aware of that ideal status, and were not uncritical of their own ideals. But the persistence of the fiction is an historical fact of substantive signification.

Young's closest affinities with classical literature were with the earliest writers of agricultural economics, Cato, Varro and Columella, in whose authority the enlightened physiocrats were (in a sense, literally) rooted. Land was the fundamental source of wealth, and cultivation of the soil (and the proximity to nature that brings) was the foundation of civic virtue. There is a direct link here between the patriot farmer warriors of Livyean Roman history and the role of George Washington at Mount Vernon as president of the Society of the Cincinnati (as well as president of the newly fledged republic) and the Jeffersonian ideal of a nation of smallholding yeomanry ('the chosen people of God'). Looking beyond this eighteenth-century version of the classical ideal, *mutatis mutandis* the *Volk* of romantic nationalism were rooted in the same tradition (witness the Nuremberg rallies). Accordingly, in the classic or romantic versions of the myth the life of the countryside is idealised in contradistinction to the artifice and corruption of urban existence (the 'Rome' of Juvenal's third satire, and the 'London' of Samuel Johnson's imitation of Juvenal). Lord Kingston (in Young) has chosen the way of virtue by leaving the sophisticated delights of Paris to improve and cultivate his estate.

This rural ideal became sophisticated when involved with 'villa culture', for the rich man in his country house was in symbolic, not actual, relationship with cultivation of the soil. (Virgil's georgic advice to Augustus to plough naked was not to be taken literally!) The normative classical examples were the Tusculan villa of Cicero (republican statesman and philosopher) and the Laurentine villa of Pliny the Younger (civil servant and aesthete), as known both through their own writings and, for Young, the eulogistic *Life* of Cicero by Conyers Middleton (1741) and Robert Castell's *The Villas of the Ancients Illustrated* (1728). The tradition was poeticised by Horace, Martial, Statius, Sidonius . . . It was at home in the countryside that the wise man (and it was initially a masculine tradition) could be 'free' (as Stoic and Epicurean philosophy would put it) and 'independent' (as Whig ideology reinterpreted the tradition). This was a dignified leisure (*cum dignitate otium*), and in that leisured freedom the wise (and accordingly happy) man could cultivate both his estate and his mind, enjoy his library and the artefacts of high culture, and with suitable modesty (not vain ostentation) cultivate his friends (chosen not for self-interest but for the greater interest of finding wisdom).

This was an ideal adopted into enlightened tradition in English via the classic status given to the recension of classical villa culture in Palladio's *Four Books of Architecture* (1570). The ancient sages, Palladio wrote, used to retire to their villas, where 'The body will more easily preserve its strength and health, and . . . where the mind, fatigued by the agitations of the city, will be greatly restored and comforted, and be able to attend the studies of letters and contemplation.' At home, attended by virtuous family and friends, the ancients, by cultivating their house, their garden, their estate and thus their virtue, 'could easily attain to as much happiness as can be attained here below'.[18] This was a tradition that descended (perhaps implicitly, as much as explicitly) to the Edgeworths and the Gregorys in Ireland, or to Violet Martin, dedicated to the restoration of Ross House, cultivating the health of her body on the hunting field, and giving her leisure hours to the pursuit of literature.

This ideology became interwoven in English literary tradition with the real, inherited presence of the 'Gothic' manor house, and thus with the native traditions of residual feudalism and the associated myth of the organic community and the justly hierarchical society. The interweaving (and conflicting) ideologies are in complex relationship, but the literary tradition possesses a number of canonical texts to supplement the Roman/Renaissance inheritance. In English poetry the foundational text for the transmission of the classic/Gothic tradition was Ben Jonson's *To Penshurst* which in substantial measure originated 'the country house poem' of the seventeenth century, which in turn continued through to at least Alexander Pope in the eighteenth century (and with remote echoes in Yeats, who was arguably the last in this long line). At Penshurst Place (in Kent) ideal civilisation (which Jonson called 'the mysteries of manners, arms and arts') is represented by the great family of the Sidneys, who are warriors, statesmen, good Christians and patrons of the arts (the link to Yeats' Major Robert Gregory is self-evident). The ancient manor house that is their home is the centre of a happy and loyal feudal community, whose tenants' prosperity, the panegyrical verse claims, in large measure depends on the bounty of their lord, who dwells among them (the word 'lord' has religious as well as economic implications). Iconographically, therefore, the great hall of Penshurst is the centre both of the house and of the poem. Jonson's eulogy is set on a great feast day in which all the members of the household are gathered at the Sidneys' tables. 'All come in', Jonson writes, 'the farmer and the clown', each bearing gifts in celebration of the fertility of the estate. It was this tradition to which Elizabeth Bowen was to allude, more than two hundred years later, at the conclusion of *The Last September*, where the 'hospitable door' of the country house still stands open, but now to the destructive fire of the insurgent republicans.

Poetic eulogy survived the transference to the more realistic form of the English novel. In Young's enlightened culture, Squire Allworthy (Ralph Allen) at Fielding's Paradise Hall and Richardson's Grandison Hall are models of a civilised ideal that directly underlies the fictions of Jane Austen in England and Maria Edgeworth in Ireland. Grandison Hall may serve as a canonical example. Sir Charles, the owner of the ancient house, is a man of taste and a Christian. As a virtuoso he collects pictures, statues, bronzes and busts when on his extensive European travels, but, as a lover of God, on his return home, he gathers his family and servants about him in an elegant chapel, and to serve as an example to all his tenantry he worships in the village church. Although he has remodelled the old house in the new classical style, the ancient Hall is still a centre of hospitality and social care. For Sir Charles' friends there are convenient 'lodging rooms', fit even for the 'best lord in the land' (at Penshurst even the king had called in!) For the tenants, or rather '*my* friends *my* workmen', there is a pharmacy and a salaried apothecary, a surgeon who lives rent-free on this welfare estate, and even a library of improving literature for the loving domestic servants (Sir Charles himself, of course, is deeply read). Grandison Hall commands delightful prospects of the prosperous and contented estate. In the park, which shows a just blend of art with nature, flourish the plantations of Sir Charles' ancestors. Flocks of fertilising sheep crop the grass; in the gardens grow apples and oranges, cherries, plums and peaches. The tenants are 'sober', 'diligent', 'housewifely', 'pious' and so on. One might well object that this is all too good to be true, but on the other hand it is a representation of an ideal order not far removed from the intentions of Richard Lovell Edgeworth at Edgeworthstown, Thomas Johnes at Hafod and even the great East-Anglian estates that are normative for Young.

For Young the 'civilisation' of Ireland meant the *translatio* of this ideal (fictional) order from the rest of Britain to Ireland and the material application of the ideal as economic reality (improvement of the land by massive capital investment). Every good landlord should be a Grandison or a Kingston. Thus Ireland would evolve (after the Williamite settlement, which Young celebrated) towards that norm of enlightened culture and material prosperity represented by the Whig propertied establishment in the rest of Britain. For Young this represented progress (from savagery). Others were to condemn the process as 'anglicisation' (the obliteration of indigenous Gaelic civilisation) or (currently) as 'colonialism' (a once positive word become pejorative).

Or one might take the stadial view, as represented by the 'patriot' Sydney Owenson, Lady Morgan, that the historical process in Ireland was ineluctable and to seek to separate Ireland from the dominant European current was 'chimerical' and 'visionary'. The landed establishment was for her, writing thirty years after Young, an historical fact 'sanctioned by time, by succession, by all that guards the privileges and claims of society, and all that serves the property and possessions of the individual.'[19] Gaelicisation was an archaic embellishment to be absorbed, but not an instrument of de-anglicisation or decolonisation (if she would even have understood the terms).

How you interpret cultural tradition depends on where you stand temporarily and/or materially in the Heraclitean flux, and the *topoi* of the fictional country house order are not absolute and permanent (as if glass beads strung in fixed order along a transhistorical chain), although the *topoi* are persistent and reiterative. No greater permanence is claimed for the country house ideology summarily reviewed here than for the material presence of the architectural forms of the real houses. This enquiry has begun with Young, cutting obliquely into historical process, because of his major status as an informative writer about Ireland (a prime historical source) and because of his influence on Maria Edgeworth, who was the first major writer in Ireland to write fiction in the neoclassical tradition of Jonson, Pope, Fielding and Richardson (although Jonathan Swift, *qua* satirist, had mocked the *translatio* half a century before. Only a fool would seek to build a country house in a land of bogs and slaves, he claimed).[20] Young and Edgeworth marked a certain point in time in a European ideology that both articulated and justified plantation culture in Ireland (and justification of possession of the land was a central issue of Irish conflict from the first Gaelic colonies to the legacy of Wyndham's Land Act), and this European ideology found its most authoritative and ideal statement within enlightened culture in Ireland.

It was a belated efflorescence and on a contested frontier. If Maria Edgeworth was the originator of the Irish variant of the tradition, she was two centuries behind the English incorporation of the European *topoi*. The historical reason for that is simple. For Ben Jonson, writing in Kent in the early 1600s, the barons' wars were a remote memory somewhere the other side of Drayton and Shakespeare. As Francis Bacon had written in his *Praise* of Elizabeth, the peace and prosperity of the newly emergent state was manifest in the erection of what later historians have called the great 'prodigy' or 'power' houses of the Tudor establishment. The queen had 'received a realm of cottages, and hath made it a realm of palaces'. You built because you were secure. At Hardwick Hall or Longleat the very walls of the house seemed built of glass – such was the security (and wealth) of landed property; whereas in Ireland, as Spenser and Davies recorded, the barons' wars were still in progress, the anarchic divisions of which, Shakespeare warned in *King Lear*, were still the substance of actual experience.

The causes (and subsequent reinterpretations) of the sixteenth- and seventeenth-century Irish wars are not at issue. But these wars were fundamentally related to the belated establishment of country house culture in Ireland. One reason given by Spenser and Davies for the conquest/pacification of Ireland (and they were canonical authorities for Edgeworth) was that the old baronial order (the savage) had to be replaced by that variant of 'villa culture' manifest in the post-Tudor order. Ireland had to be incorporated *vi et armis* into that tradition of European civilisation. That the process was itself savage, no reader of Spenser and Davies will doubt (the most shocking, and shocked, passages of Spenser are commonplaces). Thus, fundamentally, the paradoxical interrelationship between civilisation and savagery was intrinsic (genocidically even), but the idealistic imperative, the *fiat lux*, was the justification of the war. Ireland had to be brought out of the dark ages, because while it remained a heart of darkness the barbarians on a permeable frontier remained a permanent threat to the new order of the Tudor state.[21]

Accordingly, if one takes the great country house and estate as the normative sign (icon) of law and order, peace and prosperity in the unitary Tudor state, then, in contradistinction, in Ireland war was necessitated by the anarchic and violent disunification of Ireland into the competing fiefdoms of warlords. Each warlord had at his beck an instant army of young men (for whom even murder was no capital crime).

The warlords maintained their power by theft and extortion, in which they were encouraged by the bards of the warcourt, whose art celebrated the man of violence, the thief and the outlaw as the Irish role model. This system of government through private armies, had brought 'barbarism and desolation upon the richest and most fruitful land of the world'; 'desolation and barbarism' the like of which 'was never seen in any country that professed the name of Christ'.[22] Perhaps, in a time of war, Spenser and Davies exaggerated the violent tendencies of this anarchic warrior culture. Nonetheless, in general, there was a not dissimilar imperative uniting the desire of the post-Tudor establishment to 'decommission' the private armies of competing and destabilising factions and the objectives of the post-Good Friday peace progress four centuries later. As Froude once argued with some disgust, things do not change much in Ireland.

For Spenser and Davies one obvious sign of the 'confusion' and 'incivility' of Ireland was the failure of the warring septs to settle on estates around great houses, to create towns in which to market the produce of those estates, and to develop ports to export that produce. On the contrary, if Fynes Moryson were to be believed, the 'barbarousness' of the natives ('not much unlike wild Beasts') had obliterated all security of property (and all agriculture) in Ireland, which was now a land devoted merely to the marauding cattle-raids of seminaked 'nomades'.[23] Accordingly the imposition of country house culture (peaceful security of tenure and legalised control) was the aim that Spenser and Davies enunciated, and it was the belated accomplishment of that process that Young celebrated two hundred years later. But in the interim, in a time of war one does not expect 'multicultural' appreciation of the customs of the enemy. That is a romantic indulgence only to be appreciated in security. In the meantime 'tanistry', 'coshery' 'ericke' and the other 'Brehon' forms of Irish law were all attacked as aspects of barbarism. From a position outside the war one might question whether the Tudor systems of primogeniture, land ownership and tenant organisation – the operations of the country house as 'power' house – necessarily represented superior (civilised) forms of social organisation, but that would be like asking an American frontiersman, faced with tribes on the warpath, to become a social anthropologist. In war what matters is superior firepower, and as Spenser and Davies knew, Tudor society was perilously close to the enemy: 'for it is but even the other day since England grew civil'.[24] The anarchic division of the kingdom, mythically represented in Shakespeare's *King Lear*, was both a recent memory and a future threat.

If peace can only be established by successful termination of war (which is the tragic conclusion of *King Lear*), then the archetypal model resided in the very foundations of European civilisation. In a key passage Davies turned to the poets of the Roman empire: '*Fecisti patriam diversis gentibus unam*', and, again: '*Matris, non dominae, ritu; civesque vocavit, Quos domuit, nexuque pio longinqua revinxit*'. ('You have united different peoples into a common mother land, making those you have brought within your dominion citizens bound together by long-enduring justice and equity.') For Davies, just as Rome had civilised the ancient Britons, once 'rude and dispersed', now the Tudor state would operate in Ireland. His imagination at once turned to the establishment of architectural signs of transhistorical and unificatory civilisation: 'temples, houses, and places of public resort'. The argument is stadial. As our ancestors in ancient Britain became civilised, it is claimed, they 'proceeded to curiosity and delicacies in buildings and furniture of household, in baths and exquisite banquets; and so being come to the height of civility, they were thereby brought to an absolute subjection'. 'Subjection' was for Davies, a monarchist, the English equivalent of *cives* in his Latin original, a mistranslation of major historical significance. But in context, by 'subject' he means not 'slave' but the acknowledgement by the members of a state of one common overlord within the state, not the tribal diversification (*diversis gentibus*) of the clans.[25] It was an argument that was to have long development – Froude, writing late in the Union, was to argue that in the power struggles between cultures, ultimately it was 'the wisdom, and ultimately the duty, of the weaker party . . . to accept the benefits which are offered in exchange for submission'.[26]

Once the effective power of a kingdom replaced the wars of the septs, both Spenser and Davies offered a vision of the garden of Ireland. For Young it was that Ireland which, 'in the last twenty years', was now coming into being. It was a land (because of its allegiance to a common monarchy) where property was secured by the laws of England, a land divided into counties governed by sheriffs and justices of the peace, agricultural property secured between landlords and tenants, and where, in security, men 'built houses, planted orchards and gardens, erected townships, and made provision for their posterities'. As a result of the establishment of a homogeneous civility between the kingdoms of Ireland and England there would be a 'union of manners and conformity of minds, to bring them to be one people', 'a perfect union' and a universal peace.[27]

From a *post facto* enlightened viewpoint (that of Young or Edgeworth), what Spenser and Davies were describing was an ineluctable process. Feudal society had run its historical course. The forces of progress were exerting an irresistible pressure that led to the congress of commercial kingdoms that constituted modern Europe. Thus for an enlightened historian such as Hume it was the establishment of Tudor England that marked the threshold between the dark ages and a spectacle he claimed to be more worthy of our attention: 'Thus have we pursued the history of England thro' a series of many and barbarous ages; till we have at last reached the dawn of civility and science.' Much the same conclusion was reached by William Robertson when examining the history of feudalism as an oppressive and anarchic system in Scotland. As for Ireland, perhaps one might qualify enlightened optimism with a Voltairean irony: 'Avec quelle lenteur, avec quelle difficulté le genre humain se civilise, et la société se perfectionne.'[28]

Spenser belonged to the Mitchelstown landscape of which Young wrote. Kilcolman Castle was part of the locale (Elizabeth Bowen was to elaborate the significance of this in her valedictory *Bowen's Court*), and Spenser in Ireland belonged to the sequential history of Irish country house ideology. *The Faerie Queene* is deeply embued with the local experience of the land and the attempt to impose a self-nominated just order there, and the burnt remains of Kilcolman Castle (in which Spenser lost a child) are iconic of that Heraclitean flux that the poet called 'mutability'. Ideal civility is never here and now; the quest for the unobtainable must always be begun again and is riddled with ambiguous complexities; the substance of things is rarely as it seems. The very unfinished form of Spenser's poem is symbolic of unachievable closure. It begins, however, with what may be the first Irish country house poem in English, dedicated 'to the right Honourable the Earle of Ormonde and Ossory':

> Receive most noble Lord a simple taste
> Of the wilde fruit, which salvage soyl hath bred,
> Which being through long wars left almost waste,
> With brutish barbarisme is overspredd:
> And in so faire a land, as may be redd,
> Not one *Parnassus*, nor one *Helicone*
> Left for the sweete Muses to be harboured,
> But where thy selfe hast thy brave mansione;
> There in deede dwel faire Graces many one.
> And gentle Nymphes, delights of learned wits,
> And in thy person without Paragone
> All goodly bountie and true honour sits,
> Such therefore, as that wasted soyl doth yield,
> Receive dear Lord in worth, the fruit of barren field.

This sonnet is based on the same motifs as the passage from Young with which this exploration of the Mitchelstown landscape began. For both Spenser and Young there was 'brutish barbarisme' in Ireland, now the establishment of a great country house: 'thy brave mansione' establishes the 'faire Graces' of civilisation. It was to this place of peace and culture that the poet dedicated his verses, for there 'learned wits' might understand his writing. In Spenser the emphasis is on art rather than agriculture (Young's central topic), but any learned reader of book six of *The Faerie Queene* will know that the Graces and agriculture are related, and the poem itself is referred to here as a 'fruit' of the 'field'. Spenser was a mythic poet, Young an economist, but *mutatis mutandis* both shared the same ideals.

But in the poet of mutability, how much depends on that mutation? Consider the name of the dedicatee – Thomas Butler, tenth Earl of Ormond – and its suspension in history. To be merely historicist, we are concerned with a warrior who was involved both with the termination of the Wars of the Roses in its Irish dimension (the defeat of Desmond) and with the defeat of the Protean figure of Tyrone (part Elizabethan courtier and country house gentleman, part Gaelic warlord), who involved Ireland in the European wars of Spain. Those were the 'long wars' that created the 'waste' of which Spenser wrote. But one cannot hold the name of the dedicatee only within that context. Both the nominations, 'Ormond' and 'Butler', are culturally loaded. The initiator of country house fiction in Ireland, Maria Edgeworth, chose the name 'Ormond' for one of her exemplary heroes; and the last great celebrant of the country house in English poetry was given a name of which he was historically proud – W. B. Yeats was a 'Butler' (his other Christian name, William, is also not without signification on both sides of the Irish Sea).

'Minute by minute' things change (to quote Yeats in Spenserian mode). What is particularly Spenserian here is the way in which apparently discrete things meld, and as they interrelate they change signification. 'Grace' and 'brutish barbarisme' belong to the same soil. *The Faerie Queene* is seen both as a work of high civilisation (of Helicon and Parnassus) and as a 'wilde fruit'. What has fed it and fertilised it is a 'salvage soyl'. That is not mere *sprezzatura*, although modesty is part of it. Rather it is an admission by the poet that his poem is of Ireland, and expressive of Ireland. It comes out of the wars that led to 'the flight of the earls'. Perhaps 'salvage' in relation to the Gaelic septs carries with it some of the connotations it will be given in *The Faerie Queene*, where the Salvage Man has something about him that is reminiscent of the virtues of the noble savage; but one can find little optimism in the admission that the land of Ireland, potentially 'faire', is 'wasted' and 'barren' now. But it is that waste, without Helicon or Parnassus, that has given birth to this poem.

Only one 'harbour' is offered Spenser: it is in Ormond's 'brave mansione' (Plate 1). It is as though we were at the very inception of the process that Young was to celebrate as the product of the past twenty years. The building of a country house on a soil wasted with war is a sign of the establishment of peace and of the rule of the 'good Lord' (compare Jonson's 'thy lord dwells' at Penshurst) rather than that of the warlord. On cursory reading, the praise offered to Ormond may seem the usual matter of Platonic exemplary panegyric. Here are 'honour' and 'bounty', for the ideal country house is like a mirror in which virtue is reflected and like a fountain that fertilises the land (to adopt metaphors from elsewhere in *The Faerie Queene*). But here Spenser emphasises the feminine qualities of the house as a sign of peace. This is the abode of 'gentle Nymphes' and especially 'faire Graces', which signify those arts the house embodies and which best exist within its peaceful patronage. But even this exemplary panegyric is troubled. That the word 'brave' is associated with the house suggests that it is an act of courage to build this kind of dwelling on Ireland's wasted soil, and it would not be necessary to couple the word 'true' with 'honour' were there not, in contradistinction, an honour that is false (and the entire epic that follows endlessly reworks that insecure distinction). How secure, also, is the affirmative 'in deede'? It implies that elsewhere words and deeds are separable things; indeed it implies more, for the need to emphasise that this is so indicates that there are those who might see it as not so (the blatant beast of undefeatable detraction).

What a Herculean labour indeed was it to build one 'brave mansion' in Ireland, and there is no way to separate the celebrant from the savage soil on which the house is raised. Nor can the dedication be separated from the poem that follows. The Parnassian tradition in which Spenser locates his 'sweete Muses' is that of European epic. His classical masters are Homer and Virgil, and with these we return to the fundamental texts of European civilisation, and thus to the intrinsic relationship between civilisation and savagery. Like the Mosaic Pentateuch with which this enquiry began, the subject of Homer's *Iliad* is the imposition by force of one order on another. The *Iliad* is the story of the destruction of a city (*civitas*, a civilisation) by the collected armies of quarrelling warlords whose gods are as divided and vicious as themselves, and it tells of repeated acts of killing in battle, with all the details of an abbatoir. The subject is 'savagery' or a form of berserk wrath. But the story is told with the command of language, power of imagination and profundity of insight into the nature of man that established Homer (whether man or tribal discourse) as the founder of European poetry.

In this text one cannot disentangle the Kurtzian 'horror' of the subject from (let us call it) the 'beauty' of the artefact; or in Young's terms, 'barbarity' and 'civilisation' are intrinsically and inextricably one. The reinscription of Homer has been and still is one of the great cruces of European civilisation. Seamus Heaney's *Beowulf* (constructed as an Irish epic) is the latest in the series. For Spenser, between the depiction of Ireland in *The Faerie Queene* and Homer there are interposed Virgil, chivalric epic and the entire struggle of *civitas Dei* with pagan Rome. Each interpretation makes the self-questioning more complex. To choose only the most obvious example, if one places Virgil between Homer and Spenser, Virgil's recension of his Greek original has as its subject the founding, not the destruction, of a civilisation. But the *Aeneid* is both a celebration of Augustanism as the apex of the Roman *civitas* and a depiction of an expenditure of blood, toil, tears and sweat so dreadful that the civilised reader is bound to ask whether the end (the founding of Rome) is worth the cost of burning Troy, the destruction of Carthage or, climactically, even the loss of a single life, that of Turnus, unworthy (*indignus*) of death at the hands of Aeneas, no longer *pius* but berserk with the anger of blood revenge?

There is in Spenser's master Virgil, not a dichotomy between civilisation *or* savagery, but rather a deeply disturbing conjunction, civilisation *and* savagery. The words, of course, remain indeterminate and any theoretical schema operating at this level of generalised abstraction runs the obvious risk of accommodating everything by meaning nothing. It is for this reason that our argument must move from the generalisations of this introduction to the specificity of literary texts in both time and place (Ireland in the nineteenth century) and to the complex interrelations between texts, their internal episteme.

The subsequent chapters are concerned with what may be designated as 'the school of Edgeworth', an interrelated group of prose writers who chose as a subject the role of the country house in Ireland: Maria Edgeworth, Charles Lever, Anthony Trollope, Violet Martin and Edith Somerville. The enquiry ends with Elizabeth Bowen and Lady Augusta Gregory, returning, at Bowen's Court and Coole, to the iconography of real places (as in Mitchelstown at the beginning), but real places seen in the context of previous fiction, and like Mitchelstown now lost and therefore existent only in the literary imagination.

The reasons for this selection are simple, although the implications are complex (quite a different pattern would emerge if, like McCormack, one began with Burke and ended with Yeats, for instance).[29] The nineteenth-century English novel is, arguably, the refined and subtle instrument of what one might call 'the liberal conscience'. In the discursive divide between civilisation and savagery, the selected novelists belong to the ironic mode of interpretation of the *topos*. They perceived the interrelation of light with darkness. In the real world of things, of which their writing is a symbolic projection, the majority of these writers were chatelaines of country houses. Hence they were constrained by their sex to the contemplative life of the writer rather than the active world of masculinity. They were appreciative of the civilising function of their culture, participating as writers in that civilisation, and they wrote from within what they knew (a strength and a limitation). The two male writers fall outside this class. But Lever saw himself as the literary protégé of Edgeworth, and she regarded him as a man of 'genius', adding (with memories of her own career) 'how my father would have delighted to help him'.[30] Therefore, he would have fallen, within the patronage of the country house. Lastly, the inclusion of Trollope is ineluctable. He was the major writer of country house fiction of his time. The inclusion of Trollope is also strategic.

The 'racial' origin of these writers is not relevant. As writers in English they belong to the European tradition that is intrinsic in the polyglot nature of their chosen language and the multicultural nexus of English literature. The most cosmopolitan of the writers are Edgeworth and Gregory. Edgeworth's fiction belongs to the culture of the Enlightenment, and like the writer it moves between the nodes of the country house circuit and the salons of the metropolitan capitals of London and Paris. Gregory was plucked by marriage from provincial obscurity to serve as a great hostess (and patron) in an intercontinental empire. Bowen was not far removed from this context. Somerville was educated (as a painter) in Paris. Bowen, Edgeworth and Trollope did not confine their fiction to mere (*merus*) Irish settings and the European dimension of Lever's work is substantial. If Martin seems regional by comparison, that limitation does not apply to the furniture of her formidable intellect.

Since these were writers in English in a European tradition, certain familiar terms such as 'Anglo-Irish' and 'Protestant Ascendancy' are marginal to this enquiry. When these hackneyed terms arise (as they will in the discussion of Bowen) they are late and appear as historical intrusions, arising in Bowen's case from her reactive position in relation to an ascendant nationalist agenda. It tells something of the cultural history of Ireland that a racial category, that of cultural mulatto, should have been invented, and that a writer's religion should be attached like an invisible star of David to his or her work. A simple illustration indicates the tangential nature of the categories. Seamus Heaney's *Beowulf* was cited above as an example of the dichotomy between civilisation and savagery in the European epic. The *translatio* of that European work into the English language is exemplary of the way in which literary tradition develops. Although the time and place of Heaney's translation (post-Hopkins, he states) inevitably affects the immediate application of the text (is Heorot the Scandinavian Tara, and therefore are the Celtic and Anglo-Saxon traditions united?) it would be a grotesque application of new historicism to describe the multicultural and transhistorical power of the poem as merely Anglo-Irish, or merely the product of Heaney's 'Irish identity' expressing itself in opposition to Protestant ascendancy. That would be an absurd parochialism.

The unionist context of the school of Edgeworth, however, cannot be so readily marginalised. On the contrary, the résumé of Spenser and Davies has emphasised how much the imposition of the country house order upon Ireland was intrinsic to the anglicisation/Europeanisation of the island. Indeed that process was bound up in the emergence of what Young designated as civilisation. In 1800, the Edgeworths themselves were unionist by conviction (although opposed to the manner in which it was instituted). All the subsequent writers of the school of Edgeworth were born into the Union. It was a pragmatic fact that Ireland was a metropolitan integer of the British Empire. The Irish served as adminis-trators for the Union, manned the armed services, and colonised both the new and the old empires. The Union, therefore, was the conduit for writers to the entire Anglophone world and to European and imperial culture. Nationalism, on the other hand, in its Sinn Fein symbolic order, was introverted, moving towards isolationism, Gaelicisation and a narrowly fundamentalist sectarian theodicy. Therefore the partition of the United Kingdom/Ireland after 1921 was not only that of the northern and southern Irish, but also of two conceptions of culture. None of the school of Edgeworth belonged to that culturally separatist tendency. After the first Home Rule Bill (1886), for a time Somerville became a Home Ruler politically but then acknowledged the accuracy of Martin's dire warnings about the Pandora's Box of nationalism. Faced with the problem of what to do with the insurgents of 1916, Somerville recommended sending them to the line to fight the Germans! Lady Gregory, a chameleon-like survivor, moved from being an imperial liberal and liberal unionist to become the director of the self-styled 'national' theatre (un-Irish to some). Coole, however, remained an archetypal country house in its social and artistic functions. Gregory's son, Robert, died fighting in the wars of the United Kingdom (which posed interesting problems for Yeats when writing an elegy for the Irish

Sidney) and Robert's wife, Margaret, née Parry, narrowly escaped murder/death-in-war by the IRA when her tennis companions were shot before her eyes. If 1800 provides a clear beginning with Edgeworth's Irish fiction, the subsequent partition of the United Kingdom/Ireland provides an indeterminate and contested termination for the last of her literary heirs, but they remain within the cultural union.

The historical process continues. Nothing in this enquiry can be separated from the Heraclitean flux. There is 'unfinished business' as they say, and that involves not just Northern Ireland. The reconjunction of Eire and the United Kingdom under the umbrella of the European Union suggests that the imperatives that led to the earlier Union are still operative in the deep material structure of things. Long processes of historical interconnection and friendship (yes, friendship!), the continual intermixing of populations, shared language and institutions, and the economic interdependence of proximity have created nodes of connection that, although temporarily interrupted by the unpredictable events of 1916 (the deliberate sabotage of Home Rule by armed force), have now resumed ineluctable, stadial development. If this is so, then rather than seeing the Union as an imperialist monolith sadistically imposed by a tyrannical English people upon the despised and long-suffering Irish innocents, one might reconstruct unionism (not in a Paisleyite sense) as an attempt (pragmatically necessitated by the uprising of 1798, but reformist, adaptable and pluralistic in subsequent practice) to incorporate Ireland into the progressive modernism of the most advanced industrial economy in Europe. That is to say, one might reconstitute the history of the Union from the perspective of another follower of Edgeworth, Sir Walter Scott. During the nineteenth century the United Kingdom was in process of rapidly developing the liberal and democratic institutions that have become the common inheritance of 'western' capitalist and industrialised economies, including universal education, the emancipation of women, the establishment of trades unions, freedom of speech and association, and the ultimate achievement of universal suffrage. To return to 1800, Richard Lovell Edgeworth was right in principle when he argued that the Union was premature, for it did not rest on consent at that time. But democratic consent now exists to the principles that the Union, in ideal form, represented for Edgeworth and are the common culture of the European Union.

No further apologia will be offered for accepting the Union as the matrix of this enquiry. But one consequence of the incorporation of Ireland into the reformist, industrial state was a shift of power from the country house order. Once the conclusion of the (costive but ongoing) process of Catholic emancipation established a new ascendancy of the ballot box (which some would subvert by the gun) the old structures of landed dependency and patronage (the organic community, as it was idealised) became unsustainable. There are numerous accounts of the shock felt by landlords when tenants marched to the polling station and voted against the landlord's preferred candidate. Consequent land reform substituted the economics of the market place for the old system of personalised patronage (or oppression). This shift in power was not unique to Ireland. It was a cultural phenomenon from the Urals to the Americas (one could transpose any Chekovian estate to an Irish equivalent). The revolutionary change was frequently violent. The Reign of Terror in Jacobinical France, the American Civil War and the Russian Revolution place the so-called 'Land War' in Ireland in Lilliputian perspective.

The major event in Ireland was the famine, whose economic consequences precipitated a decline that Gladstonian liberalism rendered a permanent fall. This process of decline and fall was post-Edgeworth. There was no way in which she could have foreseen it and country house fiction in Ireland was accordingly, initiated in circumstances (Young's enlightened optimism) that no longer obtained by the end of Edgeworth's (long) life. The decline and fall self-evidently coloured the work of subsequent writers, but the very decline of the country house as a power house gave particular signification to its symbolic function for writers. What had it stood for, and for what might it stand? At the end of the process a number of texts, such as Somerville's *Wheel-Tracks* (1923), Gregory's *Coole* (1931) and Bowen's *Bowen's Court* (1942) were devoted to the preservation of what is now little more than cultural memory. But this decline and fall, it must be emphasised, was a product of the Union to which, paradoxically, the school of Edgeworth was intrinsically related. Legislation from the Encumbered Estates Act to Wyndham's Land Act was entirely Unionist. The IRA did not burn out a 'garrison'. Years before the 'last September' Violet Martin, earning a living in part from her writings, had been slaving with a scythe in the drive of Ross House to stop the wilderness swallowing up her all but derelict but passionately loved home. The idea that a single Victorian maiden lady with hands callused from the scythe constitutes a garrison is more of a fiction than even Violet Martin's fictions.

This cursory summary indicates the presumed Unionist context of the following chapters. It would be false to the relativistic nature of the argument to claim that this hypothetical history is 'true' in comparison with other accounts, which, accordingly, are falsified. It is no more than a strategic hypothesis, the purpose of which is to provide the argument room to manoeuvre, free from the preoccupations of other kinds of Irish national/cultural studies, for instance, the Field Day project, and all attempts to invent Ireland and Irish identity.[31] In this enquiry the Union is a mere pragmatic fact, a historical given, the historical matrix in which these writers in English entered the country house tradition.

In the current dichotomy between revisionist and postcolonial Irish history this is a revisionist position, if only by default (or to put another way, one implication of the unionist argument would be that the post-colonial phase in Ireland began in 1800!) Although imperial ideology was intrinsically bound up in the *fiat lux* conception of civilisation and the transference of civilisation to Ireland through the country house order was manifestly an act of colonisation, the use of those words in this enquiry is both classical and no more than analytical. The problem with the application of undiluted postcolonial theory is that it ultimately depends on an anti-unionist assumption in which, simply put, Ireland equals colony equals oppressed Celtic people. But this assertion is not a self-evident truth. It is heavily overlaid by appeal to the canonical authorities (Fanon and Gramsci, for instance), the argument operates by selective (non-empirical) universalising analogy (Ireland is like India, the Philippines and Mexico), and it employs a slippery generality of vocabulary ('hegemony', 'repressive state apparatus', 'imperialism' and, as Stephen Howe has pointed out, a catch-all use of the foundational words 'colony' and 'colonialism').[32]

David Lloyd's *Ireland after History* (1999) serves as a typical (and distinguished) example of the genre and represents the polar opposite to the present enquiry. Decolonisation, Lloyd argues, has not been achieved in Ireland for the old hegemony of imperialism has merely changed into its equivalent, the global oppression of capitalism. Eire (conservative, Catholic, agricultural and therefore reactionary) is now itself colonially collusive in its support for the 'repressive violence' of imperialism in Ulster, and its incorporation into the European Union has made it part of 'Fortress Europe' (a Nazi term). It is a corollary of this pessimistic hypothesis that the postcolonialist turns to the occluded subalterneity of history to find sites of resistance to racism, imperialism, capitalism and state violence (condemned from the moral high ground of the university campus). Lloyd's occluded subalterns turn out to be the Fenians and the socialist feminists of the IRA, which takes one back, the long way round, to the nationalist agenda.[33] In many respects, this argument, is the mirror opposite of the unionist hypothesis. There is an historical process that both perceive, but it is invested with a diametrically opposite interpretation. This is what one might call, in the context of this introduction, the Mitchelstown effect: same thing, radically different witness statements.

Does this make my own enquiry revisionist, if that is the only theoretical alternative? Generally speaking all new enquiries are revisionist, and the label is unnecessarily restrictive when applied only to certain attempts to write non-partisan history in Ireland. Yet if there are only two camps, this enquiry is revisionist. Ideologically its position is close to that in R. F. Foster's *The Irish Story* (2001), for its concern is with what Foster calls 'cosmopolitanism' rather than the 'introverted, autarchical' discourses of old nationalism and postcolonial apologia for nationalism's idealised victim culture. W. B. Yeats emerges in Foster as a representative cosmopolitan (and Gerry Adams as his antitype), and the chapters of the present enquiry are in some ways prolegomena to the country house poetry of Yeats.

But Foster's concern is biographical; as an historian he is subject to the discipline of empirical fact, and ultimately his cultural narratives return to the old theme of 'Irish identity'. The present study of country house iconography, although sharing Foster's revisionist base, is literary rather than historical. The narratives of culture considered here are in the main fictions (or idealised descriptions of place), and the fundamental subject (as this introduction has indicated) is the reinterpretation of a foundational European ideology in the context of Ireland. The empirical data are no more than the very words of the narrations, their literary inheritance, context, complexity and resonance. Inevitably some of the texts are the familiar subject of literary histories of the novel in Ireland (although many are not), and a general debt (warmly acknowledged) is owed to three major generic studies of country house fiction in Ireland: Genet (1991), Rauchbauer (1992) and Kreilkamp (1998). But these works are general surveys of the entire field of this fiction, subsuming unionist and post-unionist texts into one broad-brush account. Genet's and Rauchbauer's works are miscellanies by diverse hands (and with diverse agenda). Kreilkamp (a unitary voice) is equally diverse in subject, ranging from Maturin to Trevor, but, when we close in on the same passages we can see that her closely read analyses are deeply perceptive.

In line with this book's revisionist basis, the following chapters redefine the subject and approach it from a different perspective. The argument set up in this introduction is that the cosmopolitanism of which Foster writes is the necessary correlative of cultural unionism.

Moreover, as far as the political Union was concerned no one could have foreseen the absurdity of the events of 1916, nor the rewriting of history by the winners of the subsequent war. In returning to the Union, it is a European not an Irish identity with which we are concerned. To challenge the notion of Irish identity further, that Europeanisation is a sign of the (long-established) modernity that is the subject of Declan Kiberd's (1995) inventive enquiry. It is a correlative of the revisionist position that this Europeanisation in Ireland is 'complex' (a notorious word in the *Kulturkampf*), hence the emphasis in this introduction on the ironic interplay of civilisation with savagery as a leitmotif in European thought, and hence the emphasis in the following chapters on the ambivalence of empirical evidence (the words on the page) that is not subject to 'theoretical reduction' (Foster's phrase).

Many of the narratives to be considered are works of fiction. But arguably so too are all other nineteenth-century narratives of Ireland, even the 'lives' in Foster's enquiry. What is explored in the subsequent chapters is a certain kind of cultural fabrication, and no claim is made that this fabrication is the basis of any history of fact. This kind of minute verbal enquiry is of course on the horns of a familiar dilemma. One risks reducing everything to textuality (for instance, the famine, as Trollopian discourse); conversely one might end up with a numinous boom of cultural generalisation (what on earth does one mean, out of verbal context, by 'civilisation'?) To that dilemma I have no theoretical answer. I offer only such tact as the navigator possesses.

2
Edgeworthstown 'Rebuilding'

W. H. Maxwell, in his *History of the Irish Rebellion in 1798: With Memoirs of the Union* (1845), tells of a notorious incident at Scullabogue in Wexford:

> One reads, almost with incredulity, of Autos-da-fe, and Eves of St. Batholomew, and blesses God – when he finds the narrative is true – that his lot was not cast in an age of cruelty and darkness. But when he is told of scenes enacted within fifty years, and immediately beside him, he almost blushes to think that the wolfish wretches who were the actors, bore the common name of man.[1]

He is about to describe what happened on 5 June 1798 at the country house of Captain King, who had fled before the insurgents. Attached to the house was a large barn in which more than two hundred loyalists – Protestant and Catholic, men, women and children – were imprisoned. On 5 June the insurgents were repulsed at Ross and a message was sent from an unnamed priest that the prisoners should be put to death. Accordingly the barn, was set on fire and the prisoners burnt alive. A witness of 'this dreadful scene, saw a child who got under the door, and was likely to escape... when a rebel perceiving it, struck his pike through it, and threw it into the flames.' Outside the house summary executions were taking place:

> Richard Grandy, who was present, swears that the prisoners in front of the house were led out by fours to be shot, and that the rebels who pierced them when they fell, took pleasure in licking their spears.
> A gentleman present, who had a narrow escape, assured me that a rebel said he would try the taste of orange blood, and that he

dipped a tooth-pick in a wound of one of the Protestants who was shot, and then put it into his mouth.

Those were the atrocities ('war crimes') of just one June afternoon in 1798. Writing in England in 1845, Maxwell found what he was describing almost unbelievable in the here and now. This kind of thing belonged to the atavistic dark ages of religious intolerance and conflict: *tantum potuit religio suadere malorum*.[2] It is as if there had been no progress from the Ireland of Spenser and Davies. *A fortiori*, such things necessitated the Union which followed.

George Cruickshank's illustration to Maxwell (plate 2) has become notorious. The scene is dominated by the impaled body of the child held aloft towards the fiery furnace. Those who are struggling to escape through the door will be dismembered. Cruickshank supplements the horror. The semi-animal figure in the bottom left hand corner beating out the brains of a dead man with a stone was his own invention. So too was the degraded woman robbing the corpses. Psychosis and criminality combined in the insurrection.

This notorious massacre was what Eagleton might call a 'typical' event of Irish history. Like the Omagh bombing and Bloody Sunday (of more recent memory) it was a mythologised act. It has been claimed that the reference to the simian features of Cruickshank's mob betrayed racial prejudice (this is English and Protestant history), but this iconography was a standard representation of the mob violence of the time, whether the anarchy of French Jacobinism or the Gordon riots in London.[3] Compare the faces in Browne's illustration 'The Prison Tribunal' in Dickens' *A Tale of Two Cities*, and the Protestant insurrectionists in 'The Rioters at Work' and 'A No-Popery Dance' (Plate 3) in *Barnaby Rudge*. The very existence of the propertied classes was a provocation to the mob. Hence the fear of Jacobinism that haunts these illustrations. But fundamental is a sense of psychosis, the return of the repressed, the re-emergence of the savage in the civilised order.

What happened at Captain King's house at Scullabogue might equally have happened at Edgeworthstown (and Maria Edgeworth was still alive when Maxwell wrote his account). The entire countryside was gripped by terror and the life of no one – Catholic or Protestant, pauper or property holder – was safe. Among the Catholics the cry went up that the Orangemen were coming (better equipped than the rebels to burn, rape and murder). Meantime the rebels had joined forces with an army from Jacobinical France, and according to Maria Edgeworth (citing the authority of the French) even the military were shocked by the revolutionary Irish scum: 'beggars, rascals, and savages' bent on pillage but useless in battle. Faced by imminent attack from these 'savages', Richard Lovell Edgeworth endeavoured to raise a non-sectarian home guard, but the (Protestant) authorities failed to supply arms for a (partially) Catholic force. The family had no option but to become refugees and flee to the garrison town of Longford. The expectation was that Edgeworthstown would be burnt.[4]

The family were twice close to death. They were offered a military escort but it was blown to pieces. Even in Longford itself they were not safe. Among the hard-line Protestant population (who at Catholic hands might have suffered the fate of the garrison at Drogheda) the Edgeworths, as enlightened friends of Catholic emancipation, were suspected of spying for the rebels. Richard Lovell was saved from an Irish Protestant mob only by the presence of the British army.

But the British army was not needed to save Edgeworthstown itself. When the rebel forces arrived one of them, 'who seemed to be a leader, with a pike in his hand, set his back against the gate, and swore that, "if he were to die the next minute, he would have the life of the first man, who should open that gate, or set enemy's foot within side of that place"'. The reason for this was that the Edgeworth's housekeeper had loaned rent money to this man's wife. Hence 'not a soul should get leave to go into her master's house; not a twig should be touched, nor a leaf harmed', and he mounted guard over Edgeworthstown for as long as the rebels remained in the locality.

The complexity of these events, filtered through the selective and symbolic memory of a witness involved in them, cannot readily be reduced to the abstractions of postcolonial theory. If the Edgeworths were *coloni* by origin, they were long established by right of birth and legal authority (witness *The Black Book of Edgeworthstown*).[5] Their demesne was their home. There was no other, and it is with the felt experience of that home with which we are concerned, as well as the manner in which Maria Edgeworth narrated how it was preserved and what it meant to return to it. The reason why Edgeworthstown was not burnt (and the story may be true) is manifestly because the family were known as good landlords and were thus protected. She needs to believe that if all estates in Ireland were like her father's there would be no civil war. The practical economics of enlightened landlordism blends with a residual feudalism. There is a personal loyalty, as if of a clan to its chieftain (the 'master'), which is interwoven with economic pragmatism. Hence, earlier, Richard Lovell's creation of his own militia to protect his (their) estate; and also 'the entreaties, lamentations, and objurgations' of the tenantry to accompany their landlord when he fled his indefensible home. We have no means of knowing what might be the proportion of the tenantry who shared these attitudes, nor in what measure. Later, in the time of O'Connell, there came a major crisis when the tenants, for the first time, voted against the recommendation of the family, but that is a later issue. In 1798 the loyal Abdiel at the gate is an essential signifier of hope in Edgeworth's symbolic history. In the continuation of her father's 'memoir' she recalls:

> When we came near Edgeworth-Town, we saw many well known faces at the cabin doors, looking out to welcome us. One man, who was digging in his field by the road side, when he looked up as our horses passed, and saw my father, let fall his spade and clasped his hands; his face, as the morning sun shone upon it, was the strongest picture of joy I ever saw. The village was a melancholy spectacle; windows shattered, and doors broken. But though the mischief done was great, there had been little pillage. Within our gates we found all property safe; literally 'not a twig touched, nor a leaf harmed.' Within the house every thing was as we had left it – a map which we had been consulting was still open on the library table, with pencils, and slips of paper containing the first lessons in arithmetic, in which some of the young people had been engaged the morning we had been driven from home; a pansy, in a glass of water, which one of the children had been copying, was still on the chimney piece. These trivial circumstances, marking repose and tranquillity, struck us at this moment with an unreasonable sort of surprise, and all that had passed seemed like an incoherent dream. The joy of having my father in safety remained, and gratitude to heaven for his preservation. These feelings spread inexpressible pleasure over what seemed to be a new sense of existence. Even the most common things appeared delightful; the green lawn, the still groves, the birds singing, the fresh air, all external nature, and all the goods and conveniences of life, seemed to have wonderfully increased in value, from the fear we had put of losing them irrecoverably.

The 'morning sun' that shone upon this scene was that of a restorative dawn, the re-establishment of a universal order represented by the return of a father to his house and a landlord to his tenants. (One might compare, and contrast, this with Sir Thomas Bertram in Jane Austen's *Mansfield Park*.) Of course any rebel among the tenants would have already left or been expelled from the estate, but that is no reason to deny the welcome in the eyes of the 'well known faces' on the road. What was expressed was at least 'civility'. There was a communal knowledge of person for person, a welcome recognition that united these people across divisions of class, religion or even 'race' (whatever that word means). It was inconceivable that Edgeworthstown should become Scullabogue. Perhaps Maria exaggerated the degree of joy. Perhaps she merely projected onto the scene what she wanted to feel. But this was a visionary moment, for her the equivalent of a Wordsworthian 'spot of time' transfiguring even 'the most common things'. She felt, she claimed, 'a new sense of existence'. It is a passage one might set against Wordsworth's 'Bliss was it in that dawn to be alive', celebrating the false light of the dawn of Jacobinism.

Her feelings were most engaged with the regained demesne. The house and gardens had been, under the improving hand of Richard Lovell, a miniature Burkean realm. Maria's father had found an inconvenient and old fashioned house in a shockingly poor country. Gradually the conveniences of the house had been increased, the gardens landscaped and ordered, the management of the estate rationalised and capitalised. But the family had neither torn down the old to construct some magniloquent 'house of envious show' nor camped in Swiftean squalor while dreaming of Laputan schemes for Ireland.

But at that moment of heightened experience, the essential space that for her was the heart of the house, was the library. If the burning barn at Scullabogue represented savagery, the library at Edgeworthstown was a sign of civilisation preserved. It was a 'Mary Celeste' situation. The family had vanished from the scene, and all we can deduce about what they were is from the signs of communal activity they left behind. There were the books themselves, as repositories of European culture, to which transhistorical store both Richard Lovell and Maria had added. But at the moment of departure the key signifiers were a map that 'we' (she and her father) had been consulting, 'the first lessons in arithmetic' that 'the young people' had been studying, and the remains of a botanical lesson. This was a scientific civilisation, the prime signifier of which was the map. The scientific mathematics of the map concerned the delineation and measurement of space, and thus of property (whether the demesne or all Ireland is unspecified). The order that the map created was thus, related, both to the 'power house' and to the reduction of Ireland from anarchy to order. As an enlightened project the Ordnance survey had been established only seven years before (1791, although it was not extended to Ireland until 1824). At that moment, therefore, 'we' were in a space that was indeterminately delineated (as Beaufort complained in his *Memoir of a Map of Ireland*, 1792). The purpose of the future Ordnance survey in Ireland would be to delineate the rights and duties of property, to regularise the naming of places and to establish on scientific grounds the facts concerning the remains of antiquity. 'Civilisation' in this context was knowledge, and knowledge was power.

The only space in the demesne comparable to the library in symbolic importance was the pleasure garden, or rather what was described as 'all external nature', as if the norm to which the natural world aspired was the demesne with its 'green lawn', its 'still groves' (safe from political tempest) and the birds singing in the fresh air. When Maria looked for an image to describe the preservation of the house she chose a natural one: 'not a twig touched, nor a leaf harmed' as if (to return to Edmund Burke again) the house were a tree that had survived a storm. This is a familiar nexus of imagery in country house literature, where the operations of power by which property is acquired and maintained are concealed by naturalising the house in the landscape, as if it has grown there *sponte sua*. But equally familiar is the portrayal of the house as 'paradise hall' (to use Henry Fielding's designation). Perhaps the closest affinity to what Maria felt and sought to express was Marvell's description of another Maria in a garden, also after a period of civil war: he called Maria Fairfax of Appleton House 'paradise's only map'.[6]

The demesne and the library were to acquire classic status. Just as Maria returned at once to the library as the essential heart of the house, so too did visitors to Edgeworthstown, and now with conscious interpretative purpose. Two remarkable examples serve to illustrate. The first is Mrs Hall's *Ireland: Its Scenery, Character, & c.* This is one of the most important unionist texts in nineteenth-century literature, written just before the famine to confirm the English and Irish as 'one people', and celebrating the enormous advances in prosperity and civilisation visible everywhere in Ireland, spreading eastwards from the anglicised counties, although with much still to be accomplished. In some measure, this work was the nineteenth-century equivalent of Young, but written for the middle-class liberal whose sensibility was to be quickened by admiration for the ancient national landscape and whose reforming principles were to be strengthened by quickened feeling for the common people. The importance of Hall's work is obvious in the material opulence of the three magnificent volumes. *Exegi monumentum.*[7]

In Hall's itineraries the traveller is not usually invited into the demesnes of the unionist landlords. Castle and villa, wood and lake are for the delight of the eye, delighted also by the prosperity and responsible care the improved estate manifests. But Edgeworthstown is the exception. Maria Edgeworth had been one of Mrs Hall's mentors (she claimed) and one is taken across the demesne and into the library on much the same route the Edgeworths had taken in 1798. The moral commentary is explicit:

> Edgeworthstown, however, may almost be regarded as public property. From this mansion has issued so much practical good to Ireland, and not alone to Ireland, but the civilised world, – it has been so long the residence of high intellect, well-directed genius and virtue, that we violate no duty by requesting our readers to accompany us thither – a place that, perhaps, possesses larger moral interest than any other in the kingdom. (III, 276–7)

If one compares this exordium to that of Young approaching Mitchelstown, there is a striking difference between Young's emphasis on civilisation as emergent from barbarianism and the progression of Hall's text from Ireland to the whole 'civilised world'. Ireland and civilisation are now unified, and the engine of that unification is this country house, 'the residence of high intellect, industry, well-directed genius and virtue'. The claim is carried to extremes, for apart from the slight check of a 'perhaps', this house is claimed to possess a 'larger moral interest than any other in the kingdom'.

The 'Burkean' house is modestly illustrated in the text (Plate 4). It is fully naturalised, embosomed in trees that press to the very walls. In the shrubbery a genteel family group are strolling, and the older woman is inspecting one of the plants (one recollects the botanical specimen on the mantelpiece in the library in Edgeworth's description). One might guess that the central and lower window of the bay serves as a door leading directly into the garden, thus marrying nature and the civilisation of the villa by the easiest of conjunctions. The architectural form of the house itself manifests its organic growth within its restricted space. There is a minor extension on the facade to the right; an abrupt quasiclassical oriel window has enlarged what is perhaps a bedroom to the left. What is equally significant, especially with regard to the civic humanist and Whig origins of the Edgeworths' civilisation, is the imposition of classic signifiers on the facade. The Diocletian window facing the viewer and the pediment to the right are both signs that Edgeworthstown was derived from the villa culture of the ancients. Cicero and Pliny would have recognised these signs, and the imposition of the temple portico to the gentleman's country house, in Palladian tradition, united enlightened (and tolerant) religion to the ideal home (witness Alexander Pope's Twickenham).

Mrs Hall's description leads the visitor through the well-planted demesne towards the house, which is sparkling with cheering lights. The house dog warmly greets the visitors, and one is taken at once into the *sanctum sanctorum*, the library, well stored with books and pictures, a room that, of need, has been expanded in size, embellished with pillars (again 'bearers of meaning', to use Onians' phrase,[8] speaking of classical civilisation) and in direct visible contact with idealised nature in the form of the garden with its 'beautiful lawn' and 'judiciously planted' trees. This is not the solitary place of study of the writer as hermit, but the family room of the house where 'all come in' (to adapt Ben Jonson's words from *To Penshurst*), bound 'to the spot by the strong chords of memory and love' and by a love both for study and for the fine arts. But the *genius loci* is Maria Edgeworth herself, who rises in the morning earlier than her visitors and until eleven at night is constantly concerned both with the embellishment of the house and with the welfare of the estate and its tenantry, 'ministering to their wants, careful to inculcate whatever lesson they most need'.

Mrs Hall concluded her account of the house by celebrating Edgeworth as a great writer who had used her pen morally 'in the service of Ireland' by vindicating the character of her country from jeers at the 'mere Irish' (a phrase loaded with colonial overtones). She was in the tradition of Grattan and Sheridan, but Mrs Hall's celebration of Irish eloquence was unionist in implication. Thus the writer with whom Mrs Hall most closely associated Edgeworth was Sir Walter Scott, whose pen lay on her desk, for Scott was both a great 'national' novelist and a unionist historian. The lesson of history that Scott's novels taught was that different cultures (often historically antagonistic) could, in the course of time, change and, particularly through the laws of economic development, grow together into constructive union within difference. It was part of what Wordsworth was to call that 'dark/Inscrutable workmanship that reconciles/Discordant elements', and makes them 'cling together/In one society' (*The Prelude* I, 341f). Thus Mrs Hall concluded that 'Miss Edgeworth is public property, belonging to the world at large'. Hers was not a culture parochially turned inwards, nourishing old hatreds, dividing peoples. Edgeworthstown house was grounded in a great European tradition.

It is a tragic irony that this celebration was written almost on the eve of the famine. Yet half a century later Mrs Hall's panegyric was matched by Anne Thackeray Ritchie in a classic introduction to *Castle Rackrent* and *The Absentee* (1895). Ritchie wrote for Macmillan's 'Illustrated Standard Novels', itself a quasi-unionist project, bringing together Edgeworth, John Galt, George Borrow and Jane Austen, each in their different ways examples of the diversity of the regional novel. The editor, herself a novelist, belonged to the mainstream of the traditional canon of English literature, since she was the daughter of William Makepiece Thackeray and her stepniece was Virginia Woolf (whose *Orlando* and *Between the Acts* were late, elegiac, idealistic country house fictions). The 'Illustrated Standard' edition was published four years after the death of Parnell. At that time it was still entirely reasonable for a liberal unionist writer to believe that progressive land reform was successfully addressing the substantial agricultural crisis that was affecting not just Ireland but all parts of the United Kingdom. Moreover a liberal unionist might well have believed that some form of devolved government in the regions (which had been on the parliamentary agenda since 1886) would strengthen the mutual ties of friendship that bound together all the English-speaking peoples (hence the catholic choice of authors by Macmillan). Just as Mrs Hall could not foresee the catastrophe of the famine, so Ritchie could not foresee (in an enlightened parliamentary democracy) the demand of Padraic Pearse that Ireland be liberated by war from its 'slavery' to the British 'murder machine'.

On the contrary, what Ritchie perceived on her approach to Edgeworthstown were the visible signs of enlightenment and prosperity. Ireland now possessed an excellent railway system (constructed by progressive capitalisation and industrialisation) and it was no accident that she reported that 'Maynooth was a fragrant vision as we flew past'. She noticed Maynooth because enlightened tolerance had established a Roman Catholic seminary there as early as 1795. The meadows were a 'sweet wonderful green', transfigured by her imagination both as regions of 'sweet content' and, suddenly, as a magic space for 'dancing circles of little fairy pigs with curly tails' (so much for the pig in the kitchen and the dung hill at the door of another kind of narrative of Ireland). It was familiar, like England, yet different, like Europe, and she thought of the skies of France and Italy.

Edgesworthstown, however, was pure England: a great house, protected by the branches of 'century old trees' (signs of deep-rooted continuity in the family and community) close by a village (and the Roman Catholic village church) where, under the shade of sycamores, 'pretty cows were browsing the grass'. It was in a mood proleptic of her stepniece's *Orlando* that Ritchie came upon 'the old home, so exactly like what one expected it, that I felt as if I had been there before in some other phase of existence'. But of course she had been there before. Fielding, Richardson, Austen, Mrs Hall and Edgeworth herself had shaped Ritchie's sense of what she should see and feel (and Woolf and Waugh, James and du Maurier would imaginatively find similar ideal houses after her):

> There were the French windows reaching to the ground, through which Maria used to pass on her way to gather her roses; there was the porch where Walter Scott had stood; there grew the quaint old-fashioned bushes with the great pink peonies in flower, by those railings which still divide the park from the meadows beyond. (p. viii)

The enlightened nature of Edgeworth's ideal description of her coming home in 1798, with its emphasis on education and science, yielded here to a picturesque 'olde worlde' feminine sentimentality. What was most attractive about the bushes now was not the lessons they might give in botanical science but their 'quaint old-fashioned' quality. Likewise the house – with its 'winding passages and side gates', its curious enfilade of rooms 'opening from one into another' and the old long-case clock that 'Maria wound up when she was over eighty years old' – was symbolic of time past.

One aim of the ideology of picturesque aesthetic had always been to separate form and function. But another purpose was to establish those mystic chords of memory that, by binding present to past, gave to a culture that sense of identity that came from continuity. Accordingly the library remained the key room at Edgeworthstown for Ritchie. Sir Walter Scott (of course) was the first author to be associated with Maria, but then the literary canon extended to Wordsworth, Mackintosh, Barbauld, Descartes, Rogers, Hallam's *Constitutional History*, Turgeniev and 'piles of Magazines that had been sent from America'. This was a canon that one might characterise as enlightened Whig in its origins but tending towards conservativism. It was cosmopolitan (American, French, Scottish and Russian as well as English), and self-evidently was not romantic nationalist (there was no Morgan or Davis). But Hallam, to pick out an exemplary case, devoted the final chapter of his *Constitutional History* to Ireland, and his conclusion of Irish history with the reign of George II was appropriate in a unionist and international context. It was in that period, Hallam wrote, that 'the great parliamentary history of Ireland begins', terminated after half a century by that parliament's choice of the Union. There was, therefore, no subsequent 'Irish' history for Hallam because it had become part of an inherited British tradition, that of 'mixed or limited' monarchy 'which the Celtic and Gothic tribes appear universally to have established'. The conjunction of Celt and Goth in a unitary tradition represented by the English constitution needs no further comment.

It was a union that also appeared economically successful within the sphere of influence of the demesne. Ritchie's visit extended to the circum-ambient locality. Her account of Richard Lovell's improvements to his estate derived from his *Memoir*: the termination of feudal practices, the capitalisation of tenant holdings, the encouragement of security and improvement, and the obviation of sectarian division. It is a reasonable assumption that were Richard Lovell to be born again he would see the good sense of the modern 'spirit of progress', for as Ritchie noted, his experiments in non-sectarian education had been 'a sort of foreshadow-ing of the High Schools of the present'. The excellence of the public highways, the neatness of the village cottages, the fertility of the soil, the lively village shops and the newly established post office all testified to the peace and prosperity of Ireland. The post office, of course, had not yet acquired its symbolic association with man-killing Cuchulain. It was a sign, like the railway system, of the benefits of imperial com-munication for all people.

Of major symbolic importance was the one ruined cottage in the village, at a place where two roads divided, and beyond the cottage 'a falling shed, on the thatched roof of which a hen was clucking and scraping'. In nationalist literature ruined cottages were one of the most potent symbols of the evils of imperialistic oppression. There we perceive (in a typical episode) the eviction of an innocent poor family by the greedy landlord, his corrupt agent, who were empowered by the Royal Irish Constabulary and backed up by the occupying British army. But at Edgeworthstown:

These cottages Mr Edgeworth had, after long difficulty, bought up and condemned as unfit for human habitation. The plans had been considered, the orders given to build new cottages in their place, which were to be let to the old tenants at the old rent, but the last remaining inhabitant absolutely refused to leave; we saw an old woman in a hood slowly crossing the road, and carrying a pail of water; no threats or inducements would move her, not even the sight of a neat little house, white-washed and painted, and all ready for her to step into. Her present rent was 10d. a week, Mr. Edgeworth told me, and she had been letting the tumble-down shed to a large family for 1s. 4d. This sub-let was forcibly put an end to, but the landlady stops there, and there she will stay until the roof tumbles down upon her head. The old creature passed on through the sunshine, a decrepit, picturesque figure carrying her pail to the stream, defying all the laws of progress and political economy and civilisation in her feebleness and determination. (pp. xiii-iv)

A nationalist reader would recognise this figure of an old woman. It was the Shan van Vocht, the embodiment of the suffering poor of Ireland. But for Ritchie the Shan van Vocht represented the old Ireland of the rentier middlemen, who rented low from the landlord and then subdivided the land and rackrented those poorer than themselves. The exploiter here was Irish and of old Ireland, and it was now modern political economy under the Union that was trying to put an end to this. As the text states, the ruined cottage stood where two roads divided. The Shan van Vocht obstinately stuck to her old ways, refusing the neat new built cottage, neither moved by threat nor inducement, determined to defy 'all the laws of progress', or, one might say, still resolute to defy the law. Hence she was, in Ritchie's view, an utter anachronism but harmless in her self-inflicted poverty, a 'decrepit, picturesque figure'. Proleptically reinterpreted, however, she might also stand for the Ireland of de Valera, so wedded to traditional rural practices, so isolated in its refusal of 'modern political economy' that the State wrapped itself in its poverty as though this were a virtue. As Ritchie wrote, two roads divided at the ruined cottage. For her the preferred road was that which the Edgeworths had chosen.

The ideal recreation of her home in Edgeworth's novels is the Percy estate in *Patronage* (1814).[9] The ideal status of the family derives from their possession of 'property sufficient to secure ... independence'; from this depends 'the blessings of *real liberty*, and of domestic tranquillity and happiness'.[10] The 'real liberty' of the Percys was presumably set by Edgeworth, *sotto voce*, against the spurious *liberté* of contemporary Jacobinism. Mr Percy is a beloved (Grandisonian) landlord; his sons are established in 'independent' professions: the law, medicine, the army; his well-educated daughters accept the domestic ideal of marriage and motherhood. This is the 'due order' of things.

It is a cosmopolitan order, or to use Mrs Hall's expression, one that is exemplary to the 'civilised world'. The German Count Altenberg has left his country, which has been disordered by revolution and overrun by the French, married into the Percy family and settled as a country gentleman in England. He is English on his mother's side, and Edgeworth's text calls upon Hibernian Burke and Caledonian Scott in justification of a patriotism that is cosmopolitan.

An essential guarantee of independent property at that time was the rule of law, with its safeguard of the line of inheritance, and a key word in conservative ideology was 'legitimacy'. The exemplary plot of *Patronage* involves the loss and subsequent recovery of the Percy estate. That recovery is secured by the son, who is trained in law and establishes the veracity of the true deed, as opposed to the falsely postdated alternative. In the context of the contemporary revolutionary wars, take away the law (as in the rising of 1798) and one was left (in a real world situation) either with occupation by French armies (as the Edgeworths, like Count Altenberg, might have experienced) or the anarchy of a Jacquerie and a return to the savage state of nature.

There is no distinction in Edgeworth's writing between the real property of her own family home and the ideal order represented by the Percy estate in England. Both have the same symbolic status. Accordingly there is no essential distinction between the ideology of her major 'English' novels, *Patronage, Belinda, Helen* and her 'Irish' tales. The ideal ending of both the 'English' and the 'Irish' fictions is the establishment of the happily married protagonists upon a well-ordered demesne. But in all these tales the country house order is under threat. In the English versions one might instance the corrupt political world in which Lord Oldborough has to work; the libertine and ultimately criminal high society into which Lady Delacour is drawn in *Belinda* (the supposed cancer in her breast is a sign of a disease eating her brilliant, painted exterior from within); or the dereliction of Old Forest in *Helen*, where the old timber has been felled, the family portraits are gone, and the weather is breaking in. How might one 'repair this ruin, restore this once hospitable mansion, and put it in the power of the son to be what his ancestors have been?'[11] Although Edgeworth was a conservative writer, her fictions, like Austen's *Mansfield Park*, reveal that she was deeply (and satirically) aware of the corruption within the ancient social order she supported, and the need for that order to change if it was to survive. So too Disraeli, her successor.

Although there is no difference in ideology between the English and Irish fictions, the change of place endows the tales with a difference of time in the history of civilisation. To return to Young again, Ireland had emerged from cultural barbarianism to the kind of civilisation that Mitchelstown and Edgeworthstown represented. But contemporary

Europe, in historical progression, was beyond that. The present crux was that in the most advanced culture in Europe, France, the *ancien régime* (as its enemies called this civilisation) had become corrupt and disintegrated. (The supposed cancer in Lady Delacour's breast is an appropriate symbol of this.) The events of 1798 in Ireland were a remote ripple from the tempest of the Terror. England, in anti-Jacobin war, was a *tertium quid*. Edgeworth's Irish fictions move, in their symbolic order, between English and Irish estates, and between metropolitan London and Paris. Hence they are moving on an historical spectrum that extends from savagery to the emergence of civilisation, and to the decline and fall of that civilisation. In an extraordinary cycle the old Irish 'savage' joins hands across the centuries with the 'swinish multitude' of the Jacobin mob. Accordingly, where one stands geographically within these territories is related to the temporal development of civil society. This is a familiar device in the fiction of Scott and Fenimore Cooper, Edgeworth's contemporaries. Their fiction is concerned with place as chronotrope.

This is symbolic politics in Edgeworth and not politically engaged in the manner of country house writers such as Pope and Byron. The treatment in *Ennui* of the 1798 rising, for instance, is absurd, no more than an episode of Salvator Rosa banditti and loyalist tenantry scoffing at a Milesian restoration. The Parisian episode in *Ormond* merely foreshadows, by way of Burke, the revolution to come. In *The Absentee* the Napoleonic wars are no more than an adjunct to the plot that places Captain Reynolds in Austria. Subsequently Edgeworth refused to engage with O'Connellism. Her concern was with a philosophy of history – as illustrated by the symbolic use of place – not with the turmoil and the mire of war, party politics and the agitation of the masses.

A direct comparison between two country houses in *Ennui* serves to flesh out these hypotheses. One, Sherwood Park, is in England, the other, Glenthorn Castle, in Ireland. A fundamental and traditional country house motif establishes the symbolic signification of Sherwood Park. It is the Horatian *Beatus ille*: 'How happy the owner of this place must be!' remarks 'one among the party of strangers' visiting the pleasure grounds of Sherwood Park, or as Pope put it, 'Happy the man whose wish and care' is bound by his paternal acres. It is a key word that is associated in *Patronage* with the ideal Percy estate. The only trouble is that in Glenthorn's experience the ideal is simply not experientially true. He is caught 'in the middle of a desperate yawn' when he hears how 'happy' he is:

> Sherwood Park, my English country-seat, had but one fault; it was completely finished. The house was magnificent, and in the modern

taste; the furniture fashionably elegant, and in all the gloss of novelty. Not a single luxury omitted; not a fault could be found by the most fastidious critic. My park, my grounds, displayed all the beauties of nature and of art, judiciously combined. Majestic woods, waving their dark foliage, overhung – But I will spare my readers the description, for I remember falling asleep myself whilst a poet was reading me an ode on the beauties of Sherwood Park. These beauties too soon became familiar to my eye; and even the idea of being the proprietor of this enchanting place soon palled upon my vanity. Every casual visitor, all the strangers, even the common people, who were allowed once a week to walk in my pleasure grounds, enjoyed them a thousand times more than I could. (p. 4)

As the abrupt hiatus indicates, this is a parody of the description of a demesne with which any contemporary reader (of Young, for instance) would have been all too familiar and a flattering poetic tradition so exhausted (by Pope, for instance) that the commonplaces of an ode no longer pleased even the dedicatee.[12] Presumably the pleasure grounds are open (like those of Stowe) for the education of even the common people, but rather than teaching the park has become a subject of what Jonson called 'envious show', for the remark 'how happy!' is not philosophical in context, but covetous. This is a consumer society dedicated to the endless pursuit of the expensive demands of taste, fashion, novelty and ostentatious magnificence.

Commerce depends for its very existence on the creation of continual material wants, which wants can never be a source of happiness (in the true philosophical sense) for they can never be satisfied, or ever satisfy. As Glenthorn remarks, he is continually going shopping 'merely to pass an idle hour' and because he 'could not help buying something' (p. 7) and the products of his expenditure have a Juvenalesque extravagance: 'the immense cost of the fruit at my desserts was recorded; the annual expense of the vast nosegays of hot-house flowers worn daily by the footmen who clung behind my coach was calculated; the hundreds of wax-lights, which burned nightly in my house, were numbered by the idle admirers of folly' (p. 6).

The ennui from which Glenthorn suffers is a corruption of the ideal form of Ciceronian/Palladian philosophical leisure, *cum dignitate otium*. Accordingly the historical paradigm Edgeworth uses is the decline and fall of the Roman empire. Ennui is the product of what she calls 'luxurious indolence' (p. 1). Juvenal wrote, *saevior armis, luxuria incubuit*[13] – more savage than arms, the taste for luxury subverts civilisation and, he added, avenges the world that our empire has subdued. It was an enlightened commonplace, and one which Byron called in *Childe Harold* 'the moral of all human tales':

> Wealth, vice, corruption, – barbarism at last.
> And History, with all her volumes vast,
> Hath but *one* page ... (IV, 964f.)

The decline and fall analogy is explicitly spelled out. 'The wealthy and noble youths of Britain' are likened directly by Edgeworth to their Roman counterparts during the worst days of the empire (p. 15). Hence the sexual libertinism of high society (represented especially by the flight of Lady Glenthorn). The pursuit of selfish pleasure and material indulgence corrupts even marriage, the bedrock of civil society. In this respect *Ennui* is closely analogous to Austen's *Mansfield Park* and Byron's *Don Juan*. Closely related to the re-emergence of 'barbarism at last' is the taste of a decadent *luxuria* for cruelty and violence, of which the gladiatorial games in Rome were the most notorious example. Thus the death of the Irishman in the boxing ring in England is described as a 'savage spectacle' like the games in the Coliseum of old. This message is spelled out: 'the Romans were most eager for the fights of gladiators during the reigns of the most effeminate and cruel emperors, and in the decline of all public spirit and virtue' (pp. 35–6). This directly relates (in terms of plot and theme) to the scars on the head of Christy O'Donoghoe. But whereas the wild Irish boy has received his wounds in drunken faction fights at fairs, the Irish boxer has been killed in England as part of the regulated entertainment of civilised high society. In this respect civilisation is more savage than the savages.

Byron (in ironic Spenserian imitation) spelled out the implications in his monitory description of the dying gladiator: 'Shall he expire/And unaveng'd? – Arise! ye Goths, and glut your ire!' (*Childe Harold*, IV, 1268–9). No reader would doubt that for ancient Rome one might equally read modern Europe. Edgeworth perceives the same historical analogy, but unlike the rebellious poet she has no desire to call on the Goths to rise. Yet the barbarians were at the gates. Consider the squalor of Glenthorn's Irish tenantry in their 'mud-walled' cabins, literally pigsties, with the dunghill before the door and the spreading pool of raw sewage breeding deadly disease (p. 60). This is the breeding ground for the 1798 rising, which insurrection was a direct product of the decline and fall of the *ancien régime* in France. 'Ennui' itself, a French expression, indicates that Glenthorn is infected with a mental disease potentially as fatal as an Irish dunghill.

The movement to Glenthorn Castle is a step back from the *luxuria* of contemporary Europe to a period still retarded in a pre-Tudor period. When Glenthorn comes home (but to a home that, he will discover, is not his home) it is as a 'feudal' lord, someone whom apparently loyal vassals and dependants (p. 49) celebrate as a monarch who is long to reign over them. His estate shows all the disorder that Tudor administrators associated with the gavelkind and tanistry of the ancient clan system in Ireland, with its uncertain tenure, disputed possessions and hence constant demands for favour and succour from the chief of the sept. The multitudinous townlands and parks cry out for the (future) activities of an Ordnance Survey. The pleasures of exercising apparently unlimited power in such circumstances are graphically illustrated (for instance the futile attempt to provide the old nurse, Ellinor, with an improved, picturesque cottage, which is ruined in an instant by her squalid habits). The romanticism of the scene attracts the Gothic imagination – witness Glenthorn's first day at the castle:

> When I awoke, I thought that I was on shipboard; for the first sound I heard was that of the sea booming against the castle walls. I arose, looked out of the window of my bedchamber, and saw that the whole prospect bore an air of savage wildness. As I contemplated the scene, my imagination was seized with the idea of remoteness from civilized society: the melancholy feeling of solitary grandeur took possession of my soul. (p. 51)

Glenthorn's imagination, 'carried... centuries back' (p. 49) has been shaped by Irish Gothicism. The passage sets up the possibility that this is the kind of place where he might meet a Glorvina strayed from the fantasy world of Morgan, or he might himself become a Milesian chief such as Maturin invented. 'Sherwood', in England, had been the home of romantic outlaws, in remote times, but in Ireland the present-day kerns of Glenthorn's estate see him as their potential warlord (that is what the leader of the clan is for).

But once society returns to that order of things then the old feudal custom of fostering produces an alternative claimant for the estate. Edgeworth flirts knowingly with the Gothic (like Austen in *Northanger Abbey*) in her use of the motif of the return of the repressed in her interchange between Glenthorn (who is in fact of Irish peasant stock) and his foster brother, Christy O'Donoghoe (who is the legitimate heir to the Glenthorn estate). The changeling motif is representative of symbolic tanistry, and what the allegory insists upon is a strict process of legitimacy for the inheritance of the estate. Anything else is anarchy. As Edgeworth has Christy state, once you begin to question title to property in Ireland you must go back to Adam, 'the father of all', to establish possession (p. 190). Thus it is by strict process of law (by marriage to Cecilia Delamere) that Glenthorn/O'Donoghoe ultimately (in a convoluted plot) returns to the estate as a reformist landlord who deserves both his independence and proper 'distinction' by virtue of his success in his newly acquired profession of the law. This is a Ciceronian analogy in its origin, and an Irish equivalent to the establishment of the Percys in *Patronage*.

The burning of Glenthorn castle is a farewell to the old order of things in Ireland. It is the point of departure from the world of *Castle Rackrent* (to see it as foreshadowing the 1920s would be a postcolonialist fantasy!) Christy's letter, which tells of the event, *mutatis mutandis* is analogous to the discourse of Thady Quirk in the earlier fiction, and the allegory is simple. Firstly, in the nationalist context it would be disastrous to attempt a return to the 'barbaric magnificence' of the coshery and tanistry and the tribes of 'vagabond relations' of pre-Tudor Ireland (pp. 228–9). Secondly, contemporary Jacobinism is equally destructive. Members of different classes should stick to their own class:

> The castle's burnt down all to the ground, and my Johnny's dead, and I wish I was dead in his place. The occasion of his death was owing to drink, which he fell into from getting too much money, and nothing to do.... When I came to my sinses, I was lying on the ground in the court, and all confusion and screaming still, and the flames raging worse than ever.... I will go back to my forge, and, by the help of God, forget at my work what has passed. (pp. 245–7)

So much for 'romantic Ireland, dead and gone': feudal, drunken, improvident. It is 'all confusion', as Christy states, and as damaging to the poor themselves as to the property of the rich. 'My Johnny's dead', his father laments, delivering a message that O'Casey's Juno Boyle was to reiterate more eloquently at the time of a later civil war. But as Edgeworth writes, 'Glenthorn Castle is now rebuilding...'

The crux is, rebuilding in what way? The simple answer is, on the model of Edgeworthstown. Educative fiction produces potential model answers, and a romantic happy ending gives the reader a heroine whose allegorical name (Cecilia Delamere) tells that harmony will come to Ireland from over the sea, presumably by Irish blood acquiring English education and old aristocracy acquiring utilitarian middle-class skills.[14]

But as the wise and sceptical Scots economist M'Leod, observes, 'time is necessary to enforce the sanctions of legislation and civilisation' (p. 77). The word 'enforce' suggests that legality and civilisation might not be easily achieved, even in the course of 'time'. But that is future history. In the present there remain the ruins of Glenthorn Castle, somehow to be reconstructed, and the continuing presence of Sherwood Park.

This summary of *Ennui* stands to the novel like the argument to the complex allegory of a canto in *The Faerie Queene*. No more is intended than to establish the existence of the place–time spectrum, and to give a local habitation and a name to the mere abstraction of the dichotomy between the savage and the civilised. Even in summary, however, it is apparent that the loci stand in ironic relation (their significations are relative) and the frontier between them is permeable. Thus the Protean protagonist moves freely from place to place (and hence through time) and as he moves his nomination changes. He is O'Shaughnessy, a Milesian warlord, O'Donoghoe, an Irish peasant, Lord Glenthorn, an English aristocrat, and then he accepts 'the name and arms of Delamere' (p. 244). Not until Woolf's *Orlando* will one find such a (postmodern) destabilisa-tion of identity in country house fiction.

The signification of places also changes. The chronotropic dichotomy of Sherwood Park and Glenthorn Castle of this summary is not absolute, but subject to reinterpretation. Witness what happens to the civilisation and savagery theme in the Ormsby Villa episode. The villa is a version of Sherwood Park translated to Ireland, but here the patriotic Lady Geraldine swings the idea of historical progress by the tail. She addresses the country house set:

> Go on, my friends; go on, and prosper; beg and borrow all the patterns and precedents you can collect of the newest fashions of folly and vice. Make haste, make haste; they don't reach our remote island fast enough. We Irish might live in innocence half a century longer, if you didn't expedite the progress of profligacy. (p. 111)

Her diatribe opposes the noble savagery of an 'age of innocence' (her Ireland) to the transpontine corruptions of the civilisation of Sherwood Park, 'the progress of profligacy'. This places the 'savage wildness' of Glenthorn's Irish demesne in a quite different cultural context, and reverses the imperial interpretation of progress. But that only scratches the surface of Edgeworth's ironic mode. Lady Geraldine is an Irish equivalent of Shakespeare's Gonzalo, talking Utopianism to a sophisti-cated court. In practice, astute manipulation of the patronage system of the *ancien régime* secures her and her husband an imperial appointment in India. This patriot Geraldine is a proto Lady Gregory (not a latent Lord Edward). Profligate Ormsby Villa is also patriot Ormsby Villa, a place of Utopian idealism and the base for sound imperial government. Every change in signification alters with it the interpretation of the other symbolic loci tied together in their time–place nexus. (The same complexity involves Coole at the end of the Union.)

In this kind of writing, therefore, signification is unstable. One could continue to qualify this defining sketch of *Ennui* indefinitely. There is process, not stasis. In the Heraclitean flux one never sees the same place twice, since in the meantime one has become aware of other places. Rebuilding Glenthorn Castle is, therefore, a necessary process as continuing reconstruction is historically inevitable. The problem with Sherwood Park, as Glenthorn states, is that it was 'completely finished'. Hence it was both perfected and without the potential for continuation.

Like a civil society built upon a tectonic fault line, in *The Absentee* a simple moral (Edgeworthstown) is built on the shifting sands of Edgeworth's irony. Ostensibly the moral for the country house gentry is much the same as that in *Ennui*. It is made specific (with Youngian illustration) in *The Absentee* that the landed classes should reside on their estates, employ good agents and improve their tenantry. As far as enlightened unionism is concerned, Lord Colambre, the novel's protagonist, is born in Ireland of an English mother and an Irish father. He is educated in England at 'one of our great public schools' (p. 94), contemplates a military career fighting for the United Kingdom against Bonapartism, but returns to his native land to live the life of a country gentleman. His marriage to his putative 'cousin' Miss Reynolds (aka 'Grace Nugent') is a further (symbolic) sign of cultural union. Grace Nugent is a celebrated Irish name, fit for bardic song, as we are told at the wedding feast, but Grace's Protean nominations – St Omar/Reynolds/Nugent/Colambre – and her cosmopolitan ambience (conceived in Austria, the daughter of an English officer, she was reared in England and married in Ireland) make her even more transnational than O'Shaugnessy/O'Donoghoe/Glenthorn/Delamere in *Ennui*. (She even has an Irish *doppelgängerin*, another 'Grace' whose peasant marriage on the Clonbrony estate mirrors hers.) One may reasonably conclude that nationalist ethnicity is as alien to Edgeworth's enlightened sensibility as religious sectarianism. The key words for her are not national but cosmopolitan.

Characters are praised for their knowledge, letters, science and morality, (p. 335) and the attributes that go with gentle birth and breeding are politeness, noble sentiments and magnanimity (p. 124). This is to be both liberal and British (p. 113). In this kind of crude summary, *The Absentee* emerges as a (naively?) optimistic exercise in a kind of cosmopolitan and enlightened feudalism. We end with the rich man in his castle celebrated by the poor man (the Irish Larry Brady) at his gate.

This pointed moral is undoubtedly present in *The Absentee* (refine it a point or two if you wish). But, just as in *Ennui*, the rebuilding of the Clonbrony estate (which is going to rack and ruin at the hands of 'Old Nick', the bad Irish land agent) and the cementing of the union are both the work of a future time, and therefore constitute a Platonic resolution. (One might use a Spenserian analogy, for we are concerned with a quest and therefore will never actually reach the court of the 'faerie' queen). In the meantime the state of things is imperfect, relativistic, mutable.

The potential complexities of the ironic mode (the shifting of the tectonic plates) are indicated by a general summary in *Ennui*. If the existence of an ironic substructure is granted in general, in *The Absentee* details of the text can be probed more closely to explore Edgeworth's self-questioning, her sense of historical relativity and her awareness of the deep-rootedness of that problem called 'Ireland'. Our concern is both with the uncertain dichotomy in Irish history between the civil and the savage, and with the working out of that dichotomy through the intercalation of historical place, especially London, Tusculum, Halloran Castle and the Clonbrony demesne. The sense of place in *The Absentee* is far more dramatic and more realistic than in *Ennui*. For instance, the *luxuria* that threatens decadent civilisation with decline and fall (the Roman syndrome) is established in *Ennui* primarily by allegorical and literary allusion, but in the brilliant drama of the first chapters of *The Absentee* it is, as it were, sold to Lady Clonbrony by the yard by Mr Soho. Thus we see it in the oriental exoticism of the wallpaper he palms off on her, and this commercial commodity of empire – in actual experience, not just by historical syndrome – provides the *mise en scène* for Lady Clonbrony's social humiliation and financial ruin.

Accordingly the questions posed about civilisation in *The Absentee* are profounder because they are more fully realised. Rather than being naively optimistic, the imaginary ideal that fiction creates (cultural union on an Edgeworthian estate) is brought into critical juxtaposition with the recalcitrant nature of things fully dramatised. One may begin with a traditional example of the civilisation/savagery dichotomy. It is a passage closely related to Lady Geraldine's 'progress of profligacy' speech in *Ennui*. Here Lady Dashfort tells how she was bored by Irish society in Dublin:

> Yawn, did I – glad of it – the yawn sent them away, or I should have snored; – rude, was I? they won't complain. To say I was rude to them would be to say, that I did not think it worth my while to be otherwise. Barbarians! are not we the civilised English, come to teach them manners and fashions? Whoever does not conform, and swear allegiance too, we shall keep out of the English pale. (p. 197)

At first glance Edgeworth's use of such speech is apparently simple since Lady Dashfort, who is morally corrupt, is cast here in the role of a 'stage' Englishwoman and is merely wrong. As a character in the fiction she dramatically embodies 'the progress of profligacy', and obviously Edgeworth did not approve this kind of racial arrogance. But is it that easy? This is not merely an ideological statement. It is a fully dramatised speech and Lady Dashfort is 'on stage' for her auditors. Like Lady Geraldine, Lady Dashfort is knowingly playing a role. She has adopted the persona of stage Englishwoman. It is a self-aware, witty self-caricature and also a black, bleak, comic utterance. (Wilde frequently used the same device, witness Lady Bracknell.)

If this is so, then one of the potential devices of the comic mode is to speak the unspeakable from behind the mask (as any classicist would be aware). Lady Dashfort says (obliquely) what Edgeworth would not admit directly about her own position at Edgeworthstown: that 'barbarian' Ireland had been invaded by England and that the English in Ireland are both a dominant, invasive, self-nominated civilising force, and also aware of their position as a beleaguered garrison within 'the pale'. Historically Lady Dashfort's imagination is stuck somewhere about the time of the Statute of Kilkenny. One of the idealistic intentions of unionism, of course, was to move history forward. But here the historical residue of ignorance, prejudice and fear surfaces again, albeit associated with a morally corrupt character and leavened by comedy, but nonetheless something that might be interpreted as a Freudian displacement of Edgeworth's unease at how she came to be where she was in history. (There is an obvious parallel case in Jane Austen's intrusion of Sir Thomas Bertram's slave plantations in *Mansfield Park*.)

Postcolonial criticism would readily go along with this. But this is still too superficial a reading. Lady Dashfort, in her juxtaposition of civilisation and barbarity, is right as well as wrong. Ultimately she is merely repeating, in comic parody, the standard historical position of Edmund

Spenser, Davies, Young and Beaufort. But it is these authors who, in *The Absentee*, are specifically recommended by Sir James Brooke (a model gentleman) to Lord Colambre as those who 'afforded him most satisfaction' in getting to know Ireland (p. 178). In this mode of 'getting to know', the imposition of civility on Ireland (its enforcement, as M'Leod would say) was both necessary and right. We have returned emphatically to the point of entry into Irish history of the present enquiry and to the intrinsic justification for the establishment of the country house order. Moreover Sir James's list is historically progressive. What in Young was emergent has been regularised, 'mapped' by Beaufort. In this context Lady Dashfort is like Jonathan Swift's 'modest proposer'. What she says is monstrous, yet logically necessary given the ineluctable nature of things.

Ironically read, therefore, Lady Dashfort is both wrong and right. English culture was an agent of civilisation in Ireland because it was progressive. To go back would be to return to sectarian and territorial war, the residual state of things at Glenthorn Castle in *Ennui*, re-emergent (as Edgeworth depicts it) in the insurrection of 1798. Thus Lord Colambre, as a forward looking unionist, had 'formed friendships in England; he was fully sensible of the superior comforts, refinement, and information, of English society' (p. 94). The word 'superior' is directly related to Lady Dashfort's own attitude. The role model for the ideal Irish landlord (at Clonbrony Castle) is the 'cultivated, enlightened, independent English country gentleman', who is described, alluding to the classical tradition of Horace's *Beatus ille* epode, as 'the happiest, perhaps, of human beings' (p. 143). At this point in her fiction Edgeworth has entirely written out of the story the ironies that involve the 'happy man' of Sherwood Park in *Ennui*.

England, of course, is threatened by 'the progress of profligacy' (this theme is emphatic in the dramatisation of degenerative oriental luxury with which this fiction begins), but in comparison Ireland has scarcely emerged from savagery. That irony, fundamental in *Ennui*, is still operative in *The Absentee*. Without Colambre's imposition the reformed Larry Brady, whose feudal testimony ends the novel, would have become a poteen-addled vagrant, whose way of dealing with Nicholas Garraghty, the bad Irish agent, would have been to burn the villain alive (instead of his effigy).[16] Meanwhile there still exists in Ireland a dangerous residue of an underclass, 'the old uneducated race, whom no one can help, because they will never help themselves' (p. 206). They have surfaced on the bad estate of Killpatrick (an allegorical name?) According to this interpretation the old uneducated classes, whom no one can help, have placed themselves without the pale (to return to Lady Dashfort) of the new Ireland.

The clearest indication, however, that the dichotomy between civilisation and barbarity remains valid as an historical category is Sir James Brooke's description of the decline then rise of Dublin after the Union. First the city was denuded of its moral aristocracy, who either removed to London or retired 'disgusted and in despair to their houses in the country' before an influx of a vulgarian middle class (Lady Dashfort's 'barbarians'). But when the 'new men' (*novi homines*) had been reduced to their proper place by ridicule or destroyed by extravagance, then:

> that part of the Irish aristocracy, who, immediately upon the first incursions of the vulgarians, had fled in despair to their fastnesses in the country, hearing of the improvements which had gradually taken place in society, and assured of the final expulsion of the barbarians, ventured from their retreats, and returned to their posts in town. So that now ... you find a society in Dublin composed of a most agreeable and salutary mixture of birth and education, gentility and knowledge, manner and matter; and you see pervading the whole new life and energy, new talent, new ambition, a desire and a determination to improve and be improved. (p. 181)

So Sir James Brooke reports. He is using the same historical vocabulary as Lady Dashfort, and his sense of class is equally acute. But his tone is manifestly different, as is his progressive attitude. For him 'the pale' (the town) is open to all those of 'birth and education, gentility and knowledge' liberally found in Ireland, and to whose presence Lady Dashfort is wilfully blind. Accordingly, his interpretation of the dichotomy between civilisation and barbarity seems to be privileged at this juncture because, like Edgeworth, he is committed to 'improvement'. On the other hand, like Lady Dashfort's speech, this is a position fully dramatised. It is how a man like Sir James might see the world, and as McCormack and Walker (1972) have shrewdly commented,[15] we do not actually see the refined society that Sir James represents – the embodiment of his brave new world is lacking.

This lack should be fulfilled on the ideal country estate. Tusculum, Halloran Castle and the Clonbrony estate are the three major cultural sites realistically created and symbolically explored in *The Absentee*. They allude to Platonic ideals, but they are not themselves idealised. They are sites that interrogate the inherited traditions of European civilisation. (In comparison Killpatrick and Oranmore in *The Absentee* are merely brief examples of estate management and no more than utilitarian exemplars.) From what paradigm do they emerge, and how do they relate to that paradigm?

The villa called 'Tusculum' and Halloran Castle are a contrasted dyad. They represent the two great architectural traditions of the West: the classical, grounded in the Roman empire and subsequently revived in the Enlightenment by Palladianism; and the Gothic, deriving from the overthrow of Rome by the forces of barbarism. But paradoxically, that overthrow replaced the corrupt luxury of a decadent imperialism with a revitalising force. By the time Edgeworth was writing Gothic architecture (technically a major international style) had become associated with national identity, and accordingly with national liberty (witness the Gothic 'Temple of Liberty' in the patriotic Whig garden of Stowe). Therefore, Tusculum and Halloran Castle, symbolically involve a history of European culture and are variants of the relationship of Sherwood Park to Glenthorn Castle in *Ennui*. The choice between the classical and Gothic alternatives was to acquire, in Edgeworth's lifetime, substantive symbolic signification. One might instance the debate in England on whether to reconstruct the Parliament of the United Kingdom in Gothic or classical style, and the refurbishment of Windsor Castle as a national icon; and, conversely, across the Atlantic, witness the determination of the founders of the Roman republic revived in the 'empire for liberty' to build upon the classical model, the Pantheon recreated as the Capitol in Washington and the use of the Palladian villa as the model for the president's dwelling.

Edgeworth's choice of names for her classical and Gothic loci is allegorical. Tusculum alludes to the most famous of Cicero's villas and the location of the *Tusculan Disputations*. Halloran Castle alludes to Sylvester O'Halloran, the antiquarian celebrant of the pre-Norman ('barbarian') history of Ireland and the reclaimant of Ossian (the Celtic Homer) for the Irish. Ideally the two traditions might fuse into one. Thus Ben Jonson imaginatively blended the two in the *Ur* poem of the English country house tradition when using classic allusion to describe Gothic form in *To Penshurst*. So in Ireland, might diverse traditions be reconciled in union?

The experiential quality of the fiction, however, shows only the lack of ideal resolution in villa or castle. What Swift would have called 'the blunders' of Tusculum are an obvious example. It is to this that the Ciceronean ideal has been reduced by Mrs Rafferty, who is one of the 'barbarians' of Sir James Brooke's discourse. It would be a curious game to track down all the literary sources and allusions that underlie the satire, and might have no end. The 'dish of fish' brought across Ireland from Sligo (p. 186) has its origin in the giant sturgeon of Juvenal, and the failed dinner party (a parody of the Socratic symposium) derives from Trimalchio's nouveau riche banquet in *The Satyricon*. To come closer to Edgeworth's own times, perhaps the blundering Irish servants are of national invention, out of Swift en route to Somerville and Ross, and it might be difficult to end a list of contemporary passages satirising the false taste for the picturesque. But the mockery of the 'grotto full of shells, and a little hermitage full of earwigs, and a little ruin full of looking-glass' (p. 125) is just the kind of sardonic thing Swift might have written, mocking even his friend Pope at Twickenham. The moral of all this is spelled out by Lord Colambre: 'in whatever station or with whatever fortune, extravagance, that is the living beyond our income, must lead to distress and meanness, and end in shame and ruin', (p. 187) and he thinks of his own mother aping metropolitan fashion in London just as much as provincial Mrs Rafferty.

But the symbolism of Tusculum is more complex than Lord Colambre's simple moralisation. There is at the villa 'taste' as well as 'incongruity', 'ingenuity' and even 'genius', as well as 'absurdity...and blunder' (p. 184). It is not enough to claim, as Sir James Brooke does, that the shopkeeper should stick to his shop and not emulate the gentry (as the smith should stick to his forge in *Ennui*). Mrs Rafferty has a hunger of the imagination that desires something she does not understand, but ideally what she desires is the culture of the European elite. She knows that a villa should have a portico (although her own pillars are 'hollow'); her desire to create a picturesque garden identifies her aspiration with *le jardin anglais* as one of the great embodiments of enlightened culture; and before one becomes too dismissive of her 'little conservatory' and the 'little grapery' one might take an imaginary walk with Catherine Morland around the grounds of General Tilney and ask what might be the greater excellence of a big conservatory and a big grapery? Mrs Rafferty builds, we are told, merely 'for show' (which has always been a term of condemnation in country house literature, as opposed to building 'for use'), but all architecture embodies symbolism of form. What Mrs Rafferty is trying to achieve, albeit through partially misunderstood signs that no longer serve a function, is the civilisation of Ireland. Hers is the new middle-class world, the *nouveau régime* that, willy nilly, is the emergent replacement for the *ancien régime* throughout nineteenth-century Europe. If she fails, then what future for inherited civilisation, confined only to an educated elite of the wealthy?

Indeed what exactly is the basis for mocking Mrs Rafferty's blunders? To take a comparatively simple example, imagine Thomas Jefferson seeking to educate the ignorant about the right and wrong of porticos (one intention of his architectural design for the University of Virginia). The discourse of educative civilisation would begin with the modular relationship of the masculine body to the Pythagorean mathematics of the universe and the five orders of architecture, it would then proceed to a neo-Palladian moralisation of the transfer of temple porticos to the facades of country villas, and ultimately Jefferson would claim that this *sorites* constituted a universal norm. There are, however, two major problems with this: it is wrong in every instance, indeed it is no more than a preposterous fantasy; and it is pedantically non-utilitarian. All Mrs Rafferty really needs is a veranda to her house. Everything else has no relation to the everyday needs of her world.

But is Halloran Castle preferable? That Count O'Halloran is a civilised gentleman is not in question. He derives his title from the Holy Roman Empire and he can converse in Latin with Lord Colambre over the head of a Heathcock. In class terms it is appropriate that the count should own the castle, and we are specifically told that he is 'a fine old military-looking gentleman' (p. 214). This is praise, but it relates the count to the historical origins and function of the castle. His roots are in those feudal times when Ireland (like England) was divided by the barons' wars. Each warlord won and held his territory by force of arms. Indeed Lady Dashfort calls O'Halloran 'my conqueror', which leads at once to Lord Colambre's correction that these are not the times of the 'barbarous Scythian' (p. 215). The allusion is to Herodotus and to the Persian invasion of Scythia (a parallel to the English invasion of Ireland), but one that is rejected as not appropriate. The castle is now a peaceful country seat. The armed forces of the United Kingdom, in the service of the state, have replaced the old bands of kerns. Hence O'Halloran's recommendation to Lord Colambre that he defend the liberty of his country by fighting in Spain against Napoleon. That is an advance in civilisation within the state, although an advance that has replaced internecine struggle only by international conflict. The proper function of a gentleman, as the count sees it, is still to carry arms.

Because O'Halloran's country seat belongs to the old order of things, it is appropriate that it is also a museum. His extraordinary collection of anti-quities records a dead culture: brass-headed spears, urns full of ashes, old horns, golden ornaments, bones of elk and moosedeer, spermaceti ... Since there is a reasonable probability that Count O'Halloran is Edgeworth's reworking of the Prince of Inismore in *The Wild Irish Girl*, her enlightened rationality deposits all that sort of thing as so much historical sediment. There is, however, an 'almost extinct' Irish wolf-hound, still of age to breed, whose name (with obvious symbolic resonance) is Hannibal – the great foe of Rome. A present of the breed is made to England at the end of the novel, both as an appropriate expression of the old 'gift culture' to which the antiquarian count belongs and as a sign that warfare is now at an end and the Union cemented. (Hence too, appropriately, the count's suggestion that the militia – that is, the local armed forces – of each country should now be exchanged for mutual advantage.) The idea that one might back an O'Brien on the one hand or a Fitzgerald on the other belongs in a museum of antiquities.

But then so do the count and his castle. He is a curious eccentric (witness his anarchic menagerie). Symbolically Halloran Castle is analogous to the *nouveau riche* villa of Mrs Rafferty. It too fails in its intention. The count is trying to modernise the castle by turning it into an 'excellent house'. But he has failed, and will never succeed for it never will be finished. 'I live like many other Irish gentlemen', the count admits, 'who never are, but always to be, blest with a good house. I began on too large a scale, and can never hope to live to finish it' (p. 220). Once again the ideal is not present but somewhere else, not here, not now. The passage ends with a symbolic description of the landscape when Lady Dashfort and Lord Colambre, united at least in a common educated taste, admire the prospect from the castle and ask the name of a distant hill. '"Ah!" said the count, "that hill was once covered with fine wood; but it was all cut down two years ago."' Ancient timber is traditionally associated in country house literature with the continuity of ancient families and the fertility and prosperity of the estate. The denuded countryside around the castle testifies to the economic decline and transitory nature of the ancient order of which the childless count is the last scion. The kind of civilisation he represents will finish with his life. The culture of the castle is all but dead; the culture of the villa only blunders into being.

Since Garraghty's destruction and purloinment of the timber on the Clonbrony estate is one of the most shocking signs of corruption that Lord Colambre discovers, there is a clear link between the landscape around Halloran Castle and the conclusion of the fiction. Replacing old timber is not amenable to an instant fix, even by Mr Burke (whose namesake, Yeats wrote, believed the state was like a tree). Nonetheless an appropriate ending for the novel would be for classical and Gothic tradition (Tusculum and Halloran Castle) somehow to be rectified, revitalised and combined on the Clonbrony estate. This is a resolution that Edgeworth was to explore in greater detail in her subsequent Irish novel, *Ormond*. But here the importation by Lady Colambre of 'natural flowers' on the white velvet of the chairs of the drawing room (and the burning of the old yellow damask) is scarcely a convincing way of blending diverse traditions. On the contrary, it might equally suggest that the family still carries with it the very taste for luxury that had already proved so dangerous.

Presumably the literary model for the family's return is Sir Charles Grandison's homecoming (a source that Edgeworth uses more overtly in *Ormond*), and the Richardsonian stops are pulled out for all they are worth. Compare, for instance, Larry Brady's account of the family showing itself on the terrace, with the housekeeper's address to Lady Grandison in Richardson:

> My lady *laning* on my young lord, and Miss Grace Nugent that was, the beautifullest angel that ever you set eyes on, with the finest complexion and sweetest of smiles, *laning* upon the ould lord's arm, who had his hat off, bowing to all, noticing the old tenants as he passed by name. Oh, there was great gladness and tears in the midst; for joy I could scarce keep from myself. (p. 380)

> Don't your ladyship see, how all his servants love him as they attend him at table? How they watch his eye in silent reverence – indeed, madam, we all adore him; and have prayed morning, noon, and night, for his coming hither, and settling among us. And now is the happy time; forgive me, madam; I am no flatterer; but we all say, He has brought another angel to bless us. (VII, 8)

The general similarities between the two passages are obvious. At least Edgeworth is more skilled at avoiding the sense of hypocritical sycophancy that is suggested by Richardson's housekeeper. But Larry Brady's letter in Edgeworth is a swift and abrupt coda to an ironic and multivalent novel, whereas Richardson's account of the return to Grandison Hall is one of the longest passages of idealistic country house fiction in English literature. The pious Sir Charles has already achieved what Mrs Rafferty and Count O'Halloran have failed to do. He has remodelled his house in modern (that is, neoclassical) style, but has retained the ancient Hall as a centre of care and hospitality (compare the filthy 'presence chamber' at Clonbrony Castle).

Unlike Sir Charles and Lady Grandison, the family at Clonbrony castle are seen, through Brady's eyes, as if at a great distance, like remote icons where distance in space may also suggest distance in time. They are smaller than life, no longer gifted with speech, leaning one upon the other for support. They have ceased to be characters in the fiction and are now totems. Consider, in this context, how Larry Brady describes the entry of the family to the park:

> we all got to the great gate of the park before sunset, and as fine an evening as ever you see; with the sun shining on the tops of the trees, as the ladies noticed; the leaves changed, but not dropped, though so late in the season. I believe the leaves knew what they were about, and kept on, on purpose to welcome them.

This is very much a 'last September' or Chekovian image. It is sympathetic melancholy, for it is suffused with Larry's pathetic fallacy, but the meaning of 'the leaves changed, but not dropped' is clear enough. At least it is better than Lord Colambre's first sight of the family churchyard where he saw 'several boys (with more of skin apparent than clothes)... playing at hustlecap upon a tombstone, which, upon nearer observation, he saw was the monument of his own family'. (p. 261) Given these dark intimations of mortality, it would be inappropriate for Edgeworth to expatiate on the return to the estate in Richardsonian mode. The analogy is there, but there only for the trope to be shown and to be charged with the melancholy of suspended decline and fall. Here the emphasis is not on the rebuilding of the castle, but on the arrest of a latent but natural and inevitable process of seasonal change.

The process of change is critical in *Ormond*. Ostensible thematic repetition in the Irish tales is thematic variation, and thus historical complication.

The end of *Ormond* employs a familiar dialectic. The protagonist, Henry Ormond ('Prince Harry' as he is popularly known), has to choose between two estates: Castle Hermitage, the former seat of the bankrupt political 'jobber' Sir Ulick O'Shane (Ormond's former guardian), and Corny Castle, indeterminately situated in a region called 'the Black Islands', whose feudal lord, 'King Corny', has died in a hunting accident, killed by the explosion of his own experimental gun. Ormond chooses Corny Castle for two reasons. The first relates to the crucial issue of legitimacy. Since Sir Ulick O'Shane's son and natural representative is still living, Ormond, an orphan who was fostered in a Irish cabin, decides he has no right to Castle Hermitage, whereas in the Black Islands he is popularly recognised (by a form of symbolic tanistry) as the lawful representative of the deceased King Corny. His second reason is that in the Black Islands 'he might do a great deal of good, by carrying on his old friend's improvements, and by farther civilizing the people'(p. 378). Ormond chooses legitimacy, improvement (through a substantial investment of imperial funds) and civilisation.

The invocation of 'the people' in Edgeworth's conclusion suggests an affinity between Ormond's civilising mission and classic Whig Enlightenment principles. Compare the Foxite invocation of 'our sovereign, the people' in the United Kingdom, and the self-identification of 'we, the people' as the sovereign authority in the republican United States. Reference to the people of Ireland in this historical context is highly charged, for the action of *Ormond* is set on the eve of the American and French Revolutions and the concomitant movement of United Irishmen. But the people of Ireland, in Edgeworth's fiction, show strong reactionary tendencies. The demand of the Black Islanders is for 'Prince Harry' to come and reign over them, which is indicative of a regressive tendency towards the prostitute feudalism satirised in the retrospective *Castle Rackrent*. The family name of their new prince (Ormond) is, of course, that of one of the greatest feudal overlords in Irish history, the Butlers. Although 'Prince Harry', like Shakespeare's Prince Hal (to whom he is also compared), has the common touch (fostered by the people), the civilisation with which he is associated descends on his people from above. He is their sovereign (to reverse the Foxite allusion). Moreover a common designation for the islanders in *Ormond* is 'savages'. It is not civilisation as an accomplished state that is the Utopian end of *Ormond*. It is a process that is translated to an alternative social order. It is a process that in late-eighteenth-century Europe had been (and still was) subject to major revolutionary challenge.

Ormond is concerned not with Edgeworth's own post-Union Ireland, but with the historical shift that made union a necessity of state. The dyadic structure of the fiction concerns not merely two contrasted country estates (between which the protagonist chooses) but also a critical division *in extremis* in European culture between the apogee of civilisation represented by the *ancien régime* in Paris and the related, but polar opposite, Black Islands. Allegorically the islands derive from *The Arabian Nights* or from the idea of *Ultima Thule, Gezirat Thule* (isles of darkness). Accordingly they are an imaginary realm and we repeatedly described as separated from 'the continent', thus beyond the island of Ireland, beyond the island of Britain, off the continent of Europe, without location on any map. Allegorically the Black Islands, which mark something extracontinental, are essentially Irish if one understands Ireland as constituting an imaginary frontier where European culture, in crisis, comes face to face with its other.

The resolution of that crisis in *Ormond* involves an educative process as the protagonist is, as it were, a frontiersman. *Ormond* is a self-referential enquiry (for in itself the fiction embodies civilised values) into how what is wild can be made civil, and on the very cusp both geographically and historically where worlds collide. As so often in 'Irish' culture the fundamental issue had already been raised by Spenser, a poet who himself existed between two worlds. What is it that constitutes the education of a gentleman (his induction into the civil order) at a time when and in a place where the old courtly discipline seems to belong more to some ancient (faerie) realm than to present reality? So in Edgeworth, as Spenser's cultural heir, by what educative process does a Butler, Prince Harry, a hero not entirely of our time, become fitted to undertake the 'civilising' of the Black Islands of Ireland?

The specific textual analogies are initially to the reformation of Shakespeare's Hal, who like Ormond had 'run wild', (p. 11) and to Fielding's Tom Jones.[17] Edgeworth's fiction is structured on other ideal fictions that depend (of course) upon the reader being educated in a common English literary culture. Thus the drunken King Corny is a quasi Falstaffian figure whom Ormond must learn to regulate and incorporate into his development (rather than reject in Shakespeare's severer allegory). And if, unfortunately, Sir Ulick O'Shane is no squire Allworthy, better than Allworthy is the ideal figure of Richardson's Sir Charles Grandison, who inspires Ormond with a new role model as good landlord and good Christian. Edgeworth's protagonist accordingly progresses from Fielding to Richardson:

> In Sir Charles Grandison's history he read that of a gentleman, who, fulfilling every duty of his station in society, eminently *useful*, respected and beloved, as brother, friend, master of a family, guardian, and head of a large estate, was admired by his own sex, and, what struck Ormond far more forcibly, loved, passionately loved, by women – not by the low and profligate, but by the highest and most accomplished of the sex. (p. 86)

This, apparently, is simple enough. The Grandison of Grandison Hall, as in all Edgeworth's fiction, is a model country gentleman. Ormond is educated by reading model fiction, and Richardson's personification of morality is transformed through the warmth of Ormond's own passionate nature and, as one might expect from a female novelist, 'the highest and most accomplished of the sex' are elevated as the inspirational object of admiration and masculine desire. The Irish Tom Jones, inspired by the wisdom of his Sophia (Florence Annaly), will become the proper master of his family and guardian of his estate. That estate will be modelled, one may assume, on that of the Annalys themselves – itself a combination of Grandisonian idealism with Edgeworthian practical economics. Politically, it is a Whig conclusion if one reads the name 'Florence' as alluding to classical republican tradition, incorporated into the Annalys' estate in model Palladian architecture.

But if it were that simple the complexity of the dialectic would have yielded to the didacticism of the educational tract. As in the fundamental educative original, Spenser, nothing is as simple as it seems. There is something peculiarly old-fashioned about this adoption of a Richardsonian role model for a nineteenth-century fiction. Even for Ormond, in his *ancien régime* context, Grandison's 'dress and manner were too splendid, too formal for everyday use', his perpetual ceremonious bowing is alien and he seems all costume, like an 'old portrait' (p. 85f.) (This passage seems to have returned to Somerville's mind in *The Big House of Inver*.) The 'terrible array of *good people*' initially alienate Ormond, especially the long-windedness and 'perpetual egotism' of the heroine. Thus he has to learn to squeeze the juice of morality, as it were, from what seems even to an eighteenth-century reader to be an old text (and *après le déluge* of the French Revolution for Edgeworth's nineteenth-century audience). Even when Ormond has learnt to model himself on 'the good man', the lesson is at once peculiarly misapplied into a jejune idealisation of the worldly Dora as the abstract idea of a heroine who will teach him 'French, and drawing, and dancing, and improve his manners', (p. 90) or in short, provide merely the superfluities of civilisation. The Grandisonian model is morally correct, but curiously old-fashioned and misapplied.

But the implication of this literature with the culture of the country house is intrinsic. *Tom Jones* and *Sir Charles Grandison* are both country house novels. It is a set of duplicate books from the library of the Annalys' residence that first begins Ormond's education in 'the English and French classics', (p. 84) and it is in the library of Castle Hermitage that this education continues, now in juxtaposition with the social life of a great country house. At Castle Hermitage the pairing of Lord Chesterfield and Middleton's *Life* of Cicero replicates the progressive and ironised pairing of Fielding and Richardson. Chesterfield's *Letters* are recommended by Sir Ulick as a model for education (p. 224). The

Letters constitute a work that teaches manners (but without morals). This is an appropriate text for the library of Ormond's elegant, sophisticated but ultimately corrupted and soon to be destroyed guardian. Chesterfield's *Letters* represent the *ancien régime*. The example of Middleton's *Life* of Cicero is more positive. This is one of the eighteenth century's great works of classic republican hagiography. The philosopher statesman was a prototype for figures such as Washington and Jefferson. Middleton's *Life* is also one of the major vernacular sources for transmitting the country house ethos of Cicero's favourite villa at Tusculum (he had many). It is the country home:

> in which he took the greatest pleasure, for its delightful situation in the neighbourhood of Rome, and the convenience of an easy retreat from the hurry and the fatigues of the city: here he had built several rooms and galleries, in imitation of the schools and porticos of Athens, which he called, likewise, by their Attic names of the Academy and Gymnasium, and designed for the same use of philosophical conferences with his learned friends. (1810 ed. I, 151)

Middleton goes into substantial detail about Cicero's passion for furnishing the house, especially in the case of 'emblematic figures' of Greek statuary, Hercules as 'the proper deity of the Gymnasium' and Minerva 'of the Academy'. Above all Middleton tells of Cicero's empassioned commissions to his correspondent and friend Atticus in Athens, whose 'family of learned slaves' supply the Roman statesman with his 'very large collection of curious books'. This library, purchased by means of what Cicero calls his 'little rents' (!) will be 'the relief of my old age', and thus supplied he calls himself 'richer than Crassus' and despises 'the fine villas and gardens' of the merely rich. This is the ideal that Mrs Rafferty admires, but misapplies, in *The Absentee*, but although it is ideal, it is also 'self-evident' (to employ a word from the master of Monticello) that it depends on enormous imperial wealth, on the labour of others (the slaves) and (in an Irish context) on the model philosopher statesman also being an absentee.

But as with *Sir Charles Grandison* the ideal undergoes a process of change in Edgeworth's recension. The conclusion that Ormond draws from his reading undoubtedly derives from the classic idealisation of villa culture: 'The only place in the world I should wish for, sir, would be a place in the country', Ormond tells Sir Ulick (p. 217), but the word 'place' is ironised. It refers both to a country house *per se* and to 'place' in the political sense that Cicero and Sir Ulick would understand:

a position in the government of 'our country'. But reading the life of the philosopher statesman has led Ormond to reject a political career, for that would be to enter the corrupt milieu in which moves Sir Ulick, who sells principle for 'place'. Instead Ormond wishes for 'a place of my own, a comfortable house and estate, on which I could live independently and happily, with some charming amiable woman', in short, to be like the Percys in *Patronage*. This is, of course, an equally classically derived 'choice' (to allude to the title of Pomfret's once well-known poem), although sentimentally domesticated now in Christian marriage. But it is a paradoxical result of a course in reading Cicero. The historical reasons are clear, and may well have local analogy. For Cicero failed as a statesman in his desire to preserve the Roman republic. He was murdered in the civil war that followed the assassination of Julius Caesar, and he failed, so it was traditionally told, because the corruption of Rome (its *luxuria* and the concomitant decay of private and public morality) had gone so far that nothing could save the republic (a message readily derived from the opening of Livy's Roman history).

Plus ça change . . . , as the example of the political world in which Sir Ulick moves all too clearly demonstrates. Another revolution and war are on the horizon. But this is not to deny the seductive splendour of what Paine called 'the plumage' of country house culture and the *ancien régime*. Witness Castle Hermitage itself. The literary and allegorical function of the locus is made clear at once by the very naming of the house. The allusion is both to the Court of St Petersburg and to the idea of the country estate as a place of moral and philosophical retreat. A specific literary allusion establishes the relation of the place to the 'earthly paradise' described so lovingly in Spenser's *The Faerie Queene* (III, v), where an ailing knight is made well but then falls prey to another disease. Good and evil are intricately and inextricably woven together here (as Spenser's finest commentator, Milton, knew). Despite the longeurs of the great dinners at Castle Hermitage, there are other moments when the culture of the *ancien régime* blazes in all its splendour. There is a rich supply not only of material luxury, but of information on the ways of the world, 'a quick and happy intercourse of wit and knowledge' that 'quite delighted' and 'almost dazzled' the eyes of Ormond. 'Much was indeed beyond, or above, the reach of his present powers; but nothing was beyond his generous admiration – nothing above his future hopes of attainment' (p. 220). Thus to participate in the culture of a great country house is a civilising process, but that civilisation is inextricably bound up with an internal sickness.

The apex of the culture of the *ancien régime* was the court (witness Spenser), and the greatest court of eighteenth-century civilisation was that of Versailles. If the 'wild man' (fostered in an Irish cabin) is to become the agent of civilisation, then it is an appropriate culmination of his quest (to pursue the Spenserian analogy) that he should move from a country house setting to a *hôtel* in Paris when the power of France embodied the inherited and transmitted culture of Europe. Here too there is the same interplay between literature as a source of inspirational ideas and the social setting that ironises the literature. Reading allegorically, it is perhaps not without significance that Voltaire was not then in France and that Ormond does not meet the quarrelsome Rousseau. His literary guides (in a further course of literature) are D'Alembert, Marivaux, L'Abbé Morellet and especially Marmontel, and 'no evidence could be stronger than Marmontel's in favour of virtue and of domestic life' (p. 337). This is as straight a moral message as this fiction offers, but it is given at the public literary breakfasts of the Abbé Morellet towards the end of the *ancien régime* in Paris.

The induction of Ormond into Connal's 'hotel' serves to summarise the significance of the Parisian locus:

> Connal enjoyed Ormond's surprise at the magnificence of this hotel. After ascending a spacious staircase, and passing through antechamber after antechamber, they reached the splendid salon, blazing with lights, reflected on all sides in mirrors, that reached from the painted ceiling to the inlaid floor. (p. 310)

An 'hotel' is a kind of parody of a country house. It has the appurtenances of but is divorced from the organic relationship of house to productive land. One purchases in a city hotel what the country estate naturally supplies. Compare, thus, the self-sufficiency to which the dying feudalism of Corny Castle aspired under its 'king' to an hotel in Paris, *omnia cum pretio* (where all things have their price).[18] The hotel here is both an urban locale and one that is entirely inturned. There is no circumambient landscape to link house to nature. On the contrary, the only light is that of blazing candles (at great expense), which are 'reflected on all sides in mirrors'. This is a society that sees only reflections of itself – images that the same images beget – and Connal's hotel mimics the hall of mirrors at Versailles. The court also intrudes into the domestic space in the emphasis on ceremony of approach by ascending 'a spacious staircase' and passing 'through antechamber after antechamber'. This is the antithesis of democratic equality or any kind of human familiarity between people (compare the love that King Corny's people have for him in the Black Islands). The hotel has become a kind of theatre for magnificence, and given the emphasis in this episode on Ormond's experience of the theatres of Paris, the word 'painted' could be extended from the ceilings of the hotel to the whole staged artifice of face, dress and public display of hotel society. Yet it possesses magnificence, and this Spenserian word is not necessarily pejorative. This magnificent place is where Ormond feels it natural to be.

Edgeworth intrudes coming revolution into the text by means of another of those textual allusions which acquire their ironic resonance from their context. The allusion is to Burke, and the subject is Marie Antoinette, or rather not the Dauphiness herself but 'a picture of Dagote's which was at this moment an object of fashionable curiosity in Paris' (p. 329). The historical personage is known only by an image, and that image is itself subject to interpretation by a culture of fashion, and superficial fashion too, since 'curiosity' is a quasipejorative term. The picture:

> was a representation of one of the many charitable actions of the unfortunate Marie Antoinette, 'then dauphiness – at that time full of life, and splendour, and joy, adorning and cheering the elevated sphere she just began to move in;' and yet diffusing life, and hope, and joy, in that lower sphere, to which the radiance of the great and happy seldom reaches.

The (in)famous passage from Burke's *Reflections* is too well known to require comment. In Edgeworth it is incorporated into a celebration of the charities of the future queen, 'the darling of Paris; not only worshipped by the court, but loved by the people'. The two charitable acts that Edgeworth records are both obviously ominous. Her first munificence to the poor was occasioned by the collapse of 'a temporary building' at her wedding; her second was during a great frost. The 'suffering poor' raised in her honour 'a vast pyramid of snow'. The pyramid was traditionally a sign of immemorial permanence; but a pyramid of snow is both a frosty and a transitory signifier. In the context of country house fiction, a collapsing building (and a pyramid of snow) are warnings to Ormond himself. The culture of the *ancien régime* is one that has educated him, but with which he may also perish.

By returning to Corny Castle, Ormond goes back to an earlier stage in the historical process. He reverts to the more primitive culture from which the *ancien régime* derived. The analogy between Corny Castle and the *ancien régime* is specifically developed from the beginning of

Ormond's sojourn on the Black Islands. King Corny at his supper is likened to the King of France:

> The crowd ... were admitted into the dining-room, where they stood round the king, prince [Ormond], and Father Jos the priest, as the courtiers during the king's supper at Versailles, surrounded the King of France. But these poor people were treated with more hospitality than were the courtiers of the French king; for as soon as the dishes were removed, their contents were generously distributed among the attendant multitude. (p. 44)

It is part of King Corny's aspiration for the culture of Versailles that he would now prefer to call his castle a palace (thus suppressing the origins of his power in conquest) (p. 43). The unresolved historical question here is whether the 'barbarian mock-monarch', as the generous King Corny is called ('half-civilized ... a mixture of savage virtues & vices') in Edgeworth's extratextual characterisation,[19] represents a primitive parody of the high culture of the French palace, or whether the French court is merely a more sophisticated manifestation of a barbarous society that has lost its vital common touch. The giving of dole to the members of the castle household has its roots in the gift culture of tribal chieftainship, and is a traditional motif in the idealised celebration of the country house in English literature from Jonson's *To Penshurst* to St Geneviève in Disraeli's *Coningsby*. It is a sign of Marie Antoinette's goodness, therefore, that she at least tried to practise charity towards the poor of Paris. Nonetheless she failed.

Arguably, so too does King Corny, for the very existence of the poor crowding his feast is a sign of the economic poverty of his regime, which is caught between two worlds. Witness likewise his bedchamber, the traditional ceremonial location for the *grande levée* of the *ancien régime*:

> His majesty pointed to a bed in the corner of a large apartment, whose beautiful painted ceiling and cornice, and fine chimney-piece with caryatids of white marble, ill accorded with the heaps of oats and corn, the thrashing cloth and flail, which lay on the floor.
> 'It is intended for a drawingroom, understand,' said King Corny, 'but till it is finished, I use it for a granary or a barn, when it would not be a barrack-room or hospital which last is most useful at present.' (p. 43)

The unfinished confusion between the 'painted ceiling' (as in a hotel in Paris) and the subsistence agriculture represented on the floor needs no gloss. But the admission that the barn is now most useful as a hospital is a grim reminder that the caryatides of classical culture are supported by the sickness and poverty of the poor.

In the meantime the post office, he tells, refuses to recognise the claim that the castle has become a palace. (The signification of a post office as a locus has already been discussed in the context of Anne Thackeray Ritchie's visit to Edgeworthstown. It represents the superseding of the old order. The fixing of the names of places and the ownership of those places was an essential part of the settlement of Ireland in post-Unionist culture.) The emergent new order will not recognise Corny's writ to write the names of places as he pleases. Hence the castle is 'unfinished' (similar to Halloran Castle) because it cannot become a Palace. The old order has been overtaken by the new. After the feudal lord has died (symbolically, by the explosion of his hunting rifle) the words 'LONG LIVE KING CORNY' are written in living vegetation by a loyal retainer in the boglands, (p. 191), but it will never be inscribed on any map.

But if it is accepted that some kind of ambivalent symbiosis is established by the symbolic imagery between the castle in the Black Islands and the palace of the *ancien régime* in Versailles, then there exists a polar link between the 'savagery' of the islanders beyond the continent of Europe and the apex of the old civilisation of Europe in the hotels of Paris. Ormond must make this connection within himself before undertaking his civilising mission for the future. Accordingly the symbiosis exists not just between the places through which the protagonist moves but in Ormond himself, who links them. He begins as a 'salvage man' by horsewhipping his social inferior and murderously discharging a pistol at him in a fit of blind rage. This is the product of a character and upbringing that have made Ormond 'ungovernable by most . . . people' and a characteristic rudeness that amounted to insolence when faced with anything he viewed as 'tyranny' (p. 12). Likewise it is the very 'lawless freedom' of life in the Black Islands that Ormond finds most attractive. That lawlessness is more the freedom of a Daniel Boone than the violence of the wreckers who terrorise Sir Ulick's mismanaged estate (where even a lighthouse – the sign of enlightenment – is turned to disastrous ends), but change places and handy dandy this 'wild Irish boy' might well become the kind of rebellious Milesian chief of a fantasy by Maturin. What separates Ormond from the desperate lawlessness of the poor is the patronage of wealth, from which comes education and the slow climb up the pyramid of snow that leads, by ineluctable interconnection, from a barbarian court to the earthly paradise of Castle Hermitage and on to Versailles itself.

But the relationship between civilisation and savagery is as much a state of mind as it is something determinate. It depends on point of view rather than being a quiddity. Two examples serve to illustrate the flexibility and relativity of mental connection: one in Ireland, the other in Paris. Ireland first. When Sir Ulick and King Corny are brought into debate early in the fiction (chapter 6), Sir Ulick dismisses the feudal chieftain as a savage and mocks him for ploughing 'by the tail' like the uncivilised Irish of Spenser's time, and for his useless attempts to reclaim unreclaimable bog. In fact both Sir Ulick's allegations are untrue, and King Corny has gone as far as primitive self-sufficiency can go. What he needs, in practice, is a course in reading Adam Smith on the division of labour. But Sir Ulick perceives what his culture has taught him to perceive. The imagery of the debate is developed by Edgeworth into an opposition between the so-called culture of the tomahawk and what she calls the 'polished blade of Damascus' of Sir Ulick's wit. The polished blade of Damascus may be a more sophisticated tool – the product of a more refined industry and a signifier of the processes of an extended commercial intercourse that will, throughout the Empire, supplant the self-sufficiency (Sinn Fein) of the 'savage' Black Islands (just as the primitive culture of the tomahawk was superseded by the frontiersmen of North America) – but as far as the symbolism of civilisation and savagery are concerned it is merely a more sophisticated means of killing an antagonist. The owner of the blade of Damascus may perceive himself as superior, for he is empowered, but he is in symbiotic relationship with the culture of the tomahawk.

The crucial development of the motif of cultural relativity and symbiosis occurs in Paris, where the 'Irish' Dora and 'Black' Connal, having become 'French' as Monsieur and Madame de Connal, move in a more polished society than even that of England. Accordingly, from their point of view it is now the English who are the savages. Thus when Monsieur de Connal claps eyes on Ormond he adopts the same position towards him as Sir Ulick has towards King Corny:

'But, my dear fellow,' cried Connal, 'what savage cut your hair last? – It is a sin to trust your fine head to the barbarians – my hairdresser shall be with you in the twinkling of an eye: I will send you my tailor – allow me to choose your embroidery, and see your lace, before you decide. (p. 304)

This is the cultural imperative of the Kilkenny statutes reapplied (wild hair and wild Irish went together). In the eyes of Parisian society, to qualify as civilised the visitor from outside the pale must have his hair cut properly and wear the proper clothes. (He must also learn to speak the language properly, as is emphasised elsewhere.) Each civility adopts its mores as the norm of civilisation, and thus separates itself from savagery. This is not a racial characteristic (Monsieur de Connal is more 'Irish' than Ormond). It is the ancient fundamental divide in European culture between Hellas and the barbarians outside:

> You would pity us, Ormond . . . if you could see and hear the vandals they send us from England with letters of introduction – barbarians, who can neither sit, stand, nor speak – nor even articulate the language. How many of these *butors* [churls], rich, of good family, I have been sometimes called upon to introduce into society, and to present at court! Upon my honour it has happened to me to wish they might hang themselves out of my way, or be found dead in their beds the day I was to take them to Versailles. (pp. 318–19)

It is wittily done, not unlike Lady Dashfort in *The Absentee*. The tone of the discourse is that of persiflage. It would be a sign of bad breeding if Monsieur de Connal appeared to take himself too seriously. It is part of the facade of players on a painted stage that constitutes Edgeworth's image of the *ancien régime*. By playing with what, if taken seriously, would be offensive distinctions, the sting is taken out of them.

But as with Lady Dashfort, wit can also be a means of holding at arm's length something with which it is difficult to come to terms. In Paris, beyond the pale of Monsieur de Connal's wit, there is that other savagery which destroyed Marie Antoinette and the court of Versailles. When Ormond is taken on a drive to see the sights of Paris, he is alarmed that there are no pavements to separate the common people on foot from the rich in their coaches (the frontier between classes has been neglected). The coachman recklessly urges on his horses, pressing the people aside and warning them with what could be read as an ambiguous cry: 'Gare! gare!' Ormond wants him, at least, to slow down. His companion, a 'little abbé, who was of a noble family, and had all the airs of it', tells Ormond not to interfere with his servant: 'Leave him to settle it with the people – they are used to it. And, after all, what have they to think of, but to take care of themselves – *la canaille*' (p. 307). One might gloss the word *canaille* (if this were Ireland) as 'savages', but Edgeworth prefers a more provocative interpretation even than that. She translates: '"*la canaille*," synonymous with the *swinish multitude*, an expression of contempt for which the

Parisian nobility has since paid terribly dear.' But of course the term 'swinish multitude' did not originate with the Parisian nobility, but is Edmund Burke's notorious characterisation of a mob possessed by devils rushing to destruction.

This problem is not confined to Paris. 'Whether in Paris, London, or the Black Islands, the mob are, in all essential points, pretty nearly the same.' So Edgeworth, *in propria persona* (p. 75), writing a novel historically set on the threshold of the Gordon riots in London, the Terror in Paris and the 1798 rising in Ireland, thinks in the same terms as Cruickshank illustrating Maxwell's history of 1798, or Browne in Dickens' historical novels, and the warning to the propertied classes is the same in each case. Hence the extraordinary act of time-travelling (preposterous in realistic terms), in which Ormond resolves to settle in the Black Islands. It is as if, by re-entering history at an earlier period, one might rewrite history and avoid the Europe-wide revolution. Perhaps in Ireland, on a temporal as well as a geographical frontier, one might begin earlier and achieve a different ending. But the characteristic Edgeworthian fictional closure, in which the ending is merely a beginning, indicates that the outcome (being future) cannot be known. It may already be too late.

Edgeworth's famous letter on the impossibility of writing fiction about the contemporaneous state of Ireland suggests that she came to sense something of her own belated position: 'the people would only break the glass and curse the fool who held the mirror up to nature – distorted nature, in a fever'.[20] This was written in 1834, almost two decades after the conclusion of *Ormond* and after the death of her father, the mirror in which she saw reflected the best self of Ireland. A phase in her life and writing may have reached its natural termination in 1817.

But she returned to her theme one last time. The *Tour in Connemara* (1833) reassumes the method and subject of her earlier fictions. Like them it is dyadically structured between two estates and cultures. The protagonist crosses a frontier between the civilised world and the wild west, the passage in space constituting a temporal regression, and the relativity of place ironising the relationship of epochs. But the *Tour* claims to be true history. The protagonist is Edgeworth herself, and for the first time she experiences in fact what hitherto has been the subject of fiction. The proximity of manner and matter between fact and fiction shows how strongly the civilisation/savagery dichotomy informs and determines the fundamental ideology of both forms of discourse, and how difficult it is, at least in nineteenth-century writing about Ireland, to disentangle history from myth.

The *Tour* is both retrospective (revisiting Edgeworth's earlier writing) and proleptic, for the termination of the voyage is the Martin estate at Ballinahinch (*sic*) and the story of Mary Martin, the heir to the estate, will become one of the moral tales of later fiction, shaping Lever's *The Martins of Cro'Martin* and providing a source for Yeats' *The Countess Cathleen*. In real life Mary Martin was a relative of Violet Martin, a pervasive historical shadow at her shoulder, and Violet Martin eventually, on a journey to the west (mirroring that by Edgeworth), in a symbolic act was to locate herself in 'Mary Martin's seat'.[21]

The *Tour* is little known. A straightforward exposition of the text serves both to draw together in conclusion Edgeworth's work, and to look forward. The journey begins in that symbolic place to which the Edgeworths returned after their flight from savagery in 1798: the library at Edgeworthstown. This is the location of civilisation and it is here that the expedition was planned by assiduously studying maps (which order geographical chaos) and reading guidebooks. We begin, therefore, with the settled, familial, improving estate of the post-Tudor order of things. The *Tour* is in the form of a letter to Maria Edgeworth's youngest brother, Thomas Pakenham, who was in the service of the East India Company and resided in India. The wider civilisation of which the library is the focus, therefore, is that of the United Kingdom and the Empire, in which the Edgeworths (as natives of the region called Ireland) are successful participants.

At first the only major play that Edgeworth makes of the idea of Irishness is to mock that well-known character of Irish nineteenth-century fiction, the stage Englishman (Sir Culling Smith, her travelling companion), who, as a critical theorist, has stuffed his head with political and economic ideas about 'making an angel out of every Paddy' (p. 2). Edgeworth, being a native, believes she knows the country better than the whirligig Englishman, who 'did not in the least know which way he was going, East, West, North or South' (p. 3). But she is proved just as wrong as he in her cultural geography. For entry into Connemara leads to the *Ur* territory of Ireland, that land beyond the frontier (the pale) of civilisation. Here men 'lose their intellects' (p. 76) because the rules of civilisation no longer function. Instead one becomes lost in a region that is both alien and offers a nightmarish parody of the self. Consequently the perception of civilisation, when regained after a sojourn in the wilderness, has changed utterly.

When Edgeworth's journey ends it returns to its beginning (in a library), but the library to which the travellers escape is no longer the *fons et origo* of civilised knowledge, but a refuge from what has been, experientially, a life-threatening experience. The great bog of Connemara literally and metaphorically has all but engulfed them.[22] The party are with great difficulty 'safe out', an expression that Edgeworth reiterates. '"Safe out" is the common expression for "safe out of Connemara," and really it was no easy matter to get safe out' (p. 73) (as we shall see). Safely returned to the demesne, Lady Isabella Smith, physically crippled by her experience, can scarcely refrain from embracing every tree she sees, for the trees signify plantations and plantations signify security (p. 76).

Returning to the beginning, the aim of the party of romantic and picturesque tourists is to make a sophisticated peregrination of one of the remoter regions of the United Kingdom in search of 'the sublime'. The ultimate objective is to reach those remarkable volcanic extrusions known as the Giant's Causeway. The romantic landscape is conceived (from books) as a region of fantasy whose volcanic eruptions were described by the prescientific imagination as the work of giants (the legendary Finn McCool, for instance). Here be monsters. But the modern map and the guidebook will ensure that the well-equipped tourist party, as if on safari, will enjoy the savage scene with all the comforts of civilisation and the superior understanding of enlightened science.

The expedition is destroyed. The party's fundamental mistake is that its equipment is inappropriate for the terrain. Edgeworth makes great play with the cumbersome 'German Britchka' (the travelling carriage), which is equipped with all the latest accoutrements of useless civilisation:

> In this carriage there were all manner of inconvenient conveniences – a sliding table to draw out, which never drew out, to eat or write upon; and we never eat or wrote upon it – wells for holding writing-boxes and dressing boxes, out of which no power could extract them in time of need, any more than truth out of a well. And maps shut with spring catches were to let down from the top, but when down, there was darkness visible or so little light from the side panels that I could seldom make out anything, especially since the maps showed no crossroads and our Irish guide-book was indeed an Irish guide-book. (pp. 6–7)

This is the conveyance in which the representatives of civilisation seek to cross the bogs of Connemara, only to find that the fine new road on which they were to travel is incomplete. In reality it runs in sections in parallel to their transit as a kind of parody of the appliance of science in a region where only a bog trotter, familiar with the sloughs, can pass in safety. The travellers become lost in the wilderness. The key expression to describe their lot is the Miltonic 'darkness visible'. It is the nature of the Miltonic hell to show a monstrous parallel to heaven, which has been lost. The travellers would dress but cannot dress, would write but cannot write, would read, but cannot read, and even if they could, discourse of reason would be of no use because the maps show no way out of the bogs: 'our Irish guide-book was indeed an Irish guide-book'. Ireland has become not the sublime landscape they sought, nor a charming locale of romantic legends, but a nowhere of no sense, a lunatic heterotopia.

There are three major stages to the expedition. There is a period 'on the frontier' as it were, in a peculiar hybrid state between the civilisation to be lost and the savagery to be discovered; there is the stage of near disaster when the benighted party are ensloughed, but are saved by a tribe of wild men who emerge out of the darkness; and there is the reaching of the expedition's terminus, not where they planned (of course) but at an alternative estate (in a typical Edgeworthian dyad): that of the king of Connemara at Ballinahinch. This is a region where all laws other than those of the king are set at 'defiance', (pp. 3–4) and where Maria Edgeworth meets her alter ego, the famous and tragic figure of Mary Martin. It is as though the Black Islands have transmuted from allegory to reality.

What is that frontier beyond which the travellers are almost 'lost entirely'? (p. 9) Consider the first and seemingly most trivial of the successive disasters that befell the German Britchka. At the entrance to Athlone:

> we found ourselves wedged and blocked by drays and sheep reaching a mile at least; men cursing and swearing in Irish and English; sheep baaing and so terrified that the shepherds were in transports of fear, brandishing their crooks at the postillions, and the postillions in turn slashing their whips on the impassive backs of the sheep. The cocked gold hat of an officer appeared on horseback in the midst, and there was silence from all but the baaing sheep. He bowed to us ladies, or to our carriage and four, and assured us he would see us safe out, but it would be the work of time. (pp. 8–9)

There are two signifiers here that are commonplace in nationalist and postcolonialist readings of Ireland: the oppressive imperial army (in the person of the officer) and the (silenced) colonial people. But neither agent is functioning as it ought. The presence of the officer represents welcome order in the midst of chaos (and once the party are beyond the law at Ballinahinch Castle one may perceive why the 'wild country' requires order); and what is most noticeable about the common people (a 'hybrid' community speaking two languages) is the prolificness of the land, not its colonial oppression. The originary cause of the clash between the servants and the peasants is the very fertility of the soil, represented by the vast quantity of idiot sheep that block the way. The question is how to get 'safe out' of the blockage, and it is the repetition of the key Connemara term 'safe out' that suggests something emblematic in the confusion.

Hence the officer's claim that to come 'safe out' will be 'the work of time'. 'Time' is the governing historical conception here, for the 'frontier' at which the travellers are halted is (epistemologically) a temporal one. Edgeworth's mind-set remains that of the stadial history of Giraldus, Spenser or Young, and the officer becomes, in that context, an emblematic figure (like someone from *The Faerie Queene*) delivering a profound historical message. The 'German Britchka' (*Vorsprung durch Technik*) has, as it were, become a time-travel machine that has returned to a pastoral world that is both an emblem of primitive disorder (each farmer drives his individual flock) and a sign of temporal disjunction. We, the readers sharing Edgeworth's experience, do not belong to the old 'Ireland' that was, but we are also becoming separated from the new 'England' that is (hence potential conflict). By entering Connemara the party are, as it were, living out the matter of a Fenimore Cooper frontier novel, where to travel westward geographically is to travel backwards in time historically.

There are a whole series of incidents of this kind on the frontier, which is replete with signs of what Edgeworth calls the 'awful old relics of other times and other manners' (witness the Galway hanging of 1493). These things ought to be mere memories of the past, but the early pages are crowded with signifiers that are both retrospective to times past and proleptic of what Connemara portends. The ancient tribal chief who becomes a boarding housekeeper and regales the party with 'anti-Parliament' 'fire-spirit and water' (p. 20) is perhaps the most obvious manifestation of the coterminous existence of 'other times', against which one may set the absence of a magistrate, clergyman or chief of police to receive the travellers. Equally emblematic is the old woman whom the party wish to turn by romantic imagination into a figure of melodrama – 'the witch of the cavern' – but who instead changes into a ranting 'regular old Irish beggar' (or the Shan van Vocht) lying through her teeth (to earn sixpence) about high rents and cruel landlords (pp. 23–4). At this point the travellers face real danger for the first time when the picturesque landscape changes 'in five minutes to storm and cloud' (p. 25) as they embark on Lake Corrib. The storm is the objective correlative of the gathering danger and darkness. 'You have no idea of the places you are going into', the travellers are warned, for they are going 'out of the world' (p. 19), where 'the world' means civilisation as they know it. As they pass beyond the frontier they find themselves in an uncultivated land where it seems 'as if stones and fragments of rock had showered down on the earth' (p. 26), and where their benighted passage terminates at the bog holes, which the horses refuse and which threaten to swallow up both carriage and passengers. The backward journey through time has passed beyond mere Miltonic allusion to reach an experiential original chaos and old night.

From this chaos savage man re-emerges, screaming and unintelligible, fascinated, so it seems, by the arrival of strangers such as he has never seen before (p. 79). A terrifying party of 'wild Irish' descend on the benighted travellers who are stranded with the appurtenances of their culture: useless books, writing boxes and dressing cases (the Prospero myth reversed). The mind-set through which Edgeworth perceives these wild Irish is Spenserian. They are, historically, the remnants of the old feudal kerns, who are still the private army of the (loyalist) 'king' of Connemara and have been recently called out, we learn, to fight his territorial battles with his neighbours the O'Flahertys (this, in the United Kingdom, post the first Reform Act). But, ambiguously, they are also potentially a 'mob', who in another manifestation as 'Terryalts' have revolted against their king. There is now no polite and authoritative officer in his red coat to represent order. In Irish cultural context, these are the 'salvage' men of *The Faerie Queene*, but fortunately Edgeworth is cast in the role of Una rather than Serena. Seeing Edgeworth's distress, one of the wild men, a 'dear giant', seizes her in his arms, flounders with her through the bog, and tosses her to safety on *terra firma*. Finn McCool from the Giant's Causeway has a real life equivalent. Talk with the giant, as Edgeworth does, and the terrifying figure turns into the loquacious and helpful Ulick Burke, and the mob (for a price) bundle the travellers through the bog and to the safety (that word again) of Ballinahinch Castle (with a demi 'angel' at its gate) (p. 36).

This is a tale that loses nothing in the telling. Emblematically 'these wild Irish in the midst of their own bogs [at] this time of night' (p. 34) mark the crossing of the frontier from civilisation to savagery and to that other state of being which exists on the other side (the Black Islands). It is a trauma. Lady Isabella Smith emerges from the experience ill almost to death and Ballinahinch Castle is the *ne plus ultra* of the expedition. This castle becomes the locus that embodies the signification of the other world, the space across the frontier that is different from 'our' civilisation yet reflects it back in ironic parody. The extent to which Ballinahinch actually corresponded to what we are told is irrelevant, although it seems that the 'king' of Connemara (Mr Martin) still exercised a residual feudal state within the Victorian state until his bankruptcy led to the takeover of his territories by modern capitalist entrepreneurs. But what matters in the narrative allegory of the *Tour* is that the Martin demesne stands in relation to Edgeworthstown like the Black Islands to the Court of Versailles in *Ormond*. The places signify different states of historical process, and yet there is an unsettling relationship between the savage original and the civilised derivative.

Hitherto Ballinahinch had been known to Edgeworth only imaginatively, she tells us, and thus through the idealisation of picturesque art. As a safe refuge for benighted travellers in the wilderness it might have been another Edgeworthstown. The light of dawn, however, reveals that the castle is without substance:

> all that battlemented front which looks so grand in the drawing is mere whitewashed stone or brick or mud, I cannot swear which. But altogether the house is very low and ruinous looking, not a ruin of antiquity – but with cow-house and pig-stye and dunghill adjoining, and a litter indescribable in a sunk sort of backyard seen at the end of the mansion – a man throwing dung about with no air of majesty, and pigs and poultry. (p. 44)

The Addisonian allusion to Virgilian Georgic (verbatim: 'tosses the dung about with an air of gracefulness') sets Augustan ideal in allegorical contrast to the stinking backyard of the whitewashed facade of Ballinahinch. The allegory, read stadially, reverses the progress of history by means of descent from stone to brick to mud, and from venerable antiquity to modern ruin. Ultimately the castle is given the standard appurtenances of the Irish peasant mud hovel, with pigs rooting in the dunghill at the door. The same disintegration obtains within. There are splendid doors that do not close, windows without glass, bookcases without books, and the wind and rain corrupt perpetually. Edgeworth's claim that 'it is always a windy night at Ballinahinch' (p. 43) is a symbolic assertion, not an expression of meteorological science.

If this were one of Edgeworth's early regional fictions, Ballinahinch would represent the old, badly managed 'tail of a feudal state' (p. 63), set in contrast to the enlightened improvement to come after the Union. The re-emergence of the 'Castle Rackrent' mode this late in her writing suggests that her earlier progressive view of civilisation no longer pertains. There is a profoundly pessimistic element to Edgeworth's account of Ballinahinch as 'unfinished unliveable...as if the family had come down to these regions for a few weeks and were merely making a shift' (p. 43). This is Halloran Castle, unreclaimed even as late as 1833. But the fundamental question is, can it be that it is 'civilisation' itself, seeking to emerge from the wilderness, that remains 'unfinished unliveable...making a shift'? 'Ireland' (or here, 'Connemara') represents something intrinsic that denies the progress and establishment of the ideal order of things.

The crucial figure embodying the problem is the famous chatelaine (and future novelist) Mary Martin, the 'Bedouin' intellectual of this 'red half-savage people' (pp. 69 and 79). The unsettling question is, to what extent might she be a parody of Edgeworth herself? If the library in which the *Tour* begins is the place that represents that accumulated body of culture called civilisation, then bookish Mary Martin is the representative of that civilisation even in Connemara. She meets Edgeworth on common intellectual territory, being profoundly read in the foundational languages of Hebrew, Greek and Latin. As an enlightened European citizen of the world she speaks the current *lingua franca* – French. She is a Bonapartist, and hence a European unionist, a reader of both Byron and Scott and hence at the cutting edge of romantic sensibility. Like Edgeworth she is the great lady of a great country estate, and also like Edgeworth she will become a woman of letters. It is a mirror image of the narrator's selfhood, but 'through the looking-glass' where everything has changed utterly. For the library at Ballinahinch is now the 'dark closet' (p. 57) of Miss Martin's private world, and from that closeted darkness enlightenment has little chance of escape. At dinner (the classic symposium for 'the flow of reason and the feast of soul') Miss Martin mutters to herself like an idiot, and when she seeks to communicate with her alter ego Edgeworth, her English is virtually unintelligible, spoken 'so fast and so oddly in such a Connemara accent and with words so fluid, running into the other, that at first I could not guess what language it was' (p. 59). Connemara makes even English a foreign language, and the Miranda (or is it Glorvina?) of this heterotopia needs, like Caliban, to be taught the language of civilisation.

But Edgeworth herself in Connemara would be much the same. Her culture, like the German Britchka, the cause of all the party's disasters, out of time, out of place, is worse than useless. It serves only to make 'darkness visible', and once that inversion of order is perceived, civilisation cannot simply be reillumined as before. In an extraordinary moment in the *Tour* Edgeworth sets Sir Culling Smith and Miss Martin in cultural debate. Sir Culling is given the philosophical and political ideas about the improvement of estates that were, in Edgeworth's regional novels, the staple of her progressive views; Miss Martin talks of the loyalty of her tenants, the extent of her lands and her admiration for Greek literature (p. 62). It is the kind of confrontation that the progressive conservative Sir Walter Scott would have relished.[23] In the *Tour* the conversation results only in mutual incomprehension. It is as if two parts of Edgeworth herself have almost been split apart in Connemara, and are held together only by the civilised sensibility of the narrator. There is no resolution for this crisis except to get 'safe out' as best she may. The paradox is that the *Tour* is only intelligible if understood through that very culture, the intelligibility of which is brought into question by its location in Connemara.

This allegorical, quasihistorical text belongs to the tradition of ironic questioning of the nature of civilisation that, just as much as the imperial mode, is original in the formation of the European mind. The Spenserian analogy has been made repeatedly in the above explication of the text, but the *Tour* also has close affinities with what could be claimed to be the first Irish novel in English, Swift's *Gulliver's Travels*. Swift's hero also travels into remote regions that disconcertingly mirror and ironically distort the original civilisation of a complacent and ultimately deeply destabilised narrator. In the fourth book especially, Gulliver, like Edgeworth, is placed dyadically between two parodic worlds, the classical idealism of the world of the governing horses and the savagery of the enslaved Yahoos, and there is, we are told, no final solution to the Yahoo problem. One explanation of why no solution is possible is that Gulliver embodies both the divine *logos* (discourse of reason) and the heart of darkness (a reasoning Yahoo). What mediates between this light and darkness is the act of writing itself, the book being a sign of civil order, or a kind of britchka on a road through a wilderness. But as the *Tour* reveals, books are unreliable guides. To get 'safe out of Connemara' into a library, where the tale begins and ends, is a form of retreat into a pale of civilisation. The other side of the frontier is what Edgeworth called the 'distorted nature' that was Ireland. That she found unwritable.

3
Edgeworth's Heir: Charles Lever

Charles Lever's *The Martins of Cro'Martin* (1856) derives from the history of Mary Martin of Ballinahinch. Unlike Edgeworth, Lever wrote after the famine.[1] The tale begins by taking the reader on the same westward journey as that taken by Maria Edgeworth but with greater rapidity of the imagination. We leap the 'wild', the barren mountains, the rare and 'miserable hut' and the wet potato fields. Then 'the grateful sight of young timber' announces the approach to another world, and 'winding round the base of a steep mountain, the deep woods of a rich demesne appear' and armorial bearings above a gatehouse announce the approach to 'the ancient seat of the Martins'. The symbolic function of this ancient seat, at this juncture, is merely conventional, that of the 'happy rural seat':[2]

An avenue of several miles in length, winding through scenery of the most varied character, at one time traversing rich lawns of waving meadow, at another tracking its course along some rocky glen, or skirting the bank of a clear and rapid river, at length arrives at the Castle. With few pretensions to architectural correctness, Cro'Martin was, indeed, an imposing structure. Originally the stronghold of some bold Borderer, it had been added to by successive proprietors, till at last it had assumed the proportions of a vast and spacious edifice, different eras contributing the different styles of building, and presenting in the mass, traces of every architecture, from the stern old watch-tower of the fourteenth century to the commodious dwelling-house of our own.

If correct taste might take exception to many of the external details of this building, the arrangements within doors, where all that elegance and comfort could combine were to be found, might safely challenge criticism. Costly furniture abounded, not for show in state appartments, shrouded in canvas or screened from sunlight, but for daily use in rooms that showed continual habitation. (p. 2)

This initial description of the picturesque demesne, with its combination of Brownian beauty and the rocky excrescences of Salvator Rosa, might have come from a celebration by Arthur Young of the civilised amelioration of the improving estate. The conservative values embodied in the house would be appropriate in a work by Sir Walter Scott (one notes the word 'Borderer') or Benjamin Disraeli, and the rich and rare mixed Gothic, in its constitutional implications, suggests the kind of Burkean reading with which Byron played in the idealised description of Norman Abbey in *Don Juan*. Like the British constitution, the house is not the product of a rationalist imposition (of taste or of European political theory) but has grown organically over a long period of time. That process of time has been progressive in civilisation, for the watchtower of the feudal ages of warfare has united, by synthesis and incorporation, with the commodious dwelling house of what Lever calls 'our own' world. The rhetorical implication of the latter is that reader and novelist are comfortably accommodated in their view of what 'our' civilisation is and of what we 'own' within it. Equally important is the long period of time over which this union has occurred. After five hundred years the ancient seat of the Martins is as established as Traquair in Scotland and Warwick Castle in England. It belongs, because it is incorporated by history. Nor is it merely a 'show house', or, to borrow Jonson's words in *To Penshurst*, one built in 'envious show'. As the great tradition of country house literature demands, this is a place of 'daily use', or to return to Jonson again, 'use' indicates, as at Penshurst, that 'thy lord dwells'. The Martins are not absentees. On the contrary, the beauty and fertility of the demesne indicates that the family is committed to the improvement of the estate.

This is what Maria Edgeworth and her benighted party might have hoped to find at Ballinahinch if 'Connemara' had not transformed Utopia by parody (even if Utopia can only be found in the idealisations of fiction). The first of the Martins to be introduced is Mary herself, who in *The Martins of Cro' Martin* is partly the feudal ruler of real history and partly the alter ego of the other Mary/Maria – Edgeworth herself as chatelaine of the improving estate. Mary's locus is 'a remote part of the building which once had formed part of the ancient edifice', but she is very far from being the Glorvina of a feudal 'tail'. Her modest rooms, low ceilinged and opening on to a small grassy enclosure, express the conjunction of culture with utility:

> One was a little library or study, neatly but very modestly furnished; adjoining it was her office, where she transacted all business matters; and beyond that again was a large chamber, whose sole furniture consisted in a row of deal presses against the walls, and a long table or counter which occupied the middle of the room. Two large windows opening to the floor lighted the apartment. (pp. 6–7)

This is both the location of the culture of Mary's world (her library) and the centre from which, like the equally practical Maria, she manages the estate. Its comparative modesty is self-evident, as is the strong emphasis on utility. The two windows opening to the floor are potentially democratic in their implication, providing equal and level egress between the inner and outer world, from which Mary is separated not by fortification but by a mere sheet of glass. The natural light these windows admit might also be read as enlightenment. This is a space where 'all come in' (to return to Ben Jonson again) – the chatelaine herself and the poorest tenants of the estate – and from which issue plans for the improvement of the estate, model farms and school houses (as at Edgeworthstown), the draining of bogs, the establishment of enclosures, the planting of crops (as Young had recommended), and even the construction of roads, bridges and a harbour to connect the wilderness to civilisation, to nurture trade and establish prosperity.

But Mary herself is far more than an idealised variant of Mary Martin or Maria Edgeworth. She is, by connotation if not by denotation, the embodiment of an ideally united Irish culture. When first we see her she is seated. With a braid of her dark auburn hair falling accidentally on her shoulder she is 'patting the head of the wire-haired greyhound, who had reared himself to her side – a study for Landseer himself' (p. 3). This suggests one of the most famous images of Irish romantic culture, Queen Maeve with her Irish wolfhound. But Lever, writing in a unionist context, modifies the image marginally and incorporates it into 'our own' culture by choosing Landseer for his artist. It was Landseer, at Abbotsford, who painted the famous image of Sir Walter Scott with his dogs and who later, as a reward for his idealisation of the British monarchy, was buried in St Paul's Cathedral.

The image of the chatelaine and her dog is pivotal, for if the iconography suggests a connection beyond feudalism back to the heroic age itself, Mary as aristocrat and huntress is potentially also a proto-Yeatsian type, a fine horsewoman (and an equally fine sailor, as we shall learn) and an embodiment of that integrity, energy and capacity for leadership and ability to unite rich and poor which Yeats admired in Constance Markiewicz and Lady Gregory. There is also a direct connection, by blood and ideology, with Violet Martin, and thus with the world of art, writing and civil administration represented by Ross House (or Drishane).

There is an even more remarkable connection. Mary Martin is described as the 'princess' of her territory and 'ruler over the...wild people' (p. 198). The monarchical imagery is associated by Lever with the age of chivalry: 'beauty, grace, fascination – all that can charm and attract...and chivalrous, ay, chivalrous as a chevalier' (p. 495), an astonishing combination to find 'in such a spot'. In conservative (and accordingly Burkean) fiction the associations of chivalry are frequently with that lost age associated with the dauphiness at Versailles. Thus when Cro'Martin is threatened by a 'mob', Mary Martin turns on them, as Marie Antoinette might have wished to do in order to defend herself:

> '...how shall I speak my contempt for *you*' – and she turned a wither-ing look of scorn on the men...'for you, who have dared to come here to insult me – I, that if you had the least spark of honest man-hood in your natures, you had died rather than offended? Is this your requital for the part I have borne amongst you? Is it thus that you repay the devotion by which I have squandered all that I possessed, and would have given my life, too, for you and yours?' (p. 521)

The age of chivalry is dead. Lever has played with the Burkean formu-lation earlier in the text, calling it an 'age of alchemists', (p. 478) desirous, in vain, of transforming base metal into gold. But in the new world that Lever depicts, the man at the head of the 'mob' is a bour-geois capitalist and international financier, the Jew, Herman Merl. The assault on the *ancien régime* has moved on since the 1790s.

Since this is a fiction based on fact (the fall of the Martins of Ballinahinch) the tragic outcome of the story is inevitable. This is a classic example of the collapse of an encumbered estate. The central chapters of the novel describe the departure of the family from the demesne and its inundation by the tenantry upon the sale of the property. The true story of Mary Martin is altered for tragic effect, and it is she (not her father) who dies of famine fever caught in the service of her people. She 'dies for Ireland' just as much as a Padraic Pearse or a Johnny Boyle.

The economics of the situation are simple. Agricultural poverty simply cannot sustain the lifestyle of the Martins, and capitalisation of the estate (on the model of Young or Edgeworth) costs more than the returns. The novel even descends to facts and figures. Mary Martin's schemes of improvement are costing the estate £10 000 a year, but enclosure has not improved the fertility of the barren soil, the unfinished harbour is silting up, even the plantations (the signifiers of civilisation and intergenerational continuity) are useless financially for the returns are too far in futurity. Rather than Cro'Martin being a fountain feeding the land (a Spenserian image that Yeats was to adopt), the fountain is merely a drain (pp. 144, 383). The gentry do not have the resources to resolve the problem without investment from elsewhere in the United Kingdom, a conclusion that de Tocqueville also reached (and, one might suggest, those who later incorporated Eire into the new union of the EEC). The famine is the final blow, for without rental income there is simply no money to combat starvation and disease. In a diagnostic letter (p. 380 f.) Mary Martin analyses the problem, spells out the landlord's obligation and recognises the inadequacy of the means to meet the need. Accordingly, her own death by famine fever is more than a personal tragedy. Symbolically it represents the symbiotic relationship between the old feudal order, whose finest ideals she embodies, and the 'dependants' (p. 509) upon that order. Disease here serves the same function as in Dickens' *Bleak House*, where Chesney Wold and Tom All Alone's are linked by pestilential smallpox. It is an ineluctable act of union.

Politically the fiction is equally pessimistic. Here Lever is closer to the cynical objectivity of Trollope than to Dickens' sentimental ameliorism. The fall of Cro'Martin is seen as a revolutionary act, but, as in the 1790s, what succeeds that act is a descent into chaos (p. 277). Since there no longer exists a 'brotherhood' (p. 3) between the orders of society (and the word 'brotherhood' was about to be adopted by another society – secret, disruptive, committed to killing as an instrument of politics) there is merely a conflict between 'plebeian' and 'patrician', and between 'papist' and 'Protestant'. The newly emergent dominant order will consist of the Roman Catholic priesthood, the political demagogue and the land agitator (p. 260). What underpins this alliance is the 'very intelligible' issue of 'material benefit', and although it is O'Connell rather than Parnell who is in Lever's mind, the argument that playing the nationalist card is the right policy for any politician on the make is not without predictive force (p. 227). This is not yet an Ireland of 'plaster saints', but it is already a place of land-hungry and power-hungry 'cheats' and 'humbugs' (p. 250). This is nineteenth-century 'revisionist' history, and one need look no further for the cause of Lever's nationalist exclusion from the canon of Irish literature.

But this is merely the parochial context of the fall of Cro'Martin/ Ballinahinch. There is a larger matter at issue. It is typical of Lever's fiction that the symbolic action is given a European (and even a transatlantic dimension). The story moves from Connemara to Europe, where the events unleashed by Jacobinism in the 1790s are resurgent on the streets of Paris in the revolutionary 1830s. Subsequently the heir to the Martin estate, refusing to take responsibility for the insoluble problem of maintaining Cro'Martin, quits Europe for the United States. But ironically he merely moves from one tectonic fault line in culture to another. At that historical moment the United States was on the verge of civil war, in comparison with which the 'troubles' in Ireland were (as J. M. Synge suggested) a squabble with a potato spade in a backyard. The outcome of civil war in the disunited States was to sweep away the plantation culture of the great house.

The historical issue therefore involves the entire European community on both sides of the Atlantic. To adopt an Edgeworthian model from *Ormond*, Cro'Martin embodies the *ancien régime* in crisis. This analogy is sometimes stated explicitly, for example it is claimed that English society 'is gradually undergoing that change which in France was accomplished in a year or two' in the 1790s (p. 190), and the household at Cro'Martin is described as that of 'five-and-forty years ago' or (in Byronic allusion) 'when George the Third was King' (pp. 198, 309). Sometimes the mode is more allusive, for instance, when we are told, that Mr Martin's name has been coupled by scandal with that of Marie Antoinette, and when Mary Martin is suddenly accosted by a ludicrous figure in medieval costume (one of the members of the tableau vivant of Mr Crow the painter) (pp. 29, 45). In this pattern of allusion the chatelaine of Cro'Martin, Lady Dorothea, represents the unacceptable face of Marie Antoinette. (Lever, like Edgeworth in *Ormond*, balances contradictory views of the dauphiness and queen.) Although Lady Dorothea does not tell her tenants to eat cake, she dreams of a final solution to the problem of poverty on the estate – that all the cottages are demolished and the inhabitants quit for the United States. That way there will be neither famine fever nor rebellion (p. 264).

But the use of the term *ancien régime* ideologically predetermines one's attitude to events. Its use implies that the old corruption has been quite properly swept away by a better order of things. Except in this novel no better order is presented. The irony of the fiction is that old corruption is also old civilisation. Cro'Martin embodies, in symbolic architecture, the product of five hundred years of historical process, and if that is now passing away there will remain only disjunction and disunion. The symbolic description of the exterior of the house with which the fiction opens is matched in Chapter 13 by a tour of the interior, in which Lever invites the reader, as a 'stranger', to experience what it is that has been lost in Cro'Martin:

> all seemed suggestive of habitable enjoyment. The vast drawing-rooms appeared as if only waiting for a splendid company; the dark-wainscoted dining-room, with its noble fireplace of gigantic dimensions, looked the very scene where hospitable conviviality might be enacted; the library, calm, quiet and secluded, seemed a spot wherein a student might have passed a lifelong. Even in the views, that presented themselves at the several windows, there was a certain appropriateness to the character of the room, and the same importune question still arose to one's mind: Who is there to enjoy all this? (p. 130)

The point of view here is emphatically that of a 'stranger' to the world of the Cro'Martin, a tourist or country house visitor making a peregrination through the deserted principal rooms of the house and imagining, from what is seen, how this civilisation functioned. Each symbolic space alludes to well-established motifs in ancient tradition. There is, of course, the library, which is the place where long historical culture is most obviously located – in the ancient languages of Greece and Rome in which the menfolk were educated, and in the more modern tongues of Italy and Germany to which the women of the household turn, we are told, to express their art in song (p. 195). This is the place where the scholar might locate a life's work in retrieving and interpreting a great tradition. Two other traditional motifs are also incorporated into the tour: in the dining room the hospitable conviviality of the communal meal as the central unifying activity of the household; and in the drawing room the ideal of the house as a retreat from the atrabiliar cares of the outer world. If this does not aspire to depict the house as a classic of villa culture – a place of philosophical *otium* and of the good life in body as well as soul – the house is nonetheless described as the potential location of the 'great family party which is the *beau idéal* of social enjoyment' (p. 367). Except there is no family, and it is the (absent) family that would have provided continuity between generations: 'blending hopes of the future with memories of the past, and making of every heart a portion of one human biography in which many are sharers.' Lever claims that this 'little world within doors...emblematises the great one without', but with one greater advantage, for the ideal family is 'bound up in one holy sentiment of mutual love and affection' (p. 130). It is the familial ideal of Edgeworthstown.

This is a world to which the reader is a 'stranger', and to describe it merely as the *ancien régime* is inadequate. The *beau idéal* is a long-established classical and Gothic tradition, here deeply sentimentalised by the emphasis on family. It is as if the organic unity of generations of which Burke wrote and the 'unity of being' that Yeats admired pass through some transitional stage of Victorian hearth and home sentimentality, so that the 'one human biography' that all families represent acts as an emblem of what the great world outside the family might be. It is, *mutatis mutandis*, the same kind of use that William Morris was to make of houses such as Kelmscott, where the organic community, now a socialist society rather than a familial bonding, incorporated a model society. For Morris this was 'news from nowhere' in some Utopian future; at Cro'Martin it is a lost past. But there is one locus in the house where the spirit of the place lives on: a small room 'whose two windows projected beyond the walls, giving a wide view over the swelling landscape for miles of space' (p. 131). This is the housekeeper's domain. One might liken that space to Fanny Price's room at Mansfield Park, for here the house is, metaphorically 'kept'; or, more darkly ironic, one might compare it to the role of Firs in Chekhov's *The Cherry Orchard*, for only the aged servitors of the estate now carry on the otherwise lost traditions of the place.

The artefacts, just as much of the house, have symbolic function. Lady Dorothea's personal domain represents the very heartland of the *ancien régime*:

> Lady Dorothea's library occupied an angle of the building, and from this circumstance, included within its precincts an octagonal tower, the view from which comprised every varied character of landscape. This favoured spot was fitted up in the most luxurious taste – with rarest gems of art, and cabinet pictures of almost fabulous value – to supply which foreign dealers and connoisseurs had been for years back in correspondence with her ladyship. Now, it was some rare treasure of carved ivory, or some sculptured cup of Benvenuto, that had been discovered accidentally, and which, despite the emulous zeal of Princes and Cardinals to obtain, was destined for herself. Now, it was some choice mosaic, of which one other specimen

1. Ormond's 'brave mansion' (from a picturesque engraving, n.d., author's own collection).

2. The massacre at Scullabogue (from Maxwell's *History of the Irish Rebellion in 1789*, 1887).

3. A No-Popery dance (from Charles Dickens' *Barnaby Rudge*, 1841).

4. Edgeworthstown (from Mrs Hall's I*reland*, 1842).

5. 'Never opened a cabin-door without a blessing' (from Lever's *The Martins of Cro'Martin*, 1856).

6. 'Savage' Connemara (from a painting by Peter Knuttel, author's own collection).

7. The demesne of 'Ballinahinch'.

8. Tyrone House: the original of 'the big house' of Inver.

9. Marriage stones at Ross House.

10. Drishane.

11. Ross House.

12. The lake at Ross.

14. The bust of Maecenas in the garden at Coole.

13. The signature tree at Coole Park.

existed, and that in the Pope's private collection at the Quirinal. Such was her ardour in this pursuit of excellence, that more than once had every object of this precious chamber been changed, to give place to something more costly, more precious, and rarer. For about two years back, however, the resources of the old world seemed to offer nothing worthy of attention, and the vases, the 'statuettes', the bronzes, the pictures, and medallions had held their ground undisturbed. (p. 123)

Once again it is a library that is the location of culture, here linked to the usual location of enlightened aristocracy upon a high place that overlooks 'every variety of landscape'. High thinking and a high place are traditional correlatives (witness the usual iconographical representation of Truth as dwelling on a high mountain, or the choice by 'the sage of Monticello' of a hill top for his villa). What are collected in this lofty locus are the signifiers of the elite culture of European civilisation, derived from 'the pursuit of excellence'. The long roots of that civilisation are grounded in ancient Rome, and the renaissance of the values of the ancient world are represented by the taste of popes and cardinals, as patrons of the arts, and the artists who served those patrons, of whom Benvenuto Cellini is named as a preeminent example.

The cultural resonances of this are profound and can only be explicated through a knowledge of that culture. In that respect it is a closed loop of civilisation. One example serves both to explore and to test the limits of allusion and symbolic signification. Benvenuto Cellini is cited as a name with which the educated are expected to be familiar. His autobiography (for Lever's contemporaries in the translation by J. A. Symonds) exemplifies 'the civilisation of the Renaissance in Italy' (to adopt Burkhardt's expression), with its blend, so it was argued, of assertive individualism, violence and the cult of the heroic artist. Cellini (born in 1500) was a murderer, an exquisite crafter of silver and gold, a sculptor, a writer and even a religious visionary: at one time thrown into an oubliette in St Angelo, at another a courtier in the palace of Francis I. The hackneyed term 'the universal man' can scarcely contain such energised diversity (nor, in an Irish context, the Yeatsian idea of 'unity of being'). But Cellini's Perseus with the Head of Medusa in the Loggia dei Lanze in Florence serves as a symbol of the linkage of sweetness with violence (civilisation and savagery) that Yeats perceived in the old aristocratic order. As an example of the civilised man Perseus represents in Cellini a Christian humanist icon of the *fiat lux* of civilisation in the necessary application of rational force to destroy evil (the savage Medusa). Within that tradition, as an object of homoerotic celebration, he also represents the idealisation of the male body as the human image of the divine order. Might is right when thus embodied in Platonic ideal.

But for Lady Dorothea's domestic collection of *objets*, perhaps a more appropriate contextual reference is the saltcellar made for Francis I, which is as well known as the statue of Perseus. Here the care (and cost) elaborated on a mere domestic utensil indicates that there is no part of the life of the humanist connoisseur to which the pursuit of excellence does not extend. Nor is there any part of the world that the culture of the elite does not embrace, because even the saltcellar represents, in the 'grace' (Cellini's idiom) of the entwined male and female figures, the union of the ocean with the earth, in all seasons of the year and all periods of the day. On its owner the gods themselves throw incense, or more mundanely, salt is taken from beneath the bodies of the deities in an Ionic temple. The provenance of the saltcellar provides a real-life counterpart to Lady Dorothea's own passion for collection: 'After narrowly escaping being melted down in 1566, the salt-cellar was presented by Charles IX, in 1570, to the Archduke Ferdinand of Austria on the occasion of the King's marriage to Elizabeth of Austria at Speyer, and until its transfer to Vienna [Kuntshistorisches Museum] was preserved at Schloss Ambras.'[3] It is essential to know the path of owner-ship of the rich and rare so that its authenticity can be verified and its value (aesthetic and financial) preserved, although now only in the culture of a museum.

As significant as the choice of Cellini as the artisan of Renaissance humanism is the location of culture upon the Quirinal in Rome, to which Lady Dorothea's library at Cro'Martin is linked. To explicate Lever's text in full would be to engage in an essay on the history of humanist culture. The Quirinal, the northernmost of the seven hills of Rome, was once the site of a Sabine settlement and one of the four regions of the Roman republic. Accordingly, the place, was sacred (and rich in places of worship) to all that was implied by the expression 'Sabine virtue'. This was the Rome of these republican founding fathers: farmers whose simple piety sprang from the cultivation of the soil, patriots who served the state and not their own self-interest, and models for the ideology of the early United States of America. But the Quirinal was later to become notorious for the 'luxury' that corrupted the empire, the place where Narcissus (apt name) made his home (he made a vast fortune as private secretary to Claudius), where Domitian raised a temple to the glory of his own family (the *templum gentis Flaviae*) and Sallust acquired notorious but beautiful gardens financed, it was claimed, by imperial plunder (the accusation could not be made to stick). Hence this was an appropriate site for the private collection of artistic rarities by the Renaissance papacy, where again the holiest of associations were combined with the excess and corruptions of dynastic power. The Quirinal, therefore, is directly associated with what Lever calls Lady Dorothea's 'luxurious taste', and thus with that corrupting degeneracy which saps empires (the Roman or the British) and which, as we have seen serves as a leitmotif in the earlier pages of Edgeworth's country house fiction.

But Lever's description is proleptic as well as retrospective, for the description of Lady Dorothea's library as a repository of fine things is suggestive of things to come. One thinks of the country house fiction of Henry James, for instance. Lever is concerned with what James would have called 'the spoils' of Cro'Martin. Or to choose another example, the passionate aestheticism that has inspired Lady Dorothea is not, in principle, far removed from the exquisite sensibility revealed by Walter Pater's 'gem-like' invocation of culture in *The Renaissance*. Her collection embodies a form of secular religion as art, for contemporary culture, in Arnoldian fashion, replaces religion as the substance of the soul. Lever goes on to refer to the 'sanctity of the spot', 'the threshold of the tabernacle' and the custodian of the collection as possessed of a kind of 'sacred character'. But in Lever the temple of art is now closed. It is shown to no one, and is no longer enjoyed even by the once avid patroness of dead artists. 'The resources of the old world' no longer offer Lady Dorothea anything 'worthy of attention'. Satiated taste is left without appetite (*ennui* in Edgeworth's categorisation); the 'spoils' of Cro'Martin are sold (like the contents of Jefferson's Monticello or the pride of the Cobhams at Stowe). The moral of this might seem clear enough for there is nothing to recommend the bored apathy and help-less prejudice of Lady Dorothea (and her husband). But where might be found the next generation of patrons of the arts? The resident artist at Cro'Martin, Mr Crow, is advised to seek support from the O'Connellites and the vulgar expediency of the nationalist political agenda (pp. 312–13). The implication is that a dumbed-down political correctness will not be concerned with the pursuit of excellence. As for 'taste' as the true criterion of excellence, as Herman Merl observes taste waxes and wanes as fashion dictates: 'We are all modern to-day, to-morrow we may be "Louis Quatorse," the next day "Cinque Centi" in our tastes.' The one thing that never changes is the might of wealth: 'Religions might decay, and states crumble, thrones totter and kings be exiled, Cuyps might be depreciated and marqueterie be held in mean esteem, but gold was always within a fraction at least of four pounds eleven shillings the ounce!' (pp. 453–4). *Omnia Romae cum pretio.*

The central chapters of the novel depict the power of gold to buy out house and estate. The new moneyed order replaces the Martins. This event had been foretold in the historical painting by the resident artist of the house, entitled 'The Abdication of Charles V' and already recorded in fourteen variants (p. 48), and 'the end of the Martins' is accordingly reflected through a double sequence of symbolic forms: the tale itself and the painting described in the fiction. As Holy Roman Emperor, Charles embodied the active form of that continuum of European-wide civilisation of which Lady Dorothea's cabinet of spoils is the archaeological detritus. The old order has 'abdicated', leaving only artistic forms as its record. In this transhistorical and European context the abdication of the Holy Roman Emperor might also be compared with the more brutal and more recent termination of the *ancien régime* in France, and later in the novel the voice of Fenian violence surfaces in Magennis's complaint, 'It was false pity for individuals destroyed the great revolution of France' (p. 469). The abdication of the saleroom, in this symbolic structure, obviates the revolutionary violence that had been latent throughout Europe since the 1790s. Charles V himself lingered on for several years after his surrender of power, just as the present monarchies of Europe still linger (the story moves to Paris in the 1830s) and as the Martins will. There is yet another layer to this penumbra of ironic allusion. Mr Crow, the painter of the 'Abdication', is a wretched late exponent of the great Renaissance tradition of history painting, and many of the paintings at Cro'Martin, we later learn, are mere copies by inferior hands of the masterpieces of old. From that sense of belated inferiority the nineteenth-century novelist himself might not be entirely free, a populist parasite at the end of a great tradition of aristocratic art.

'The end of the Martins' depicted in the great sale of Cro'Martin is not a mere Irish event, therefore, but is representative of a crucial moment of transition in European culture, or what Lady Dorothea calls 'the world of civilization and refinement' (p. 282). That world abdicates from power at Cro'Martin and is carried (towards France) in three large and stately travelling carriages, the appurtenances of an ancient social order as out of date technologically in the new world as their civilisation and refinement is outmoded socially. The first and last of the carriages require little comment. The first, of course, contains

Lady Dorothea and her husband, and the last the servants for whom the aristocracy are 'the same all the world over' whether 'at Vienna ... in London; at Rome ... so, too, at Naples' (p. 290). The central carriage carries the extraordinary dependant of the Martins, Kate Henderson. In the dialectical structure of the novel she represents for the aristocracy an alternative pathway to that tragically chosen by Mary Martin. Rather than dying in the service of an impossible ideal of feudal service, as Mary does, Kate Henderson embodies the new, revolutionary intelligentsia of socialism. She is, perhaps, historically derived from Mary Wollstonecraft, who had served for a while at Mitchelstown (or, *qua* revolutionary intellectual, she is a Constance Markievicz in waiting). Her simple function here is merely to spell out the argument that a seismic shift in ideology has eroded the *raison d'être* for the residual forms of aristocracy that were reconstituted after the earlier failure of 'the work of the French Revolution'. 'Nobody', she claims, believes in the civilisation to which the Martins belong:

> Society is reconstituted just as a child constructs a cardhouse to see how high he can carry the frail edifice before it tumbles. The people – the true people of the Continent – look at the pageantry of a Court and a Nobility just as they do on a stage procession, and criticise it in the same spirit ... then, some fine morning, they'll dash down the whole edifice; and be assured that the fragments of the broken toy will never suggest the sentiment to repair it. (p. 287)

What stands in the way of 'the true people', she claims, is a capitalist class eager to inherit 'the divine right of misrule', whereas those who are 'truly noble' have become, like her, socialists. Wrenched from its context this appears simple enough. Placed within the dialectic of the fiction, however, Ms Henderson's location in a midway carriage of the abdicating order she criticises suggests a strangely symbiotic link between her and that order. She is, as it were, a kind of Gucci Marxist, supping at the high table of Oxbridge and deconstructing the semiotics of the pageant of power from a chair of privilege. One might also enquire why, in her invocation of 'the true people of the Continent', she excludes Ireland, which she quits with the Martins (like her fellow socialist O'Casey after that other 'abdication', the treaty of 1921). But the crucial country house signifier in her discourse is in her allusion to the 'cardhouse', the 'frail edifice' that the people will 'dash down', and which she sees as an irreparably 'broken toy'. Implicit in that imagery is the deliberate destruction of the houses of the gentry and rejection of the culture embodied in those houses. Ms Henderson is an initiatory voice of what academic jargon now calls 'the culture war'.

The departure of the coaches is followed by the inundation of the demesne by 'the people', to adopt Ms Henderson's socialist nomination (for her 'the people' signify something fundamentally different from Ormond's Black Islanders). But Henderson's nicely correct political term requires more precise definition. The people who buy up and buy out Cro'Martin are not the poor of course. The poor are Mary Martin's people, depicted in the initiatory description of the house as bare-footed, ragged and desperately hungry dependants on the charity she has not the means to provide, 'low-browed, treacherous-looking, and almost savagely cruel' as they gather round her, partly slavishly servile, partly threatening revolt. Lever asks *in propria persona* (in contradistinction to Ms Henderson), 'Who would dare to call them kind-hearted or malevolent, grateful or ungrateful, free-giving or covetous, faithful or capricious, as a people?' (p. 8) These are not the proletariat of socialist theory, nor the *Urvolk* of romantic nationalism, nor the subaltern culture of post-colonial theory. 'Regeneration', Lever claims, is not to be found here. On the contrary, this multitude is about to die by cold and famine and filth and vermin (as Jonathan Swift had reasonably predicted more than a century before).

The inheritors of Cro'Martin, by right of purchase (which has supplanted right of conquest), are the emergent middle classes – petty gentry, strong farmers, urban bourgeoisie:

> Vast crowds of people...now came pouring in, all eager in their curiosity, but somehow all subdued into a kind of reverence for a spot from which they had been so rigidly excluded, and the very aspect of which so far transcended expectations. (p. 296)

The auction chapter (15) is an ironic variant of one of the most funda-mental motifs of the literature of the country house: the celebration of the great house as a place where 'all come in' (the king and the peasant), as in Ben Jonson's idealisation. In nineteenth-century context, how-ever, the auction sequence suggests comparison with the two invasions of the country house that Benjamin Disraeli uses in *Sybil* (1845) to contrast the unacceptable and the positive face of country house culture. In one Disraelian variant of the Jonsonian *topos* the 'House of Pride', Mowbray Castle, which is representative of the 'Norman yoke' of class conquest, is attacked by an enraged mob of the poor, led by 'the Liberator of the People' (an English O'Connell); the owner of the castle is stoned to death, the artistic treasures of the house scattered, and then, in a promiscuous fire, the invaders and the castle burn together. In Disraeli's alternative sequence the hungry people are met by a Mary Martin figure, who charitably serves their needs. The people then ask permission to view and admire the house, and progress in admiring order through the beauties of the demesne. Disraeli adds, 'the writer speaks from circumstances within his own experience'. His conservative imagination foresees the distant coming of The National Trust, and thus the conservation of something of the forms and substance of past civilisation in the present.[4]

In comparison there is a more astringent pessimism in Lever. His choice of the word 'reverence' to describe the gaze of the newly ascendant class might suggest some affinity with Disraeli (and the choice of the word 'transcended' to describe the people's expectations has similar mystically religious implications). But the place where this orderly tour takes place is the stable yard. This is the 'luxurious abode' of the livestock of Cro'Martin, and there can be no doubt of the pejorative use of the concept of *luxuria* here, applied to the ornamental troughs for watering the horses, the 'beautifully designed fountains' and 'the sculptured medallions...emblematising the chase' that adorn the walls. The animals of the demesne are better housed than the tenantry. Nonetheless every farmer in the yard, Lever claims, is struck by a 'hearty and sincere' admiration for the superb quality of the livestock in the yard. The same is true of the demesne without, the timber more finely grown, the fields 'more highly cultivated than anything they had ever before seen'. 'There's everything can make a demesne beautiful – wood, water, and mountain!' exclaims one of the prospective purchasers, to which his companion replies, 'And, better than all, a fine system of farming...that's the best field of "swedes" I ever beheld.' (p. 294) The Young/Edgeworth principles still apply. Capital investment, properly applied, makes the country house both a source of improved agriculture and a place of beauty.

But what of those things Ms Henderson called 'toys'? They have been reduced merely to items of financial trade and covetous desire. We are observing an historical process that has moved from the auction room in the nineteenth century to what has now, become, the detritus of an 'Antiques Roadshow':

> The visitor wanders amidst objects which have occupied years in
> collection: some, the results of considerable research and difficulty;
> some, the long-coveted acquisitions of half a lifetime; and some – we

have known such – the fond gifts of friendship. There they are now side by side in the catalogue, their private histories no more suspected than those of them who lie grass-covered in the churchyard. (pp. 292–3)

The word 'objects' is, in some measure, less pejorative than 'toys', but Lever does not credit his 'visitor' (the equivalent of the 'stranger' who earlier toured the empty house) with a fine Jamesian sense of the aesthetic pleasure of these things. The sensibility of the text (separated from the purposes of the auction) is sentimental, suggesting that the person of feeling (the reader) will see here the break-up of a home, and loss of home is a situation that can be universally recognised: 'Ay, this selling-off is a sad process! It bespeaks the disruption of a home; the scattering of those who once sat around the same hearth, with all the dear familiar things about them!' (p. 293). Hence the work of a Cellini is of no more value than a 'little sketch in water-colour' made by some member of the family, since it is familial association not aesthetic rarity to which the heart responds. If this were a conventional nationalist nineteenth-century fiction one might expect the sentimental depiction of the loss of hearth and home to centre on the eviction of an impoverished and starving tenant, not on the fall of a great family and civilisation. But that is another subject.

The question is what, if anything, remains of a civilisation reduced to what Yeats was later to depict as a beautiful and rare shell but which Lever reduces merely to 'objects' in a sale catalogue (and a house wanting even a tenant)? The simple answer is that Mary Martin is excluded from the family's 'abdication' and retired to a 'Swiss cottage' (a European republican signifier?) on the estate, where she endeavours in vain to sustain the house and the responsibilities of the house. In an Irish context this makes her a Countess Cathleen figure, an aristocrat who gives her life for the 'people' (by which is meant the starving poor) (Plate 5). But in the wider context of country house fiction in English, Mary Martin belongs to a long series of female figures who originated in the English country house tradition with Maria Fairfax, the only hope of her family in Marvell's 'Upon Appleton House', and which closes, perhaps, with the unnamed heroine of du Maurier's *Rebecca* recalling the memory of burnt Manderley. Maria Edgeworth, Edith Somerville and Elizabeth Bowen belong to this tradition, and *a fortiori* Violet Martin, who is related to the real-life original of Lever's heroine. The role of the woman in this variant of country house tradition is that of custodian of the house. This is a leitmotif that at this juncture is touched upon only lightly in Lever's text, but if one were to locate Mary Martin within this cultural nexus, the obvious figure to relate her to is Austen's Fanny Price as the moral custodian of Mansfield Park. Although Austen was not dealing with the material bankruptcy of the Bertrams, the moral bankruptcy of the *ancien régime* is at issue in her novel, and the Jacobinical context is as acute there as the class issue is in Lever. The axe has been laid to the ancestral tree. The parallel between *Mansfield Park* and *The Martins of Cro'Martin* is that in both fictions a spiritual, not a material, 'inheritance' of the country house occurs through the person of a woman who takes up (modest) residence within the ambience of the demesne. She becomes the *genius loci* because she alone understands the essential genius of the place: traditional order, traditional moral responsibility and traditional manners.

Why is it a woman to whom this particular signification is given? Although the connotations of symbolic narration cannot be contained by any totalising 'theory', one possible reason is the traditional association of women with the domestic sphere. They belong within the house rather than representing the 'house' (meaning the family) in the public sphere. Accordingly women, often serve (in fact or fiction) as *figurae* for disempowerment, marginality and suffering. From that domestic confinement and political disenfranchisement there has been repeatedly generated a desire for imaginative empowerment, achieved in the real world through entry into the public sphere via literature. Maria Edgeworth, Violet Martin, Edith Somerville and Elizabeth Bowen can in some measure be seen as representatives of this type, and all, like Lever's fictional/real-life heroine, were chatelaines of country houses.

Mary Martin's place in this socially elite company is not something that is directly available to the 'vulgar'. 'The Hall entrance is not to be invaded by . . . vulgar visitors', one of Cro'Martin's purchasers critically complains (p. 296). The *vulgus* to whom Lever alludes are the common, multiheaded mob (the 'swinish multitude'). In contradistinction Mary Martin, like her real-life counterpart, with whom Edgeworth conversed as an equal, belongs to 'elite' culture. The implications of this are made clear by Lever when Mrs Nelligan, one of the 'vulgar', loses her way and finds herself in the still perfectly kept gardens of Cro'Martin. Purchasers have been kept away from here by 'a strong paling across the avenue', and thus are placed beyond the pale and, by historical analogy, are the equivalent of savages separated *vi et armis* from the protected place of civilisation. But the paling, like the famous locked gate in Austen's *Mansfield Park*, is merely a symbolic barrier, and Mrs Nelligan, eager to see a friend within the house, leaves behind her 'the sounds of the multitude', and traversing the *selva oscura* of a shrubbery emerges 'upon a beautifully-cultivated "parterre," whose close-shaven sward and flowery beds flanked a long range of windows opening to the ground'. (p. 297) This is the locus of Mary Martin's departure from the house, where Mrs Nelligan and Mary meet 'just as if . . . equal' (in Mrs Nelligan's words) and as compatriots linked by 'mutual esteem' (Mary Martin's expression). The place is both the correlative of a (vain) wish for equality and union and the expression of the divide between those within and those without 'the pale'. The parterre and close-shaven sward are the nineteenth-century equivalent of the allegorical close-mown meadow of Andrew Marvell's 'Upon Appleton House', which 'Leveller's take measure at', and the enlightening windows 'opening to the ground' are places of easy and level access and egress between house and lawn.

The meeting between Mary Martin and Mrs Nelligan in this locus is an ideological encounter between the reciprocity of feudalism and the democracy of socialism. But it is not on common ground. The paling, the separation from the multitude, the setting of the level space without the house, even the formal elaboration (and cost) involved in the construction of the parterre still divides the elite and the common. This suggests something akin to Forster's subject in a later country house fiction, *Howard's End* – 'only connect' – but Lever also raises a Yeatsian theme. How might one replace the lost elite? The last word on that subject is offered by Mrs Nelligan's husband, a committed enemy of the Martins: 'we may pull them down – we may humble them – but we'll never fill their places!', and he hands Mary Martin to her little carriage 'with all the respect he could have shown a Queen'. That 'queen' is not Cathleen Ni Houlihan (as Maud Gonne was to embody her) but the Burkean figure of the morning star of Versailles (doomed, like Mary Martin, to untimely death).

Perhaps a more positive hope is implied for the next generation. The Nelligans' son Joe has neither the party and class interests of his parents, nor their religious concerns. He is a member of the Catholic bourgeoisie, educated at the Protestant stronghold of Trinity College in Dublin and rising to become the Lord Chief Justice of Ireland, thus bringing the rule of law even to 'the wild west'. Joe Nelligan is not a major figure in this novel since he is, self-evidently, merely a fictional hope for the 'progress of civilization' (p. 14). Others see Ireland as condemned by 'nature' itself to poverty and ignorance, for which legislative improvement is impossible, and attractive only as the subject of picturesque art (pp. 444–5). But Joe Nelligan retains a different picture in his rooms at Trinity College.

The only thing like ornament to be seen was a lithographic print of Cro'Martin Castle over the fireplace; a strange exception would it seem, but traceable, perhaps, to some remote sense of boyish admiration for what had first awakened in him a feeling of awe and admiration; and there it now remained, timeworn and discoloured, perhaps unnoticed, or looked on with very different emotions. Aye! these pictures are terrible landmarks of our thoughts! (p. 246)

It is only by refraction through the medium of art that Cro'Martin finds its way into the university, and that refraction is itself a mere copy (a lithograph of little monetary value) of an 'original' refraction. The interpretation of this timeworn artistic image is problematical, subject to varied emotions, if noticed at all; yet there it is, intrinsically evolved with the development of the new generation and carrying with it both a sense of almost religious veneration, 'awe' (for a man little concerned with the usual discriminations of religious sectarianism), and a source of reiterated 'admiration' (where the word carries, it is possible, both the English sense of esteem and, coded into the history of the language, the older Latin meaning of wonder and superstitious astonishment). But there is a further and more complex refraction of Cro'Martin. The lithograph of the picture is translated through the medium of Lever's own work of fiction, and that fiction is concerned with a Cro'Martin created only by the imagination, derived from a Ballinahinch still existent but changed utterly, and changed each time its story is narrated.

It was Yeats who wrote of 'those images which yet fresh images beget'. The image of Cro'Martin belongs in a kind of hall of mirrors that history refracts from Edgeworth to Lever, and from Lever to Violet Martin. Although the story of this place is grounded upon real persons and a familial catastrophe that overwhelmed a (still-existent) house, it is obvious that the sequential recension with which we are concerned is a symbolic fiction. Nor does that symbolism correspond even to the general social or political history of country house culture in Ireland at the time when Lever was writing. On the contrary, rather than the land-lord classes being in decline and fall, the postfamine period in which the story of Cro'Martin was published was a time of substantial renewed economic prosperity and confidence (if not quite the golden era of Edgeworth's lifetime). The investment managers of Maynooth, for instance, made extensive loans against (Protestant!) property (unable to foresee the slump and consequential troubles of the 1880s and 1890s). At Kylemore Abbey (the abbey of the great wood), only a few miles from Ballinahinch, a massive investment of Mancunian money raised a magnificent mansion and pumped some £40 000 a year in maintenance costs into what we would now call the tourist industry and agricultural subsidy. Ballinahinch itself was to become the country seat of an Indian prince (a peculiar twist for postcolonial theory), and even now (as a luxury hotel) provides the usual pleasures of country house living: fine food, fine sporting opportunities and dedicated service.

This is merely to reiterate the distinction made earlier between the empirical complexities of history and the symbolic order of fiction. The proviso is repeated because of the seductive mimetic mode of the realist nineteenth-century novel and Lever's commitment, in his later years, to writing serious historical fictions. But the concern here is with the rhetoric of the mimetic mode. The country house loci (the symbolic use of architectural *topoi*) form part of an historical sequence in Lever's writings and constitute what one might describe as an epic design that involves Ireland from the 1790s to the 1870s. The sequence of fictions extend from the revolutionary 1790s (*The O'Donoghue*, 1845), through the controversies over the Union (*The Knight of Gwynne*, 1846–7), the Napoleonic Wars (in which *Tom Burke of Ours*, 1843–4, foreshadows Yeats' 'An Irish Airman Foresees his Death') and thence to the contemporary history of the Union in *The Martins of Cro'Martin* (1854–6), *Luttrell of Arran* (1863–5), *The Bramleighs of Bishop's Folly* (1867–8) and finally *Lord Kilgobbin* (1870–2), a dark farewell to a darkening scene. Once Lever had abandoned the earlier sub-Smolletian mode for which he became notorious, his affinities were first to Maria Edgeworth, then Lady Morgan and Sir Walter Scott in an uncertain blend of enlightened historicism with romantic melodrama, and then to his contemporaries Anthony Trollope and Charles Dickens, blending the cynical naturalism of Trollope with the symbolic (rather than sentimental) mode of late Dickens.

The architectural *topoi* cover the entire post-Norman history of Ireland. The Abbey in *The Knight of Gwynne* (which is the country seat of the improvident knight) and O'Donoghue castle in *The O'Donoghue* embody a pre-Enlightenment romantic Ireland that is 'dead and gone'. In the latter novel the castle is formally contrasted with a modern villa (in Tudor style) known as The Lodge, which is the centre of an anglicised and improving estate. In *The Bramleighs of Bishop's Folly* the architectural *topos* is derived from the eighteenth century. The folly, called Castello, is a Whig Palladian mansion reared in the wilderness by an Anglican prelate. Under the Union, Castello has become the home of an English capitalist, Mr Bramleigh, who wants to do something for Ireland (p. 70).[5] Lever's ultimate novel, *Lord Kilgobbin* is proto-Yeatsian for the country house here, set on the edge of the Bog of Allen, is an ancient fortified tower. Such is the violence of the times that the tower reverts to its original function when the family have to fight and defend their property from Fenians (within as well as without). In order to indicate the rich matrix of interrelationships between the fictions it is sufficient to sketch the nature and function of the loci. The common theme is the passage of the old order: 'That the age of chivalry is gone, we are reminded some twenty times in each day of our common-place existence' (*The Knight of Gwynne*, p. 597).[6] The process of history (the progress of civilisation) is towards the incorporation of Ireland into the matrix of international capitalisation and industrialisation, but in Ireland it is a process of disruption and disjunction.

The civilisation/savagery paradigm remains the fundamental structuring myth. One passage from *The Knight of Gwynne* serves to illustrate the dark pessimism of the opposition. The story opens with Lord Castlereagh at dinner in Merrion Square on the eve of the Union. Accordingly, Ireland is first seen through English eyes.[7] One of the guests, Dick Forester, shortly afterwards seeks an assessment of the situation of Ireland from an old Mayo squire. The Englishman is aghast at the poverty he has seen, and amazed to be told that this in fact represents improvement:

> 'It is hard to conceive a people more miserably off than these,' said Forester, with a sigh.
>
> 'So they seem to your eyes; but let me remark, that there is a transition state between rude barbarism and civilisation which always appears more miserable than either; habits of life which suggest wants that can rarely, if ever, be supplied; the struggle between poverty and the desire for better, is a bitter conflict, and such is the actual condition of this people. You are young enough to witness the fruits of the reformation; I am too old ever to hope to see them, but I feel assured that the day is coming.' (p. 10)

This is a late variation of Arthur Young's enlightened view of the progress of civilisation, but it is the darkest of preludes to the projected benefits of Union. The transfer from one state of things to another, through 'bitter conflict', will get worse before it gets better, and the old order in Ireland will not survive to see it. The old man has already outlined the problems to Forester in a string of negatives: the absence of a transportation system and of markets (one thinks of Sir John Davies' insistence on the establishment of market towns); the tyranny of the landowners and the slavish condition of an exploited people; the violence of faction – 'those barbarous vestiges of a rude time' – and hence, ultimately, a land 'nearly famished' (Lever was writing in 1846–7).

Traditionally the sign of an improvement in the state of things had been the plantation of a demesne. It is to this that the ancestral home of the patriotic Knight of Gwynne is related. It is an ancient abbey and thus rooted both in the old religion of the *Volk* and in a deep-rooted social order. The abbey is compounded of elements of Scott's (mythologised) Abbotsford and the 'young England' idealism of the contemporary novel, represented for instance by Disraeli's St Geneviève, a secular seat of social welfare, tradition and culture. The external walls of the Knight of Gwynne's country house are 'decorated with saintly figures', true signifiers of its owner's moral principles; its hospitable hall, hung (like Abbotsford) with ancient armour, shows how ancient wars have yielded to the social concord of modern peace ('all come in', as at Penshurst, to be feasted here). The culture of the owner of the house is manifest both in the architecture of the locus – the tracery of the fenestration, for instance, is 'not rudely chiselled, but with high pretension as works of art' – and, of course, in the actively employed and excellent library. The jewels in the crown are the former prior's house, a treasure house of the arts of eighteenth-century French culture, and a belvedere, looking towards the Island of Achill, from which the pious, patriotic and cultured owner can survey his beneficently controlled estates, extending from the formality of his well-tended gardens to the circumambient villages, the local market town (p. 246) and the sublime landscape that links man to God. This is an ideological ideal that, to take an actual Irish locus, is embodied in the Gothic order of Kylemore Abbey.

There is nothing else in Lever's country house fiction like this. But it is an ideal order seen from a distance. Whereas Edgeworth, at the end of *The Absentee*, makes that distance spatial (we look up at the country house through the eyes of an outsider), in *The Knight of Gwynne* the distance is temporal. This fiction is placed in that supposedly golden age before the Union when men like Grattan (and the Knight of Gwynne) were idolised as 'all the Olympians' (to borrow a phrase from Yeats). The contrast between this idealised *ancien régime* and the famished society described to Forester is abrupt, and strategic, for *The Knight of Gwynne* is Lever's reworking of the thematic material of Edgeworth's *Castle Rackrent*. The basic economic substructure beneath the ideal superstructure of the abbey is unable to sustain it. The hospitality of the knight is the ruin of his estate, and another 'Jason Quirk' is waiting to seize the property. The novelist himself, as the sympathetic recounter of the tragedy of the knight is, as it were, a more historically informed version of Edgeworth's 'Uncle Tom' figure, Thady. The fall of the knight is assisted (paradoxically) by his very Grattanesque integrity, for it is his refusal to join the gadarene herd (a different kind of 'swinish multitude') swilling at the trough of the Union that leaves him without any financial lifeline (unless, as the Neanderthal Bagnel Daly suggests, he defends his home *vi et armis* – a theme to which Lever returns in *Lord Kilgobbin*).

This is a far bleaker view of the old order in Ireland than Edgeworth's retrospective comedy in *Castle Rackrent*. The knight is driven to a cynical realism about the future of the Union when he advises the new generation ('young enough to be plastic') to commit itself to Castlereagh, for 'the honour of the empire lies next his heart', (p. 586) and it is in the empire that chivalric patriotism will find its outlet, as the knight shows at the battle of Aboukir (p. 513). But the knight also perceives that the very chivalric ideal for which imperial war provides the appropriate outlet for his caste is symbiotically related to the very barbarism ('lawless outrage') with which, at home, society is involved. This is the story of Ireland's 'misery and degradation':

> The owner of the soil has diffused little else among the people than the licentious terror of his own unbridled passion; he has taught lawless outrage, when he should have inculcated obedience and submission. The corruption of our people has come from above downwards; the heavy retribution will come one day; and when the vices of the peasant shall ascend to the master the social ruin will be complete. (p. 252)

It is characteristic of Lever's dialectical method that this historical judgement is limited by the historical location of the speaker (it is not necessarily authorial), but this prediction of what is to come is a serious projection of the conclusion of *Castle Rackrent*. More specifically, the knight has already indicated that a new generation of landgrabbers (masquerading as patriots – the last refuge of the scoundrel) will succeed to the estates of the old order. The abbey manifested, at least, the graces of civilisation, so when that is taken away the common people, their last links to inherited culture severed, will turn their appetites, the common wolf, upon the houses of the great. 'We had a distinct and defined duty to perform, and we neglected it,' he says. 'Instead of extending civilisation, we were the messengers of barbarism among the people' (p. 66).

The expression 'licentious terror', which the knight uses, has a particular historical resonance that should not be suppressed by parochial limitation to the 'mere Irish'. The allusion is to these European events that immediately preceded the Union and spilled over into Ireland in the 1790s, and which in Lever's view remained intrinsically related to the class conflicts of unionist society throughout his lifetime. While Grattan and the knight debate great principles of statecraft in the Irish parliament, outside the streets of Dublin are already in the possession of the 'half-naked wretches' of a drunken and violent Irish jacquerie. The most popular lyrics of the mob, Lever claims, are those which celebrate 1798, and the leader of the mob is (in Irish context) the Shan van Vocht. We have already seen her equivalent in the imagination of Browne and Cruickshank:

> The chief chorister appeared to be a fiend-like old woman, with one eye, and a voice like a cracked bassoon; she was dressed in a cast-off soldier's coat and a man's hat, and neither from face nor costume had few feminine traits. This fair personage, known by the name of Rhoudlum, was, on her appearing, closely followed by a mob of admiring amateurs, who seemed to form her bodyguard and her chorus. (pp. 182–3)

'The French are on the sea', sang the Shan van Vocht, and 'hurrah for liberty!'

A similar figure marks the closure of Lever's fiction set in the revolutionary 1790s, *The O'Donoghue*. The Shan van Vocht is now called 'mad Mary' and wanders the desolate land between the ruined castle of the O'Donoghues (the former seat of the ancient feudalism) and an abandoned villa, the sign of the failed modernisation and improvement efforts by the English family Travers. But the villa now is 'a ruin like the rest', mad Mary states. '"Nobody knows who owns it, and they say it will never be found out; but," said she, rising and gathering her cloak around her as she prepared to move away, "there's neither luck nor grace upon the spot. God Almighty made it beautiful and lovely to look upon, but man and man's wickedness brought a curse down upon it"' (p. 485).[8] It is not just the villa she has in mind. Her allegorical function as an embodiment of Ireland expresses three traditional themes relating to the place: the loveliness of the landscape, the uncertainty of the possession of the land, and the ineluctable misery, the 'curse', of Irish history. If Lever's choice of the name O'Donoghue is an allusion to Edgeworth (it is the familial name of the protagonist in *Ennui*), once again he is pessimistically rewriting his original.

'Man's wickedness' has its elemental correlatives in *The O'Donoghue* in the great storm that destroys the French fleet and the lightning strike that completes the ruin of Carrignacurra Castle. The fire in the heavens above is matched by the destruction of the villainous expropriator of revolution's principles, the evil land agent Hemsworth, who is blown to pieces when the inadvertent discharge of his pistol destroys the rebels' powder magazine. In Lever the great storm is not the providential 'Protestant' wind (of one reading of Irish history), rather it represents the 'mere anarchy' (to borrow from Yeats) that has been loosed upon the world, whether that anarchy is the 'delirium of the brave' embodied in the Byronism of a rebel O'Donoghue, or exists in the actions of a revolutionary army compounded, so Lever claims, of the refuse of the jails of France united to a mob bent on pillage and rapine (p. 478).

It is the failure of *both* the potential sources of civilisation in the fiction, the castle and the villa, that create the vacuum of anarchy. The melodramatic storyline (which is not our concern) is underpinned by a formalistic treatment of the social function of place, in which the castle and the villa (like the Heights and the Grange in Emily Brontë's *Wuthering Heights*) represent antagonistic forces and different phases of historical process.

The castle requires least consideration for it is merely another 'Ballinahinch', a stronghold decayed to become half farmyard; a would-be demesne stripped of its woodlands; a semifortified anachronism of barbarian ideals midway between the Homeric Cuchulainism of bardic flattery and the Morgan/Maturin wild Irish boyism of romantic nation-alism. (pp. 17–19; 182–3; 50–1) Historically Carrignacurra has not evolved even as far as the 'Abbey' in *The Knight of Gwynne*, and as far as Lever is concerned the lightning strike (which symbolises the destructive nihilism of the 1790s) that destroys the castle marks the end of that kind of barbarian culture. (The resurrection of Cuchulainism in the twentieth century would have been taken by Lever – as it was by Somerville – as a sign of cultural recidivism.)

The failure of the villa, on the other hand, brings into question the progress of unionist modernity. At first sight it 'seems' (to employ a Spenserian key word) ideal, in contradistinction to the castle:

> The neat but unpretending cottage had...been converted into a building of Elizabethan style; the front extended along the lake side, to which it descended in two terraced gardens. The ample win-dows, thrown open to the ground, displayed a suite of apartments furnished with all that taste and luxury could suggest – the walls ornamented by pictures, and the panels of both doors and window-shutters formed of plate glass, reflecting the mountain scenery in

every variety of light and shadow. The rarest flowers, the most costly shrubs, brought from long distances, at great risk and price, were here assembled to add their beauties to a scene where nature had already been so lavish. (p. 356)

Even the 'salvage man' of the fiction, Terry of the Woods, has been moved to admire the scene, commending the grass walks of the garden ('as fine as a carpet'), the beauty of the flowers 'and a fountain, as they call it, of cool water spouting up in the air, and coming down like rain' (p. 344). This is what an estate agent might describe as a 'highly desirable' property. The villa's 'neat but unpretending' structure distinguishes it from the folly of some Timonesque, rackrenting overreacher. Historically, its architectural style deliberately unites it to the golden age of the greatest of Tudor monarchs, but with no regressive antiquarianism. The ample windows, 'thrown open to the ground', democratically unite house and demesne (like the 'Mary Martin' apartments at Cro'Martin), and the plate glass shutters call the landscape into the house itself. Within the villa, civilisation has united taste with the luxury that wealth supplies. Most significant of all, however, is the fountain, which sparks the wonder of the salvage man. That imaginal association of a fountain with a great house is from the Renaissance tradition, where it was a sign of both the generosity and the fertility of the house, and (perhaps by way of Spenser) was to acquire elegiac signification in the country house poetry of Yeats. The designation of this *locus amoenus* is 'The Lodge', a name that might suggest, in progressive history, an entrance gate leading to something even better beyond. Such indeed is the social purpose of the owner, Sir Marmaduke Travers, whose superabundant wealth is directed to the improvement of his estate, in the manner of Young and Edgeworth, as much as to the embellishment of his house.

If only this were not Ireland. Any reader versed in nationalist or postcolonialist interpretation will have picked up the ironic signification of a house in Ireland called a 'lodge'. A lodgement is no permanent place of residence, especially for the Travers family, which is accordingly 'traverse', crossing backwards and forwards, or 'over in England' (p. 344). This reading indicates the degree to which interpretation is subject to ideological prejudice. The word 'Elizabethan' provides another crux, for the adoption of Tudor motifs for The Lodge locates the house specifically in an era of colonial (and Protestant) plantation. For any nationalist insurrectionist that is a red rag to a bull.

The failure of the Travers' plantation is as much the subject of *The O'Donoghue* as the Jacobinical/jacquerie nexus of insurrection. There is nothing intrinsically wrong with the theory of plantation improvement. Sir Marmaduke, like the travellers in Edgeworth's *Tour in Connemara*, has equipped himself with the best available literature on the subject. His aim is the 'regeneration and civilisation' of Ireland, and Dorothea Brooke, as much as Edgeworth, would have approved of his religious ecumenicism and his practical schemes (on 'Norfolk' principles) for the erection of model cottages, a (non-sectarian) school, enclosure, drill cultivation, piggeries, beehives, dovecotes... The schemes fail, and Lever's tragi-comic account (Chapter 15) is a late exercise in a literary tradition that originated as early as the Swiftean disasters of Quilca.[9] This failure has little to do with the current background of civil unrest, although the situation in Ireland is certainly not conducive to capital investment (a subject that Trollope was to consider at length in *The Landleaguers*). It is simply that Youngian theory and Irish practice (in this fictional tradition) do not unite. The Irish pig that uproots the English beehives serves as a typical (and allegorical) example.

Whether this failure should be blamed on English ignorance or Irish recalcitrance is a pointless issue, as is whether it corresponds to actual agricultural experience. This is a fictive work, not a plantation diary (compare for instance the journals of 'the Highland lady' in Ireland). What succeeds in nullifying the plantation is what the protagonists still call 'barbarism'. The symbolic landscape (what Ireland appears to be in the imagination) is still that of a region beyond the pale of reclamation. It has, a visitor finds, 'a wildness all its own', a wildness so extraordinary that the visitor is drawn to ask of the native, 'surely you cannot mean that people are living here' (p. 5). But the people there, we are told repeatedly, are 'barbarously ignorant' (pp. 42, 110, 129), indeed so ignorant that Sir Marmaduke, driven to despair, cries that such barbarism is beyond the conception of man. This is the fodder of resistance to improvement and the seedbed of insurrection. This is 'a country, in which the resident sits down overwhelmed... and utterly despairing of solution', wrote Lever in his Preface to a reprint of this novel in 1872.[10] He wrote his comments in Trieste. By that time the wise man had quit what was irreclaimable, although he did not give his flight from the nets of Irish nationalism and sectarianism the same aesthetic significasion as a subsequent resident of Trieste, James Joyce.

The fiction flirts with a conventional (symbolic) 'solution' of the Irish problem by invoking the 'union' of a marriage. Feudal castle and Edgeworthian lodge are united by the marriage of the younger O'Donoghue son (civilised by education at Trinity College, a fine Latin scholar and an acolyte of imperial civilisation) to a Travers daughter. But they quit Ireland at once for a position as administrators in India. Conversely the O'Donoghue heir (the rebel leader) becomes a latter-day 'wild goose' in France, and his cousin Kate, rejecting an English marriage, herself quits Irish 'barbarism' – as her family describe it (p. 155) – for the civilisation (and sterility) of a convent in France. Hence the castle and the lodge are both left abandoned. There is no home for a cultural elite in Ireland.

The fiction also evokes a familiar Edgeworthian *vir bonus*, a wise Scottish economist called Sir Archy. He has seen the success of Unionism and believes it might succeed again if given the opportunity to work by gradualism and grow through time:

> It is time to outlive the evil memories of the past; we want here – time, to blunt the acuteness of former and long-past sufferings – time, to make traditions so far forgotten as to be inapplicable to the present – time, to read the homely lesson, that one-half the energy a people can expend in revolt will raise them in the rank of civilized and cultivated beings. (p. 236)

Ernest Renan would have agreed, for a nation is built, so he famously claimed, on the ability of people to choose to forget the conflicts of the past. But Sir Archy is himself, by the end of the story, a relic of forgotten conciliation and union.

Underpinning the conventional melodrama of the story there is an economic analysis, suggested by the novelist in *propria persona*. The argument is that what once held together the fissile society of Ireland was a residual feudal bond, a link between aristocrat and people based on reciprocal loyalty. It provided the cultural coherence of a barbaric polity (the castle). But its destruction, by improvidence within and new plantation without, has opened the land to the new world represented by the lodge. The Travers family now operate an agricultural order based on a cash nexus between landlord and tenant, which, to succeed, is dependent on improved economic productivity (the improvement of the estate), thus providing increased income for the tenant, higher rents for the landlord and the surplus value needed to purchase the works of 'taste and luxury' of country house culture. This is a not unreasonable economic analysis. But when that economic nexus fails (and failure was glaringly obvious to a novelist writing in the 1840s) there is no social bond (or even mutual self-interest) to hold together what Lever called in the Preface of 1872 'the new civilization' that was emerging in Ireland.

The Bramleighs of Bishop's Folly carries the theme forward to the post-Edgeworthian world of high nineteenth-century capitalism. The improvement of the estate is no longer the main concern. Rather it is the kick-starting of an entire regional economy by the injection of international capital. Mere agriculture will not provide the money either to maintain the civilisation of the great house or to liberate an entire people from the barbarism of poverty and ignorance. An Irish coal industry is the El Dorado of the Bramleighs, a merchant banking family who own Bishop's Folly. Of course in Ireland this plan of industrial modernisation is a 'folly', like the very country house the Bramleighs inhabit. To this new subject Lever adds the old Irish motif of disputed title to the land. This motif has been particularly attractive to those looking for confession of colonial guilt in 'Ascendancy' literature. But it is typical of Lever's method that he raises the old issue only to give it a new signification. The estate had been thrown into chancery, and the Bramleighs legally purchase (and ultimately hold) their land despite legal challenge (compare Edgeworth's *Patronage*). The disputed title motif is used here to emphasise the shallow-rootedness of the new capitalist order. The dispossession of some glorious bardic and barbaric caste of warlords is not an issue within the parameters of Lever's interpretation of Irish history.

The locus is a Palladian villa. Accordingly it represents, by symbiosis, the golden-age mythos of Grattanism. But that myth is another of those commonplaces which (inevitably present in the cultural subtext) are satirically rejected. Bishop's Folly, as the locals call it, or Castello, as its owners nominate the villa, is the closest Lever comes to introducing into his fiction the ideology and idealism of European and Renaissance villa culture. It stands in the symbolic order of his imaginary world in the same relation to the circumambient wilderness as Jefferson's Monticello, for instance, in the culture of the United States. A major act of will and expenditure beyond the capabilities of the owner in both cases impose the signs of an elite humanism on a place where humanism has no history. The original builder of this folly, the bishop:

> had passed many years in Italy, and had formed a great attachment to that country. He liked the people and their mode of life; he liked the old cities, so rich in art treasures and so teeming with associations of a picturesque past; and he especially liked their villa architecture, which seemed so essentially suited to a grand and costly style of living. The great reception-rooms, spacious and lofty; the ample antechambers, made for crowds of attendants; and the stairs

wide enough for even equipages to ascend them. No more striking illustration of his capricious turn of mind need be given than the fact that it was his pleasure to build one of these magnificent edifices in an Irish county! – a costly whim, obliging him to bring over from Italy, a whole troop of stucco-men and painters, men skilled in fresco-work and carving – an extravagance on which he spent thousands. Nor did he live to witness the completion of his splendid mansion. (p. 1)

This is a novelistic variant of Popeian satire, with the bishop as an Irish Timon. There is a disjunction here between morality and art. For the bishop the *translatio* of Renaissance culture involves the imitation of picturesque form rather than moral content, and art is seen in relation to its monetary value as treasure. Villa culture, in its ideal manifestation, was once seen as the site of 'the good life', witness the Palladian ideal or Alexander Pope at Twickenham; but for the bishop it is valued as 'essentially suited to a grand and costly style of living'. The staircases are wide enough for a coach and horses, and the foreign workmen are not the agents of the extension of European civilisation in this remote fringe, but the creatures of mere extravagance. Castello has not even the justification of Jefferson's Monticello. It has no educative function. Like Count O'Halloran's castle in Edgeworth (and the memory of old conquest remains in the name Castello) the inability of the owner to complete his dwelling is indicative of a culture rooted only in the forms of the past and without the ability to vitalise the future. When the fiction begins the folly is a ruin, fragments of it having been carried off by the poor: 'the doors and windows had all been carried away by the peasants, and in many a cabin or humble shealing in the country around shards of coloured marble or fragments of costly carving might be met with, over which the skill of a cunning workman had been bestowed for days long' (p. 2).

The fragmentation of European culture, represented by the partial dismemberment of the folly, is worked out subsequently in the plot by the dispersal of the Bramleighs. At the end most of the family are scattered around the (original) Mediterranean world. Augustus (an imperial name) is in a consulate on the Adriatic coast – *beatus ille* at least in a retreat from the cares of his paternal acres! Temple is a wooden functionary at the Foreign Office; Marion is married to a climber of the slippery slopes of establishment patronage; their mother, Augusta, separated from her family, sponges for a livelihood. Of course, this being a nineteenth-century novel there is a happy marriage to resolve the plot. 'Jack' gets his 'Jill' (or here, Julia) and also Castello. But that is a mere convention. If one were to extract signification from Castello surviving with a new chatelaine it might be to conclude that new money will stick by the outer forms of old property as long as it is able.

The holding of old property (by whatever means) is the subject of Lever's last fiction, *Lord Kilgobbin*. The locus here is a 'short, square tower, battlemented at top', which is the ancestral home of the ancient O'Caharney family (now Kearney). It was once seized from the O'Caharneys by the invading Norman forces of Sir Hugh de Lacy, but subsequently recovered from them by an act of murder. From the beginning Lever takes up the subject of the nineteenth-century land wars (his contemporary theme). In Ireland you kill or are killed for possession of a (fortified) place. The central episode of the novel (in thematic contrast to the departure of the family in *The Martins of Cro'Martin*) is the defence of the tower by the Kearneys against Fenian attack, aided by an Englishman, Walpole, who is wounded in the defence. As an emblem of the divided and violent history of Ireland the episode needs no comment as Ur chieftain and Ur folk descend to civil war. That division is reflected in the diversity of discourses by which the fight is described. The main polemicist is Joe Atlee (an Ulsterman – so is he 'Irish'?) who has a similar function to the Southey figure in the poetry of Byron. His pen 'makes increment' of everything and he is Fenian or Tory as the wind blows. This complex political imbroglio is Europeanised (characteristically by Lever) by the location within the tower of an exotic Greek nationalist, Nina, for whom the 'Saxon' and the 'Turk' are common enemies of freedom (pp.146, 87).[11] But this is not a view privileged by the fiction. The discourse of anticolonialism is merely yet another way of seeing things. Nina romanticises the history of Ireland in a picturesque and Morganesque manner in a celebration of 'the wild old life of the savage chieftains and scarcely less savage conquerors' (she is working on a drawing entitled 'The Return of the O'Caharney'), but for the daughter of the Kearneys, Kate, the old warriors of Ireland were 'a selfish, worthless, self-indulgent race, caring for nothing but their pleasures, and making all their patriotism consist in hate towards England' (p. 36). Kate sees the present situation as one in which her family is caught between an inoperable (because alien) system of English law and the anarchy of Fenian insurgency (p. 223).

There are obvious affinities between Lever's choice of the tower as the central locus of his ultimate fiction and Yeats' meditations in a later period of civil war. There is a proto-Yeatsian desire, in Kate at least, to find some form of sweetness and light (Yeats' honeybee) emerging from savagery and barbarism. She has planted a garden beyond the tower, (p. 82) and it is in the traces of the lost ideal of the country house as a *paradeisos* that the son of the house resolves never to surrender his birthright:

> It was a wild, neglected sort of spot, with fruit-trees of great size, long past bearing, and close underwood in places that barred the passage. Here and there little patches of cultivation appeared, sometimes flowering plants, but oftener vegetables. One long alley, with tall hedges of box, had been preserved, and led to a little mound planted with laurels and arbutus, and known as 'Laurel Hill'; here a little rustic summer-house had once stood, and still, though now in ruins, showed where, in former days, people came to taste the fresh breeze above the tree-tops, and enjoy the wide range of a view that stretched to the Slieve-Bloom Mountains, nearly thirty miles away. (p. 108)

The 'little patches of cultivation' are the microcosmic equivalent of the demesnes of civilisation that punctuate the 'wild, neglected' nature that is Ireland; and the fruit trees, 'long past bearing', are signs of a culture that was once fruitful but is now dying. The 'little mound' is the trad-itional representation of the Mount of Paradise in garden iconography, and perhaps the name 'Laurel Hill' links Christian allusion to human-ism, for the name suggests the haunt of Apollo and the Muses. (Lady Gregory was to use her garden at Coole as a sign of a Renaissance *redi-vivus* in the west.) The summer house in ruins is a seasonal emblem (proleptic of 'the last September'), but it still preserves that high, wide and equal prospect that was the attribute (it was claimed) of the independent man of property (the Monticello syndrome).

One might still catch some vestigial inspiration even from the traces of such civilisation. Accordingly one visitor to the garden reflects on what such a situation might inspire in the owner (he sees the scene in enchanted moonlight):

> What would I not give to be the son of a house like this, with an old and honoured name, with an ancestry strong enough to build upon for future pretensions, and then with an old home, peaceful, tranquil, and unmolested, where, as in such a spot as this, one might dream of great things, perhaps more, might achieve them! What books would I not write...the mind elevated by that buoyancy which comes of the consciousness of being free from a great effort. (p. 98)

Free from the cares of poverty, from the compromises that poverty entails and from 'vulgar interruptions', a mind might bring the powers of philosophy to bear on the issues of religion, politics and society, and, in the field even of belles lettres, the visitor ruminates, might create novels whose ideal heroes would embody the aspirations of the heart. The Burkean ideal of ancestral continuity joins hands across the ages with the Ciceronian humanist at Tusculum and the new clerisy for which Coleridge yearned. Alternatively one might link Lever's text with the (ironised) idealism of Henry James' *The Princess Casamassima* or Evelgn Waugh's *Brideshead Revisited*. The irony is that these country house visions are the 'mere dreams' (to return to Yeats again) of an outsider, and an outsider who, in *Lord Kilgobbin*, has to act in contradistinction to this ideal of what he might be. The visitor is Joe Atlee, the most opportunistic voice of the heteroglossia of the story. He thinks of the books he might have written had he been the son of a great house, but here in the tower the library has been reduced to a mere agglomeration of antiquated almanacs in a den of top-boots, driving whips and so on.

Set against the tower is the other major locus of the fiction: the Great Bog of Allen. The tower is on the edge of the bog, in a 'border-land between fertility and destitution', on soil 'which had probably once been part of the Bog itself' (p. 1). This is the contested 'frontier' (p. 209) between the holders of the tower and the Fenian insurgents. As is characteristic of other frontiers, this frontier marks the boundary of territory where the law no longer operates, and a direct analogy is made with 'Indian tribes' of that other Wild West (p. 231). But the Bog of Allen, like the tower, alters its signification depending on the point of view. When the English seek to cross the bog, for instance, they lose the right road, or rather there are so many possible tracks and no established road that no man not born there can choose the right way (pp. 56–9). This is a Leveresque reworking of a theme in Edgeworth's *Tour in Connemara*. For Nina, who knows the Mediterranean world (that is, she is a classical humanist), the bog offers only a terrifying inanity. 'I see nothing out there but bleak desolation. I don't know if it ever had a past; I can almost swear it will have no future. Let us not talk of it' (p. 167). The inane is ineffable. Hellas cannot speak barbarism. But the 'desolation' of this 'desert' is the natural element of the Fenian named Donogan, and if the 'great expanse of dark bog' is a symbol of the darkness about to engulf Ireland, (p. 126) for him it is both a refuge beyond the reach of the law and his *paradeisos*, which thrills his heart like the 'throb of youth itself' (p. 171). As a native he loves every detail of the land, a sentiment that even Kate, his class enemy, can respond to as a native of the place. One might compare Edgeworth's use of the bog with the unpronounceable name in *Castle Rackrent* as a signifier of the elemental in Ireland, or alternatively, Hardy's Egdon Heath.

The tower stands as a frontier post marking the division between cultivation and a lawless wilderness, but on land that was probably once part of the wilderness itself. As it was seven hundred years before, so is it now. The tower is still standing (p. 305), and as Joe Atlee concludes, in an ending where nothing is concluded, 'Life here, I take it, will go on pretty much as before' (p. 474), as the present, retiring into the past, becomes the past returned. The story began with a dispossessed O'Caharney regaining his stronghold by killing a de Lacy. It ends with the Fenian rebel (united with the Greek anticolonialist, Nina) retiring across the Atlantic to continue, one presumes, from a safer base a cycle of killing justified by the discourse of anticolonialism.

As for the present world and the tower beyond the Yeatsian symbol, at the turn of the twenty-first century one might have looked up from the town of Dundalk and seen, marking another frontier, another line of towers upon the horizon, the watchtowers of another unionist army that had been at war with those recalcitrant forces that the Chief Constable of Ulster (an ancient historical title) had likened to 'savages'.

4
Trollope as Mr Kurtz

For Lever, the tower was a regressive icon, returning Ireland to a symbolic order that preceded the establishment of the country house. There might have been other architectural signifiers of the history of the place. Had Wolf Tone in the 1790s become the Washington of the United Irishmen, the Palladian villa might have become the locus that embodied the rational culture of the national *aristoi*, in the same way as Monticello, Mount Vernon and the White House in the United States. (Castletown, appropriately, is now the headquarters of the nascent Irish Georgian Society.) Alternatively Christian Gothic might have provided an ecumenical architectural symbolism for a vigorous and conservative unionism. Kylemore Abbey, it has been argued, embodies many of the ideals of Lever's 'Gwynne' Abbey, if only in subliminal suggestion, and by appropriate historical mutation Kylemore has become a (Roman Catholic) school, a fountain of culture. But the tower, as icon, takes one back historically beyond even Ormond's 'brave mansion' at Carrick-on-Suir to the *Ur* place, the fortified site that Ormond, in vain it seems, wished to transform into an open manor house. Ireland is a locus that denies the progress of (that kind of) civilisation.

This is a pessimistic reading that is both allegorical and Platonic. The schema, derived from Lever, is concerned with the literary interrelationship of icons, not the extratextual causes of the pessimistic iconography. All texts have causes of course, but causes do not explain texts. Historically the fiction of Lever, and that of the classic realist Trollope (our present concern), is located between the famine and the Land League, subjects that Trollope specifically addresses. These are causes that self-evidently relate to the pessimism (darker even than Lever's) with which Trollope's fictions are invested. But they are causes that are related to other historical mythologies – the fictions of genocide, for instance, or of nationalism. The historical matter of Trollope's texts is historically concomitant with these symbolic orderings (ideologically driven), which are merely other stories, not Trollope's. The story he tells, like that of Lever, is one of regression and, in terms of the dialectic of civilisation and savagery, of a brutal return of atavistic dark powers, or what a familiar formulation would call the 'return of the repressed'. It is as if Caliban were to be empowered. Allegorically interpreted, is the desire of 'salvage man' to kill Prospero and rape his daughter the (justified?) revenge of an oppressed 'other', or an expression of that intrinsic heart of darkness which religious mythology has called 'original sin'? In Shakespearean romance the interpretation of the symbol is multivalent and irreducible to the specificity of one historical story (a postcolonial reading of colonisation, for instance). Even a classic realist such as Trollope may be read in the same open way.

A representative example serves to illustrate. In Trollope's *The Land-leaguers* (1883) the Fenians murder a child, Florian. He is killed because he knows which of the Fenians flooded the meadows that had been brought into productive use by his father, Philip Jones, an improving landlord on the Edgeworthian model who had bought the land under the Encumbered Estates Act. It is a minor act of violence (of Catholic upon Catholic) in the history of the times, but the murder of a child is a potent anti-Fenian symbol.

But in the Platonic order of country house fiction, reclamation of the bog is a fundamental sign of the advance of civilisation. By developing bog into meadow two functions are fulfilled. Originally, by denying 'salvage man' the untractable wilderness in which he might find refuge (witness the Spenserian theme as late as *Lord Kilgobbin*) the pacification of Ireland might be more easily secured. Thence, with the rule of law established, the drained and enclosed meadowland becomes the basis for the progressive prosperity that is derived from security and capitalisation. But in *The Landleaguers* the destruction of the meadowlands on the Jones estate (by inundation with salt water, which will render them long useless) is a wilful act of destruction in which newly fertile land is returned to aboriginal wilderness. In Edgeworth's 'Connemara', the bog is a region beyond the frontier of civilisation from which the writer retreats back to the ordered world of wooded demesne, social great house and library. In Trollope the bog reassumes the demesne in an act perpetrated by people who have known the famine but nonetheless wilfully destroy the productivity of the land. In addition the killing of the devout Catholic child is a sign that even the future is cut off. 'Ireland' is in the grip of a regressive psychosis.

The 'horror' of his vision cannot be explained away, as a nationalist might wish, as merely the product of Trollope's conservative/unionist prejudice. Something else is at work on his imagination. For Trollope there is a failure of all normal, scientific or historicist causal explanations of what is happening in Ireland. Hence the notorious invocation of divine providence as the ultimate cause of everything in *Castle Richmond* (1860). It is God's wrath that is punishing us for our folly and wickedness by sending the plague of famine; then God's mercy, by reducing the size of the population, will regenerate the land (since we cannot). This is an absurd evasion, it might be claimed, for a social novelist and periodical essayist. But it is the nineteenth-century equivalent of the 'mutability' cantos that concluded, by not concluding, Spenser's Irish epic *The Faerie Queene*. For Spenser, as for Trollope, we must believe that there is an order that structures apparent disorder, because if there is not, anarchy will be loosed upon the world (and it is only that anarchy we perceive). Yet it is not within our power, or myopic comprehension, to make, move or ultimately comprehend that order ourselves. Or to 'progress' from Edmund Spenser's religious order to that of economics, Trollope's justification of the famine bears a similarity to that of Jonathan Swift's modest proposer: it is better that the children in Ireland die now than grow up to starve. There is no other expedient. In practical terms both Swift's and Trollope's counsels are those of despair (and Spenser's 'faerie' world is also close to despair). If the function of literature were to shape political action by ideological persuasion, all this writing would be useless as causal explanation or practical instruction. But that is the point. We are beyond what can be explained or controlled either by faith or reason. Accordingly if what is apprehended is inexplicable and uncontrollable, it is (paradoxically) only made comprehensible by imaginative symbol.

A graphic illustration may make the point more readily than abstracted argument. The maiming of Keegan by the Ribbonmen in *The Macdermots of Ballycloran* (1847), Trollope's first Irish fiction, is a *locus classicus*.[1] A merely political reading might fit the passage into a simple dialectic: the oppression of the tenantry by Keegan has provoked concomitant violence in return. But that is an abstract (quasi-Hegelian) theorisation. The experiential quality of the episode cannot be so easily rationalised. Keegan, having drawn his pistol on the Ribbonmen, is knocked from his horse by a stone:

> The blow and the fall completely stunned him, and when he came to himself he was lying on the road; the man who had stopped his

horse was kneeling on his chest; a man, whose face was blackened, was holding down his feet, and a third, whose face had also been blackened, was kneeling on the road beside him with a small axe in his hand. Keegan's courage utterly failed him when he saw the sharp instrument in the ruffian's grasp; he began to promise largely if they would let him escape – forgiveness – money – land – anything – everything for his life. Neither of them, however, answered him, and before the first sentence was well out of his mouth, the instrument fell on his leg, just above the ankle, with all the man's force; the first blow only cut his trousers and his boot; and bruised him sorely, – for his boots protected him; the second cut the flesh, and grated against the bone; in vain he struggled violently, and with all the force of a man struggling for his life; a third, and a fourth, and a fifth descended, crushing the bone, dividing the marrow, and ultimately severing the foot from the leg. (pp. 446–7)

This is akin to what is now called a 'punishment beating' (containable in Ireland, so it is claimed, within the 'peace process'). But no process of negotiation is possible for Keegan. No one answers him. The faces of the 'punishment' beaters are not darkened merely as disguise. The blackness of the faces suggests that these are forces of the night (rather than of the Enlightenment), and as 'black' men they are in opposition to 'whites', thus by commonplace cultural association, they are savages rather than civilised men, negro slaves rather than freemen. They fight with stone-age weapons, and the small axe that is used to sever Keegan's foot is the Irish equivalent of the Apache tomahawk. It is grossly inefficient (Semtex has marked a great advance in the science of civilisation.) The realist mode suppresses any of the epic idealisation with which Homer, for example, celebrated the skilled despatch of an enemy, and any aesthetic pleasure in language in the depiction of killing (which transhistorically links Homer to Lady Gregory's Cuchulain epics in the language of the *Volk*). There is only the crude, protracted, graphic and gross description. To prevent the amputation Keegan offers what are (read in terms of historicist allegory) typical elements of liberal (Gladstonian) reform: money (that is, capital investment), land (tenants' rights), or 'anything', including (in vain) forgiveness (the liberal guilt of the postcolonial conscience). But the blacks have only one purpose, to hack the foot from the leg, which allegorically interpreted is to dissever the union of the body politic by removing a useless limb from a maimed carcass. There is nothing of progressive dialectic in this attack. It is a savage act in what Trollope calls a 'lawless' region upon an oppressive agent of the law.

   This is one of the most horrific examples in Trollope's fiction of the effects of the cult of violence in the 'distant and wild' (*The Landleaguers*, p. 2) regions of Ireland. The violence of the *Volk* is matched by that of the aristocracy: the murder of the revenue officer Ussher by Thady Macdermot (heir to the great and ancient house of Ballycloran) on the drive of the house. Once again Trollope, as with the attack on Keegan, dwells on the act itself: the smashing in of Ussher's skull by repeated massive blows from Thady's stick. Extended quotation would be redundant. We feel the blood lust as the skull smashes and the body falls. Thady is psychotic at this moment, possessed, like Achilles or Cuchulain, with blood-anger for a personal, familial enemy whom he meets in the dark (pp. 370–1). As with the severing of Keegan's foot, the act may be read allegorically. Ussher is killed to prevent his union by marriage to Feemy, the daughter of the house of Ballycloran. She is the only daughter of an old aristocratic family, an avid reader of the romances of old Ireland, a 'Glorvina' figure transferred from the romantic Gothic of Lady Morgan's pulp fiction to the social realist novel. If this were Morgan, Ussher would be the 'English' other who would learn to love romantic (and Catholic) Ireland, not dead or gone but embodied in an heiress. Instead one Irishman kills another (or to be more specific, a southern Catholic kills an Ulsterman). The prevention of union by murder is merely negative. Love is extinguished, Feemy dies in pregnancy, and the law, although it must punish murder, is unable to determine whether Thady attacked because of his associations with Ribbonism or to prevent the rape by abduction of his sister, or whether it is all a tragic accident. Or perhaps, to return to the providential mystery again, human law is unable to encompass the nature of events in Ireland. What remains of the ancient country house is Thady's father, 'the last of the Mohicans', an old Milesian chieftain in senile decay, and the house falls into ruin. It was the sight of those ruins that, Trollope claims, led him to write the tale.

   To enquire, by process of reason, what it is in 'Ireland' that provokes this self-destruction is invalid. Something atavistic, beyond reason, is operating in the symbolic order of Trollope's fiction, beyond the frontier of civil explanation or civil solution, not to be rationalised, for instance, by analysis of undercapitalisation, subletting, exploitation, and the apparatus of Gladstonian liberalism. This something is internal to Ireland, not merely shifted onto the shoulders of that evil other known as 'England'. *The Macdermots of Ballycloran* is concerned with a self-contained Irish community. It is Trollope's equivalent of that other community in Mayo who, in Synge, rejoice that the folk hero Christy Mahon has split in half his father's skull, or who, in Brian Friel's *Faith Healer* (1980), drunkenly castrate (like Apaches, it is said) a failed saviour in the back yard of an Irish pub.

In the central symbolic scene of *The Macdermots* Trollope takes Thady across the kind of frontier that Edgeworth traversed in her tour of Connemara. To escape from the pale of the law, Thady retreats into the territory of the Ribbonmen, the wilderness called Aughacashel (chapter 23). It is a phantasmagoric episode, perceived through Thady's increasingly disturbed imagination (Dickensian in this respect). The phantasmagoria is dominated by the presence of an old man from a cabin, taciturn, motionless as a Wordsworthian solitary, and ultimately terrifying. He exists outside civil society in a condition of permanent animality (or what Shakespeare called 'the thing itself...unaccommodated Man'):

> There he sat on the bed, quite imperturbable; he had not spoken ten words since Thady had got up, and seemed quite satisfied in sitting there enjoying the warmth of the fire, and having nothing to do. How Thady envied his quiescence! Then he began to reflect what had been this man's life; had he always been content to sit thus tranquil, and find comfort in his idleness? At last he got almost alarmed at this old man; why did he not speak to him? why did he sit there so quiet, doing nothing – saying nothing – looking at nothing – and apparently thinking of nothing? it was as sitting with a dead body or a ghost – that sitting there with that lifeless but yet breathing creature.

This figure is an embodiment of savage 'Ireland'. If he spoke, his words (Gaelic) would be unintelligible to the Anglophone listener. Thady, being Irish, is bilingual, yet the old man will not speak even to him. Because of this wordlessness, his signification is ineffable and thus inexplicable. He simply is, and his meaning is projected onto him by Thady's imagination, which runs across a gamut of interpretations. At first he is sentimentally pastoralised – how happy the poor man, if only he knew his own happiness (*fortunatos nimium...*).[2] Then, equally conventionally, the man is seen from the empathetic historicist point of view (liberal and hence reformist) – can one understand what it is in society that has reduced this man to idleness and concomitant torpid indigence? But ultimately the man becomes *unheimlich* – what dead body, what ghost of the past does he represent, what is it that is unspoken or unspeakable? To which questions there is no answer. What brings this speechless Caliban to life is lust for food: 'Then the man's apathy and tranquillity vanished, and the voracity with which he devoured ... showed that though he might have no demon thoughts to rack his brain, the vulture in his stomach tortured him as violently' (pp. 422–3). What moves the savage is a great hunger, and the literary image is Promethean. If this figure is what represents the Promethean in man (a deeply regressive image) what, then, represents that force called 'Jupiter' who bound the old man? No abstract answer is offered, but rather an experiential contrast. Thady, the heir to Ballycloran, has been brought better fare than that received by the old man. As Thady eats 'he saw the old man's greedy eyes glare on him, as he still sat in his accustomed seat, it was quite horrible to see how greedy and ravenous he appeared'. The situation is simple and elemental: the desire of the have nots to take from those who have. The concomitant is Ribbonism, a society devoted to 'all schemes of vengeance and punishment' against the haves, and enmity to any force of law that prevents the have nots from taking: 'magistrate, or policeman ... or any court of law'. It is a return to the Hobbesian state of nature, the war of each against the other. There is great hunger, and great and greedy hatred.

The famine is the ultimate sign of that great hunger. According to Trollope, beyond the word 'famine' is the thing for which no language is adequate, no human explanation ultimately possible, and which, involving a whole people, is the antithesis of civilisation within the very heart of that civilisation. In Chapter 33 of *Castle Richmond* (Trollope's 'Mitchelstown' fiction, for that great house was in his mind) the protagonist, Herbert Fitzgerald, scion of the ancient Geraldines, is brought face to face with a family dead or dying of famine in a cabin:

> Squatting in the middle of the cabin, seated on her legs crossed under her, with nothing between her and the wet earth, there crouched a woman with a child in her arms. At first, so dark was the place, Herbert hardly thought that the object before him was a human being. She did not move when he entered, or speak to him, or in any way show sign of surprise that he should come there. ... Her rough short hair hung down her back, clotted with dirt, and the head and the face of the child which she held was covered with dirt and sores. On no more wretched object, in its desolate solitude, did the eye of man ever fall. ... For a while Herbert stood still, looking round him, for the woman was so motionless and uncommunicative that he

hardly knew how to talk to her. That she was in the lowest depth of distress was evident enough, and it behoved him to administer to her immediate wants before he left her; but what could he do for one who seemed to be so indifferent to herself? He stood for a time looking round him till he could see through the gloom that there was a bundle of straw lying in the dark corner beyond the hearth, and that the straw was huddled up, as though there were something lying under it. Seeing this he left the bridle of his horse, and stepping across the cabin moved the straw with the handle of his whip. As he did so he turned his back from the wall in which the small window-hole had been pierced . . . and he could see that the body of a child was lying there, stripped of every vestige of clothing. (pp. 369–71)

Visual media have made scenes like this domestically familiar. The camera team moves in, pictures are beamed to the domestic living room, a few pence rattle into the next Oxfam collecting tin. The image connects, but also distances. So too does the text of the 'consumable' fiction of *Castle Richmond* (which is basically a conventional shilly shally story of romantic wooing, spiced with melodramatic blackmail). But Trollope extends the gap between the famine and us even further by his choice of point of view. The observer is a scion of the ancient Geraldines. The romantic protagonist, Herbert Fitzgerald, *qua* gentleman, is mounted on a good horse. He dismounts and leads his horse into the cabin, as though it were no more than a stable. When he examines the bundle of straw lying in a dark corner he keeps his distance from it by moving it with the handle of his whip. This is a sensible precaution against contamination by filth and disease, but this use of the whip also carries a clear indication of the relationship between Geraldine and peasant. This locus is so 'dark' (a reiterated word) that the Geraldine eye (which the reader shares) can scarcely translate 'object' into 'human being', and this something has 'nothing between her and the wet earth'. This being without a name is dissolving into the very bogland that was the aboriginal condition of 'Ireland'. Her naked, dead child is indistinguishable from a bundle of straw. To return to Shakespeare again, this is the 'thing' itself. This ultimate vision of hunger is linked to the condition of the old man in the cabin at Aughacashel by the extraordinary apathy of the woman, who is seemingly 'indifferent' to her condition, 'motionless and uncommunicative'. Compared with a Wordsworthian solitary, she is beyond any vestige of resolution or independence. As at Aughacashel, there is no communication, but this time it is the other way round – the Geraldine has nothing he can say, the situation is ineffable.

It 'behoves' us to 'administer' to the woman's wants. The vocabulary acquires a religious resonance, but even for this specific case it is too little too late. Beyond that, there is nothing that can be done about it (to adapt a phrase from another historical fiction, Paul Scott's *The Jewel in the Crown*). Herbert Fitzgerald's horse ride has already taken him beyond the pale and into a 'poor, bleak, damp, undrained country, lying beyond the confines of his father's property' (p. 367), where division and subdivision of the land has obliterated all signs of improved enclosure, imposed in vain upon the ineluctable bog. The conclusion of the episode is Fitzgerald's offer of 'a silver coin or two' (has Trollope in mind the more generous offer of thirty pieces of silver?) and (bleak irony) his offer to find transport to take the woman to the workhouse. Even if it is not a cold eye that this horseman casts on life and death, having looked he passes on (p. 287). He has his own misfortune. The (temporary) loss of the ancestral estate requires that he seek a career (like the hero of Edgeworth's *Ennui*) in the indigent circumstances to which a few thousand pounds reduces a Geraldine.

In Irish fiction the cabin as locus is the antithesis to the country house. It usually serves one of two (potentially contradictory) functions. It is the sign of the gross impoverishment of the dispossessed *Volk* by tyrannical and exploitative forces, whether one calls those forces the Protestant Ascendancy, British/English colonialism, international capitalism, and so on. A typical cabin scene (Carleton for instance) shows armed police, agents of rapacious landlordism, evicting the innocent and desperate poor. Alternatively the cabin is conventionally idealised as the well of Gaelic undefiled, that hidden Ireland where Douglas Hyde or Lady Gregory (or Daniel Corkery) would find the fertile roots of the *Volk* and from which was to arise a spontaneous contemporary literature (quasi Homeric when fostered by attentive nationalist expectation, and thus rooted in the origins of European civilisation).

By comparison, Trollope's treatment of the locus is radically unusual. As centres of consciousness, Thady Macdermot of Ballycloran and Herbert Fitzgerald are not alien dispossessors, since the first is a Gaelic-speaking 'Milesian' and the second, at least, an 'old Irish' Geraldine. (Likewise the central characters of *The Kellys and the O'Kellys*, 1848.) Their position, therefore, is intrinsic. They are not alien possessors, although their viewpoint on the cabin is that of men of landed property. Accordingly the usual premises of political anti-unionism are not granted, and even less the attractions of romantic primitivism (for the well-heeled researcher). Rather than the country house being an alien importation, therefore, its presence is as intrinsic to Irish history as that of the cabin. The relationship, rather than being seen as that of oppressor and oppressed, is symbiotic. The most obvious example is the elaborate theme-setting description of the ruins of the country house in *The Macdermots*. The narrator, Trollope *in propria persona*, discovers the ruins on a would-be picturesque walk from 'the well-wooded demesne of Sir G[ilbert] K[ing]' in search both of the 'beautiful' and of 'improvement' (his discourse is firmly located in the tradition of Young). But the road is 'retrograde' and the deterioration is indicative of a backward shift in time into the feudal world of the Milesian aristocracy, characterised by 'useless expenditure, unfinished pretence, and premature decay!' (p. 3) (The intertextual reference is partly to Morgan, partly to Edgeworth's *Castle Rackrent*). What the narrator finds extraordinary is that the ruin is so recent:

> Poor old Time will have but little left him at Ballycloran! The gardens had been large; half were now covered by rubbish heaps, and the other half consisted of potato patches; and round the out-houses I saw clustering a lot of those wretched cabins which the poor Irish build against a deserted wall, when they can find one, as jackdaws do their nests in a superannuated chimney.... There were two or three narrow footpaths through and across the space, up to the cabins behind the house, but other marks of humanity were there none. (p. 5)

The wretched cabin and the ruined country house here are in a dependent relationship with one another, but it is a parodic variant of the organic and hierarchical society of conservative fiction. The house props up the 'out-houses', which are seen as parasitic lean-tos; the chimney, signifier both of social status and of the hospitality of hearth and home, is merely a place where jackdaws nest, and that nomination reduces the Irish poor to an animalistic status, like birds of the air. Whether Trollope uses 'jackdaw' in the derogatory sense (recorded in Brewer) as 'a prating nuisance' is uncertain, but it is an unattractive metamorphosis. The improved road on which the peregrination began has retrograded now to 'two or three narrow footpaths' that intersect the garden running wild. The absence of all other signs of humanity suggests (imaginatively) a postfamine landscape; but it also suggests (morally) that other kinds of humanity may be hard to discover in the tale of Ballycloran.

This is a simple, static image of mutuality in decay. Cabin and country house depend upon each other, and the decay of one will cause the fall of both. This historical process is more fully developed in *Castle Richmond* in the iconography of Desmond Court. This locus is the fictional recreation of Mitchelstown, the place celebrated by Arthur Young as the sign of emergent civilisation in Ireland. There are also, in Trollope's story, fictional parallels to Edgeworth's tale of Mary Martin of Ballinahinch. Trollope also follows Edgeworth in using the resonances of ancient family names, for the Desmonds were one of the great ancient families of Ireland. In this story the Desmonds (like the Martins) 'had been once kings over these wild mountains', but that wilderness has been resistant to feudal cultivation. The miles of bleak, unadorned penury that constitute their estates are both the objective correlative of the sterility of their pride and the actual source of that poverty, which symbiotically impoverishes the rich and, by famine, kills the poor. (p. 5f.) Clara Desmond, heiress to the castle, like Mary Martin is heiress to nothing. Only the prosperous marriage that her proud, lonely and bitter mother demands can refertilise the land by financial insemination. Thus, Desmond Court is in some respects an Irish Satis House, a place where time has stopped and love has died.

As a House of Pride, it also resembles those 'proud, ambitious heaps' of which Ben Jonson wrote in *To Penshurst*, which are raised on the 'ruin' of human suffering and complaint. The stories told at Desmond Court of walls 'built with human blood' are of course false, but none-theless, they are symbolically true. The Earls of Desmond ruled their people like 'serfs', but these 'bitter and violent men' (to use the Yeatsian phrase) now possess their land, but without the original force of power. Trollope employs not the Yeatsian image of the 'mouse' but the Miltonic and Popeian image of the 'toad' to describe the scion of the house at the beginning of the nineteenth century: a 'toadying friend, or perhaps I should more properly say, the bullied flunky, of a sensual, wine-bibbing, gluttonous king'. The target is retrospective, for Trollope alludes to George IV. For the conscience of liberal Victorianism the former age was the unacceptable face of the *ancien régime*. Fortunately the regime is now impotent, and Desmond Court is 'green' (a loaded word in Ireland) with the mildew of decay: 'an unwholesome growth upon the stones', 'bleak', 'ugly' and, like the famine-stricken country-side, 'desolate'. This is what remains of what Maria Edgeworth called 'the feudal tail', or what Ezra Pound was to call 'an old bitch gone in the teeth'. This familial sterility and decay is the correlative of the famine that infests the estate.

There is no need to elaborate on this. Conventionally, in country house fiction there should be set against the evil estate an alternative great, good place. In Spenser the House of Holiness is set in contradistinction to the House of Pride; in Jonson, Penshurst Place shows things as they should be in comparison to the 'proud, ambitious heaps' of the Tudor prodigy houses; in Edgeworth the improved estate is always contrasted with the unimproved; even in Lever, 'Gwynne' Abbey, Joe Nelligan's image of Cro'Martin and Joe Atlee's idealisation of the garden of Kilgobbin at least provide a dream of the good life. But the alternative is marginally rarer in Trollope. Of course there is Mr Jones' estate, but improvement is wrecked by the terrorist activities of the landleaguers. Castle Richmond, in contrast to Desmond Court, is a benevolent albeit senescent estate (and that story knits up an ending by intermarriage between Geraldine and Desmond), but since the famine (like the smallpox in Dickens' *Bleak House*) affects good and bad landlord alike, a fatal symbiosis contaminates both. Ballycloran is already in ruins.

There remain Grey Abbey and Kelly's Court in *The Kellys and the O'Kellys*. One is empowered, the other restored to prosperity. The chronicler of Plantagenet politics recognises that the country house order remains a major historical presence and is still empowered with major cultural authority. But he describes this as a *vis inertiae* (p. 134), not as an ideal. It is there because it is there, but it is a presence rather than a function. While that inert power remains it is a major subject to be addressed, but it is an anachronism not only in local (Irish) context but also in the entire culture of the modern European world.

Thus at Grey Abbey the favoured work of literature of the sterile pride of Lady Selina is Gibbon's *Decline and Fall of the Roman Empire*. It is an obvious symbol. The extinction of *Romanitas* by barbarian invasion is a European trope and the decline of empires a Volneyan theme. It is also a trope whose signification is beyond the consciousness of the owners of Grey Abbey. We see what they cannot. For Lady Selina, reading Gibbon is the equivalent of pursuing her worsted work. Both are ritual pastimes (belonging to passed times) that distract her from the ennui of her life (p. 148). Lord Grey himself is reduced at a crisis in the action to mere motion without meaning between what should be (but is not) the meaningful world of books and the empty activities of dressing and eating that sustain a functionless life:

> As my lord went from breakfast-room to book-room, from book-room to dressing-room, and from dressing-room to dining-room, his footsteps creaked with a sound more deadly than that of a death-watch. The book-room itself had caught a darker gloom; the backs of

the books seemed to have lost their gilding, and the mahogany furniture its French polish. There, like a god, Lord Cashel sate alone, throned amid clouds of awful dulness, ruling the world of nothingness around by the silent solemnity of his inertia. (pp. 351–2)

Out of context one might easily mistake this for a passage from Dickens, although its ostensible intertextuality is to the world of Dulness in Alexander Pope's *The Dunciad*. However the play on 'watch' in death-watch is Dickensian in its metaphorical resonance, combining with its literal signification a sense of hidden, inner decay in the structure of the house, the passage of time by the watch, and of watching over death. The 'French polish' of this culture and the reduction of literature to mere 'gilding' are equally moral metaphors for a decline and fall suspended only by its own *vis inertiae* (the difficulty of moving an object so vast). The only source of hope is the rich heiress (our heroine), Fanny Wyndham. We are told that she cannot get beyond the first volume of *Decline and Fall*, which might suggest (interpreted optimistically) that the younger generation has a prospective rather than retrospective view of history.

Grey Abbey itself has become a mere show house. What is remarkable in Trollope's description of the locus is the way in which his satiric parody of a standard guidebook description strips out of the history of the place everything that idealised country house ideology might have used to justify the showing of the place. Substantial quotation is necessary to establish the remorseless sense of the progress of dullness:

Grey Abbey is one of the largest but by no means one of the most picturesque demesnes in Ireland. It is situated in the county of Kildare, about two miles from the little town of Kilcullen, in a flat, uninteresting, and not very fertile country. The park itself is extensive and tolerably well-wooded, but it wants water and undulation, and is deficient of any object of attraction, except that of size and not very magnificent timber. I suppose, years ago, there was an Abbey here, or near the spot, but there is now no vestige of it remaining. In a corner of the demesne there are standing the remains of one of those strong, square, ugly castles which, two centuries since, were the general habitations of the landed proprietors of the country, and many of which have been inhabited even to a much later date. They now afford the strongest record of the apparently miserable state of life, which even the favoured of the land then endured, and of the numberless domestic comforts which years and skill have given us, apt as we are to look back with fond regret to the happy, by-gone days of past periods...

The present mansion, built on the site of that in which the family had lived till about seventy years since, is, like the grounds, large, commodious, and uninteresting. It is built of stone, which appears as if it had been plastered over, is three stories high, and the windows are all of the same size, and at regular intervals. The body of the house looks like a huge, square, Dutch old lady, and the two wings might be taken for her two equally fat, square, Dutch daughters. Inside, the furniture is good, strong, and plain. There are plenty of drawing-rooms, sitting-rooms, bed-rooms, and offices; a small gallery of very indifferent paintings, and a kitchen, with an excellent kitchen-range, and patent boilers of every shape. (pp.131–2)

This is the gem that his lordship opens every Tuesday and Friday for the heritage industry (and the park daily), through every room of which the housekeeper drags the visitor at a fee of half a crown.

This is remorselessly dull writing, satirising both the romantic nostalgia for the world of abbeys and castles and also the complacent modernism of these 'domestic comforts' represented by kitchen ranges and patent boilers. (The castle, by the by, is now a cowshed.) The satire would be as applicable at Dickens' Chesney Wold as at Grey Abbey, but in the Irish context there is a local undercurrent. Those 'happy, by-gone days of past periods' whitewash a far from happy past, and the 'Dutch' quality of the house might suggest provocative Williamite resonances. Witness also the casual treatment of the issue of Catholicism – 'I suppose, years ago, there was an Abbey here, or near the spot...' – which merely shrugs off the penal laws. If this is so, there is a kind of strategic nihilism to the irony that reduces the long process of historical conflict merely to a half-crown show, the signification of which has become insignificant. To progress from a state of war to a state of domesticity ought to be an advance in civilisation, but, like the books in the bookroom, all that we are aware of is form, not content, an applied 'gilding' of wealth that gleams superficially.

Again if this is so, Fanny Wyndham's inability to read Gibbon is symptomatic of more than her prospective vision. There is in this fiction a rejection of history *per se* as the province of 'the dead' (to place Trollope by James Joyce). Consider for instance the title of the owner of the abbey, Lord Cashel and Grey. On the surface it is resonant with historical signification (a familiar Edgeworthian device): 'Cashel' is derived from the regal seat of the kings of Munster; the name 'Grey' is that of the master of Spenser (although it might also, such is the complexity of Irish history, be derived from Lord Leonard, whose military ambitions provoked the Geraldine League). One might write much of Irish history from Trollope's choice of names, except that he sets them up only to deprive them of signification. The main point about Lord Grey is that he is physically grey, both indeterminate of colour, and old and grey. His title carries the same (in)signification as that of the racehorses that feature so largely in the tale and carry names such as Brien Boru (closely connected to the Rock of Cashel), Finn M'Goul and Granuell. All these charged nominations are discharged – 'empty cisterns' of a wasteland of history.

Grey Abbey therefore represents a kind of cultural nihilism, and it is propagated politically through the 'great influence' (p. 27) of its grossly misapplied wealth and its cultural self-projection as a icon to the *hoi polloi*, the half-crown visitors who think it is worth seeing Frederick the Great's snuffbox and the Prince Regent's bed (p. 133). (Compare the signification still adhering, for instance, to the work of Benvenuto Cellini at Lever's Cro'Martin.) Trollope calls Grey Abbey 'the Dead Sea', a place where all the waters of the land gather in bitter stagnancy, the utter antithesis of the fountain of munificence of country house panegyric. Lady Selina is the living embodiment of this sea – unmarried, hence sterile. Hers is a life of 'horrid, weary, murderous, slow security' (p. 352) where what is murdered is the very point of living itself.

Fanny, however, marries out of this house and her union with Lord Ballindine (Frank) liberates her wealth from waste at Grey Abbey to the improvement of Kelly's Court by a returned absentee. It is a conventional ending, and one that Edgeworth might have chosen. But with a writer as ironic and self-aware as Trollope, one must ask whether, by this time in country house fiction, marriage, domesticity and an inheritance are so obviously signs of formal closure that the convention itself is brought in to question.

When we are first introduced to Kelly's Court it is uneasily poised on the cusp of decline and fall. It is an ugly house on bare land towards the west, impoverished by absenteeism and litigation. This might be another Ballycloran. Some attempt has been made by Frank's father, a man of 'practical sense' and 'education' to 'humanise' the place. 'He planted, tilled, manured, and improved; he imported rose-trees and strawberry plants, and civilised Kelly's Court a little' (p.21). But without further substantial investment civilisation will go no further. The potential 'Irish' future is represented by the presence of the salvage man in the emblematic figure of the 'fool', Jack Kelly (who carries the family name), the 'dirty, barefooted, unshorn, ragged ruffian, who ate potatoes in the kitchen of the Court, and had never done a day's work in his life'. (p. 20) Jack's function in the fiction is emblematic. His presence parodies the nature of the 'court' (of which he is the fool), which is suspended between the nether abyss of savage Ireland and the equally repulsive upper world of the greater English court, at which the elder Lord Ballindine wastes his time as a useless parasite. Frank, when first we meet him, has also never done a day's work and is a useless spendthrift. He is, therefore, as parasitical as Jack Kelly.

Thus Kelly's Court is set in parodic relationship to a courtly ideal that is not present in the world of the fiction. The daughters of the house have been named Sophia (Henry Fielding's heroine) and Augusta (Lady Gregory's name) in imitation of the wise and great of the court, but in 'Ireland' they are reduced merely to Sophy and Guss, unendowed daughters of an encumbered estate, isolated from members of their own caste in provincial ennui (p. 264). Trollope's review of the unattractive roll call of the Dillons and Browns of Mount Dillon and the Bourkes and Blakes (or the rector and his wife!) is a parody of the social world in Jane Austen's fiction, and suggestive of the tragicomedies of Anton Chekov and Ivan Turgenev.

But how much is Kelly's Court humanised and civilised by Frank's marriage to Fanny and the introduction of the inherited wealth that the court itself cannot generate? What is being propped up? Appropriate symbolic acts are routinely performed. The newlyweds take the European grand tour, the ritual rite of passage of humanist civilisation (and one which will acquire a crucial role in Martin and Somerville's *The Real Charlotte*). Fanny's money disencumbers the estate and is ploughed into improvements, and, being as faithful and fertile as the mistress of Penshurst was, the young bride produces legitimate heirs for posterity:

> Great improvements have been effected at Kelly's Court. Old buildings have been pulled down, and additions built up; a great many thousand young trees have been planted, and some miles of new roads and walks constructed. The place has quite an altered appearance; and, though Connaught is still Connaught, and County Mayo is the poorest part of it, Lady Ballindine does not find Kelly's Court unbearable. She has three children already, and doubtless will have many more. Her nursery, therefore, prevents her from being tormented by the weariness of the far west.
>
> Lord Ballindine himself is very happy. He ... has the hounds, and maintains in the three counties round him, the sporting pre-eminence,

which has for so many years belonged to his family ... Sophy O'Kelly married a Blake, and Augusta married a Dillon, and, as they both live within ten miles of Kelly's Court, and their husbands are related to all the Blakes and all the Dillons; and as Ballindine himself is the head of all the Kellys, there is a rather strong clan of them. About five-and-twenty cousins muster together in red coats and topboots, every Tuesday and Friday during the hunting-season. It would hardly be wise, in that country, to quarrel with a Kelly, a Dillon, or a Blake. (pp. 509–10)

This ought to be a satisfactory conclusion. Legalised settlement, patriarchal inheritance, improved communications, plantation of the wilderness and treaties of alliance improve and pacify Ireland in a manner that Spenser and Davies would have approved. Likewise the appropriate architectural forms of civilisation emerge even in Connaught (once notoriously likened to hell): 'old buildings have been pulled down, and additions built up'. Yet how does one judge the tone of this? The very ritualisation of Trollope's account (as in the guidebook account of Grey Abbey) suggests something sceptical and ironical. What is implied, for instance, by the statement that 'Connaught is still Connaught'? There is still the sheer dullness of provincial isolation. Fanny's continuous production of babies is an attempt to prevent herself 'from being tormented by the weariness of the far west'. And Lord Ballindine has his horses. Is it coincidental that the two days on which the hunt meets are the same days of the week that Grey's Abbey was open to the public – an equally useless ritual? Lord Ballindine, as General Tilney in Austen's *Northanger Abbey* might remark, is a 'happy' man. The context of this is that long tradition of idealised philosophical retirement in the country memorialised in Horace's *Beatus ille* (a poem, at least in the original, that is sceptical of the self-sufficiency of the very happiness it seems to celebrate). But is riding horses to hold ennui at bay what classical tradition meant by *cum dignitate otium*? If fox hunting represents an improvement in civilisation (compared with fighting on horseback), Trollope's text emphasises the residual presence of the 'clans' of the west, and his claim that it would hardly be wise to quarrel with these people is not without latent resonances of historical violence. 'Connaught is still Connaught.'

5
Only Connect: Violet Martin and Edith Somerville

With his invocation of Gibbon in *The Kellys and the O'Kellys* Trollope linked the decline and fall of the country house order in Ireland to a greater historical theme. In 1848 it was only a visionary prolepsis. 'Imperialism' was still far from its apogee (indeed it still awaited Disraeli). The emergence of the Land League was unpredictable, let alone the distant absurdities of 1914, the Easter Rising of 1916 and the stock-market crash of 1929. A retrospective imposition of historical teleology is always false to the necessary myopia of historical agents. Nonetheless it is easy (but facile) to find parallels to Trollope's decline and fall motif. William Allingham's country house verse novel, *Laurence Bloomfield in Ireland* (1864), raises the imperial issue, which also informs the early political prose of Aubrey de Vere. Perhaps most remarkable is the proleptic vision by that vigorous historian of the imposition of 'civilisation' upon 'savagery' and 'anarchy', J. A. Froude, who nonetheless claimed in 1882 to have been aware from the beginning of the degeneration of the post-Union Irish ruling classes. He wrote: 'All things have their appointed end, and English dominion over Ireland must come to an end also.... We can govern India: we cannot govern Ireland. Be it so. Then let Ireland be free.' In the Biblical resonances of 'all things have their appointed end' Froude invokes a divine teleology that takes him back beyond Gibbon to St Augustine as a historian of decline and fall.[1]

These are numinous, transhistorical resonances back to the roots of European culture. Yet in Trollope the visionary suggestion is counter-balanced by the mundane depiction of the *vis inertiae*, and the very Latinity of Trollope's phrase insists on the continuing presence of the old order, for even the middle-class reader is expected to understand that much Latin. *The Kellys and the O'Kellys* terminates, conventionally, in propertied marriage and the return to an original estate that mirrors (albeit ironically) the 'Paradise Hall' motif of the *Ur* country house fiction of Fielding's *Tom Jones*. If Trollope's landlords are reduced, in comparison with squire Allworthy in *Tom Jones*, to being those who are merely *fruges consumere nati*, his view of country house culture is as old as that of Horace, satirist but celebrant of the Augustan *imperium*.[2]

There is, therefore, an ironic eddying about a cultural crux in the invocation of Gibbon, rather than an (accidental) visionary forecast of things to come. Gibbon functions in Trollope rather as Homer functioned in the culture of the previous century. He is a revered canonical classic (now in the vernacular rather than the decent obscurity of a learned language) whose placing within culture determines the mind-set of that culture. For the adherents of 'ancient' civilisation (to employ the old, neoclassical vocabulary) Gibbon is a palladium of value; but for the 'moderns' he is unreadable (and for Lord Cashel himself, ancient books and their authors are merely the furniture of wealth). Accordingly, Gibbon is himself part of the *vis inertiae*, an empowered cultural tradition that is 'there' but going nowhere, and 'there', the locus, is the library of a great country house. This text and that place are inextricably related; the library carries the text, and the text transmits the constituents of the idea of civilisation that created the library in the first place.

In relation to our own theme, the (inter)relationship of civilisation and savagery, Gibbon is an exemplary text. His subject is the eruption of barbarianism into the *imperium* of the Graeco-Roman world; but it is also the inner failure of civilisation itself, physically weakened by internecine war, intellectually corrupted by the primitive recidivism of sectarian superstition. To tie that subject merely to the local history of landlordism in mid-Victorian Ireland would be to fail to see the wood for the trees. It is European culture that is at issue in the invocation of Gibbon. The paradox of Gibbon's text is that it preserves the idea of Graeco-Roman civilisation as a textuality and a metaphysic embodied in an ideal form (the rise of the republic) that was prior to Gibbon's chosen period and now entirely vanished. Yet modern European civilisation exists as the reinterpretation and reincorporation of that textuality and metaphysic, indeed it can only exist because the original is not there.

It would be an easy progression from here to the 'culture wars' of Victorian Britain (or even our own age), but our concern is only with the country house as textualised icon. It is a reasonable reading of Trollope (and of Lever) to claim that in the Irish novels the inherited culture the house incorporates 'hits the buffers', as it were. It is tempting to relate that interpretation to Trollope's (and Lever's) 'bourgeois' window on the world. If writers constitute their own ideal readers, it might be argued that here the Victorian middle classes question an old aristocratic hegemony (even 'ascendancy' in the original sense of the word), and in doing so betray both a fascination with the ascendant other and an awareness of the inextricable interrelation between 'modern' middle-class culture and the originary 'ancients'. One might also argue – to pursue the issue in class terms – that the nationalist desire in Ireland to return to the *Volk* represents an attempt to break that inextricable connection. But the nationalist movement itself – part bourgeois, part aristocratic – cannot escape, witness the Ossianic/Homeric nexus (Gregory and O'Sullivan) and the adulation of the courtly society of the aristocracy (Hyde and Corkery).

The fundamental point concerns the survival of the idea of civilisation, its textuality and metaphysics, after the disappearance of the material power that embodied that civil order. This is the issue that emerges in the fictions with which the final chapters of this enquiry are concerned. In moving from Lever and Trollope to Martin and Somerville, Bowen or Gregory, one enters historical territory in which decline and fall is no longer an intertextual prolepsis, but where successive hammer blows (from above as well as from below) deliberately dismantle the country house order. Ultimately in Ireland country houses are burnt (as they were in France and the United States), and those acts may be read not just as hatred of landlordism but as total rejection of those concepts of civilisation which are embodied in European civic architecture, painting, literature and hierarchies of elite value and dependency: the houses and their contents.

Since the real homes of our last group of writers were such houses, the meanings of the locus are crucial. Put simply, as Edith Somerville does in *Wheel-Tracks* (1923), there is a felt need to record a vanishing world (and Gregory's lost Coole Park, now regained as a theme park, is the *terminus ad quem* of our own enquiry). But to develop the paradox of decline and fall, as the country house order politically, economically and visibly passes from the (dis)United Kingdom, the house as icon (and the metaphysics of the house) is liberated as an ideal (a Platonic form, for Spenser is still relevant as an originary author). Thus in canonical English literature (or what was once a great tradition) there are the examples of James, Forster, Woolf and Waugh, among many others. In Ireland, of course, one is at the frontier where worlds collide. For instance, the material fact of the Wyndham Act, by isolating house within demesne (by facilitating the selling of tenancies), finally dissolved the feudal bond of landlord and dependant (this process is painfully revealed in Martin's correspondence with Somerville) and left the house exposed to that class as a symbol, with sectarian or cultural hatred being rationalised and justified by nationalist ideology. But it also liberated the house for correspondent idealisation. The country house poetry of Yeats lies outside these essays (which in some ways are prolegomena to that poetry), but there is a progression in idealism from Somerville to Martin to Bowen and ultimately to Gregory's Coole Park. It is a different idealisation from that of James or Forster, for instance, because it is autobiographical, and thus more deeply and personally aware of the difficulty of holding a guttering candle against the wind. Hence the locus becomes deeply and sentimentally involved with the writers themselves.[3]

One remarkable example may serve to indicate how persistent and intense the abstract Platonic ideal might still be (separable from autobiography). It is from a book published in 1924, when the burning of the houses terminated, and the text is a classic of Irish cultural history. The second chapter is a paen of praise for the great houses of the eighteenth century, the 'gateway' to 'civilisation' (so the writer claims) organically related both to the landscape from which they originated and to the mutuality of hospitable community that existed between the householders and their feudal tail, a 'unity of mind' only rarely vexed by property disputes. This was both a national and a European culture (rooted in the Greeks) in which the owners of the country houses were as much at home in Paris or Vienna as in Ireland. Thus each house was 'a landmark, the centre of a little world; built of local stone after local traditions; selfsupporting, seating a hundred at its tables', deeply grounded in 'a sense of historic continuity' and, the writer adds, 'scores of those old houses remain to us'. It would be difficult to find a clearer example of what has been called in English culture, 'the return to Camelot', albeit belated and out of context.

The writer has a strong theoretical base for his claims. His text is an admirable example of that kind of cultural history which claims to reveal what has been hidden in culture by the official hegemony of history (Lecky, in this instance). Moreover, the writer's position is impeccably postcolonialist. He is no lackey of the 'Ascendancy'. The security of his position is based on good textual authority, works of literature that provide true guides to the mentality of a culture when correctly interpreted (just as Emily Brontë's *Wuthering Heights* and Bram Stoker's *Dracula* inform us of the nature of nineteenth-century landlordism).

The panegyric to country house culture in Daniel Corkery's *The Hidden Ireland* is a typical example of 'the two civilisations' cultural war in Ireland.[4] Corkery's houses are Gaelic and Roman Catholic, of course (not English and Protestant), and his authorities are Irish court poets who tell the truth (rather than English poets who lie). But that is neither here nor there as far as the foundational ideology is concerned. His chapter on 'The Big House' is an encyclopedia of *topoi* shifted across the frontier between the 'civilised' and the 'savage'. We have a mirror image of a tradition; an example of the *vis* (power) that is within *inertia*. Accordingly it is in keeping with that tradition that the savage too is shown, for if Irish civilisation is Greek in affinity, than Hellas is defined in contradistinction to the barbarian. Thus outside the hidden Ireland there is the wilderness of 'plantation' culture, and Corkery uses Edgeworth(!) to make his point, turning the alternative country house tradition against itself. The dunghills of Nugentstown in Maria Edgeworth's *The Absentee* are the signifiers of the savage outside. Plantations are an 'earthquake' that have devastated the land: 'anti-Christ governed the Catholic poor...but the Lord of Misrule governed everything'.[5] Corkery, doubtless, would have had no difficulty in correctly reading the truth of another country house text preferred to Edgeworth by current post-colonial theorists. For the 'hell' of Count Dracula's Transylvania, read post-Cromwellian Connaught.

In the end there remains the beginning, for the decline and fall of civilisation in Ireland, as in Rome, still involves a contested frontier. Let us begin the ending there.[6]

In 1895 two writers from country house culture, Violet Martin and Edith Somerville, crossed the 'frontier' into what they referred to (repeatedly) as 'Indian territory'. Their visit to the Aran Islands is described in an essay by Martin, 'An Outpost of Ireland', subsequently collected in *Some Irish Yesterdays* (1906). For them, like Edgeworth in Connemara, the journey westward was a symbolic crossing into the wild west, not a return to the well of Gaelic culture undefiled (as the islands were romanticised by nationalist ideology). The shift in place involved a regressive shift in time. At the heart of the essay is a quasi-poetic meditation on diachronic history between the now of the visitors (their domestic world of Ross House and Castletownshend) and an earlier, violent, history of the land. The meditation is provoked by the ruins of Dun Aengus:

> The outermost rampart girdles eleven acres of rocky hillside, and here the unwearied savage labour constructed a *chevaux de frise* by

wedging slabs and splinters of stone into every crevice. Hardly now, in the intelligent calm of sightseeing, can the invader make a way through the ankle-breaking confusion, where, in the gloaming centuries before St. Patrick, bloody hands clutched the limestone edges in the death stagger, and matted heads crashed dizzily down, in unrecorded death and courage and despair.

After those days Danes and Irish and English plundered in their turn, but the stillness of the rock and the loneliness of the sea closed in again on the islands, while on the mainland rebellion and conquest alternated in a various agony, and the civilisation thrust on Ireland was a coat of many colours dipped in blood.... It is a pleasant descent to the village of Kilmurvey, down through the buoyant air of the hill side; the grass steals its way among the outposts of rock, till the foot travels with unfamiliar ease in level fields. Near Kilmurvey the Resident Magistrate's house shows a trim roof among young larch and spruce, a miracle of modernity and right angles after the strewn monstrosities of the ridge above; passing near it, a piano gave forth a Nocturne of Chopin's to the solitude, a patrician lament, a skilled passion, in a land where ear and voice have preserved the single threads of melody, and harmony is as yet unwoven.[7] (pp. 28–30)

There are three phases of history recorded here by the 'intelligent calm' of the writer, whose intellectualism, it seems, separates her from the violence of the past. First there was a savage epoch of *Ur* conflict and unrecorded death (before the savage knew the intellectual culture of letters). This world is now entered by the modern intellectual as an 'invader'. But Martin's confession that she comes from the modern world as an invader is strategic. She displaces any sense of postcolonial guilt, for her argument is that *all* the peoples who have entered Ireland were invaders: the Celts as much as the Danes and the English. This was the second phase of Irish history.

As a paradigm for this history of invasion, Martin invokes the story of Israel: 'the civilisation thrust on Ireland was a coat of many colours, dipped in blood'. She alludes to the story of Joseph and his brothers, who said to Joseph, 'Shalt thou indeed reign over us? or shalt thou indeed have dominion over us? And they hated him' (*Genesis*, 37, 8). They would have murdered him, and they presented his coat of many colours to his father as a sign that he was dead, for 'an evil beast hath devoured him' (ibid., 37, 33). The story of Joseph is an apt emblem for Irish history and loaded with implication. Rather than emphasising racial division (as nationalist history would have it), this is a parable of fratricide in a family that is united by blood just as much as it is divided by bloodshed. If one were to carry the implications of the story further, Joseph not only survived but also was enriched by the civilisation of a great imperial power (for Egypt read Great Britain?), although he never lost his love of his native land, and traditional typology would compare 'the coat of many colours, dipped in blood' with the seamless unity of the garment of Christ. (This was an ideal unity divided by the soldiers on the first Easter, a typology Martin might have developed ironically had she lived to witness the Easter Rising in 1916.)

The third phase of history is represented by the passage from the 'outposts' of time, signified by the rocks of Dun Aengus and the fields and plantation that mark the coming of the rule of law. The sign of the imposition of law is the resident magistrate's house, 'a miracle of modernity' in contrast to 'the strewn monstrosities of the ridge above'. The modernity/monstrosity antithesis is, historically, the nineteenth-century equivalent of Arthur Young's enlightened civilisation/savagery dichotomy. But Martin is writing in a more darkly ironic mode and the progress of civilisation represented by the magistrate's house appears an alien excrescence in the symbolic landscape of Aran, its 'right angles' (the word 'right' carrying moral as well as scientific connotations) out of kilter with the rocky landscape above. But the prime emphasis of the description is neither on the coming of law to replace war (which would be a Kiplingesque theme) nor on the development of modern science. This isle is full of music. There is a pianoforte in the wilderness and the viewless artist has chosen to express herself 'to the solitude' through a nocturne by Chopin. European art has reached even Aran. The nocturne, by implication, stands in comparison with any folk or 'national air'. But again, as so often in this meditation, there are darker undercurrents. A nocturne belongs to nightfall (not enlightened daybreak), and in Martin's text the performance is indicative of the 'skilled passion' of a high art that is also 'a patrician lament' for a 'harmony ... as yet unwoven'. (The seamless garment is as yet not woven.) And is the choice of Chopin as musician merely accidental? For Chopin, like Joseph, left his native land to immerse himself in the culture of greater powers, and the history of his native Poland and that of divided Ireland are not dissimilar.

One further irony might be latent in Martin's history of the invasive presence of modern culture. If the appliance of science (the 'right angles' of magistracy) is a sign of the imposition of law on anarchic violence, violence is also yoked to science. When describing the ruins of Dun Aengus, Martin instinctively draws on her own Europeanised culture and employs a French term to fix the scene precisely. Her words *chevaux de frise* would not have been understood by the aboriginals. It is a term of science, but the science of war. It would be familiar, one presumes, to inhabitants of Ross House or Castletownshend because the men of such families were the officer class of the armed forces of their country.

This darkly vulnerable meditation on history is far removed from the more familiar comic treatment of resident magistrates for which 'Somerville and Ross' are best known. The wider implications of Martin's theme had already been broached in a remarkable essay, 'Cheops in Connemara', written in October 1889 (reprinted in *Stray-aways* in 1920). This has affinities in contemporary Irish culture with W. B. Yeats' 'Among Schoolchildren', and in English literature with the first chapter of Charles Dickens' *Hard Times*. The question that Martin asks is, what relevance, if any, do the traditions of European education possess now, in this land at this time? The 'Connemara' in her title, like Aran, is a locus beyond the frontier of Europe, not Indian country now, but somewhere that suggests the Central Asian steppes, a region so 'bereft of life' that the very boulders suggest the forms of 'fossil . . . cattle' and the road by which she has travelled is instinct, by transference of epithets, with the 'solitary daring' she feels. Ultimately Connemara represents the protoprimeval chaos: 'a brown and billowy waste without any hint of boundary, its farthest ridges fading into haze, its nearer hollows seamed with a black or green swampiness' (pp. 26–7). This is the same bog that threatened to engulf the enlightened Maria Edgeworth. But here late nineteenth-century civilisation has planted a 'National School', which, in the indeterminate waste, has something of the same signification as the out-of-place house of the resident magistrate in Aran. Here Martin picks up a book (like Marlow in Joseph Conrad's *Heart of Darkness*). It is a compendium of literary culture: 'extracts from *Paradise Lost*, from Pope's *Essay on Criticism*, from Paley's *Relation of Animated Bodies to Inanimate Nature*, from apparently most of the recognised classics' (a nineteenth-century 'Norton' anthology), and the teacher, to impress her visitor, calls upon one of the schoolchildren to recite Horace Smith's 'Address to a Mummy'. Martin tells how it is 'rendered, carefully, correctly, but as in an unknown tongue, the guesses of modern erudition coming in a staccato sing-song' from a bare-footed boy, as obedient to command as a circus dog walking on its hind legs, but who knows nothing of (and can scarcely pronounce) the litany of Egyptian names: 'Cheops and Cephrenes, Cambyses and Osiris' (p. 29).

The anthology has been assembled with an Arnoldian idealism, for it contains examples of the best that has been known and thought, and the schoolchild's recitation returns to the roots of European culture in the power and wisdom of the empire of the Egyptians. The two (English) classic poets to whom Martin alludes, one Protestant the other Catholic, cross the religious divide of Christendom (thus becoming a seamless coat of culture). Martin's allusion to William Paley, and hence to the evidences of religion from the laws of nature, might suggest an enlightened advance beyond sectarianism towards a harmony of faith by means of science. If such culture were meaningful here, the school might be (to use a later image from the essay) 'a strip of civilisation existing and growing between the wilderness and the sea' (p. 31). But the tenor and the imagery of the essay instead create a feeling that the best that has been known and thought is – in this place at this time – merely mummified culture, 'Cheops in Connemara', and the 'unknown tongue' is an unintelligible, Marabar-like 'boom'. The example of Paley may clinch the point. Fundamental to Paley's philosophical position was the familiar argument that the existence of universal law testified to the existence of God, just as the existence of a watch demonstrated the existence of a watchmaker. (He wrote at a time when the invention of the marine chronometer had reduced the wilderness of the oceans to the fixities of longitude and latitude.) But Martin has set Paley in Connemara, a symbolic region of 'waste without any hint of boundary' and a wilderness in which the bogland merges with the indeterminate sea. The evidence of Connemara is that nature here is scarcely emergent from the original 'chaos and old night'. But for these schoolchildren, these are the elements among which they move.

What then of the position of the writer herself, the mediating consciousness between unintelligible culture and the wilderness, a presence 'solitary' and 'daring' in this place, but not confined to this place? The most extended exploration of the presence of the civilised intellect in the wilderness by Martin (now in conjunction with Somerville) is the ostensibly comic *Through Connemara in a Governess Cart* (1892).[8] But there is a clear literary pedigree to the text that is far from comic. The cousins prepared themselves for the journey by reading Charles Lever's *The Martins of Cro'Martin* and the real life, tragic history of Mary Martin makes imperative a visit to Ballinahinch. Maria Edgeworth's account of her own tragi-comic expedition was probably not available (Augustus Hare's *Life and Letters of Maria Edgeworth* did not appear until 1894), but Martin and Somerville, by class and cultural affiliation, saw themselves as Edgeworth's heirs. Hence the ambience of the cousins' tour is serious. Therefore no apology will be offered for reading 'against the grain'.

Like Edgeworth's visit to the same place, the tour maintains the traditional typological dichotomy between the civilised and the savage within the landscape (Plates 6 and 7). Now, in the progressive 1890s, the coming of the signs of 'civilisation' (p. 194) can be seen in the development of roads through (some) of the wilderness (compare Edgeworth's tour), the thin line of telegraph poles beside the roads and (here and there) the presence of clean and comfortable hotels. At Renvyle House there are even the basics of a library (Prospero's books?) reaching out to that wider civilisation represented by *The Field* (for the sporting tourist), *The Illustrated London News* (for the metropolitan taste) and Sir Walter Raleigh's *History of the World* (an imperial text). In this progress of civilisation the country house remains the ultimate sign of 'civilisation' (and it is by that key word that the prospect of Kylemore Abbey is greeted). But Ballinahinch is the crucial locus. It was the origin of the Mary Martin story, and Violet Martin is a daughter of that extended ancient clan. The house is not what they expected:

> As we drove along the high ground . . . Ballinahinch came slowly into sight; a long lake in a valley, a long line of wood skirting it, and finally, on a wooded height, the Castle, as it is called, a large modern house with a battlemented top, very gentlemanlike, and even handsome, but in no other way remarkable.
>
> It was not the sort of thing we had expected. We had heard a great deal about Mary Martin, who was called the Princess of Connemara forty years ago. . . . We were prepared for anything, from an acre of gables and thatch to a twelfth century tower with a dozen rooms one on top of the other, and a kerne or a gallowglass looking out of every window, but this admirable mansion with plate-glass windows, and doubtless hot water to the very garrets, shook down our sentimentalities like apples in autumn . . .
>
> For the first time in our travels we were in a large plantation. Some local genius once said that 'Connemara got a very wooded look since them telegraph posts was put up in it,' and after many a drive in which the line of black posts dwindling to the horizon was the only break in the barrenness we began to understand this. Here at all events the civilising hand had done its work, and we slackened pace in the greenness and shelter, and fortified by the knowledge that the present owner of the place was far away, we began to think of luncheon. (pp. 63–8)

Later a 'kindly giantess' (who is, *mutatis mutandis*, a variant of the 'giant' in Edgeworth's tour) shows them the house. The showing of the house is a familiar programme (for the fame and fate of the Martins drew tourists to Ballinahinch), and within all is clean, well-ordered and domestic.

This is a radical revision of both Edgeworth's and Lever's works, and of the tragic tale of Mary Martin, the famine, the fall of the family and her exile. Arguably this domestically disappointing Ballinahinch is merely the thing as it is, stripped of the excrescences of fiction. The kernes, gallowglasses and Norman tower are merely the Morganesque appurtenances of Gothic fiction and Gaelic fantasy. Martin and Somerville are not Irish Catherine Morlands and Ballinahinch is manifestly neither a Castle Rackrent nor a Cro'Martin. Billiard room, drawing room, dining room, library – the programme of the dull tour (this might be Trollope) – are indicative not of decline and fall, but of secured comfort and prosperity. The usual critique of the absentee landlord does not apply here. It is not a problem that the owner is away; rather it provides a better opportunity to view the house and grounds. The most terrible aspect of the Mary Martin story, the famine, is now merely history (forty years gone) and the forward march of the telegraph poles is a sign of the connection even of Connemara to progressive modernity. The 'hand of civilisation' is doing its work even in this barren land. The very dullness of Ballinahinch is therefore progressive. This castle needs no fortification and visitors may break in and picnic undisturbed. Or put another way, why fight the land war?

It is only when the 'kindly giantess' takes Martin to Mary Martin's seat in the demesne woods that the mood darkens. Uncertainty creeps in. The walk to the seat takes Martin and Somerville along the margins of a lake. Here the writerly eye 'became ... giddy with the double world', and, in instinctive protection, their vision clings 'to the silver smear on the glassy surface or the golden gleam in the shallow that testified to where illusion began' (p. 77). Although it is a vain task to distinguish Martin's writing from that of Somerville, this is symbolic writing reminiscent of the mode employed by Martin in 'Cheops in Connemara'. The comfortable, mundane superficiality of things (the Trollopian world) becomes confused by illusion and a giddying mirroring. That sense of 'doubling' between a real and an illusionary world has something of the quality of the refracted vision of Edgeworth's *Tour*, or read allegorically, the 'silver smear' and 'golden gleam' in the illusionary refraction suggests Spenser in its questioning of whether all that glisters is really gold.

It is in this unsettling ambience, outside the fortification of the house, that history reasserts itself. The tourists are confronted by an ancient Irish woman (the Shan van Vocht?) who is a living testimony to the famine, and the tour abruptly ends. Martin and Somerville refuse the offered extension of their visit to the Martin stables, where £15 000 was spent on housing the horses and the floors were paved with Connemara marble. They cannot extend 'intended admiration' to a place where horses were stabled in a palace while human beings starved.

Between the doubtfully mirroring waters of the lake and the reassertion of darker history, the narration sets what is the climactic moment of the visit, the reassumption by Violet Martin of 'Mary Martin's seat', the famous setting in the landscape from whence the tragic heroine viewed the demesne. It acquires a disturbing transhistorical resonance, as if the Martin blood link to the tragic past is something that cannot be erased by the progress of modernity. At this juncture Somerville writes:

> I remember hearing how Miss Martin had taken a guest up the mountain that should have been soaring into the heavens before us, and making him look round the tremendous horizon, had told him how everything he could see belonged to her. If the weather had been like ours, it would not have been a very over-powering statement, limited, in fact, to the cloud of mist and Miss Martin's umbrella; but as it was, with the inland mountains and moors clear to the bluest distance, and the far Atlantic rounding her fifty miles of sea-coast, it was a boast worth making. Perhaps it was the vision that was clearest to her failing sense when she lay dying on the other side of the Atlantic without an acre and without an income, a refugee from the country where her forefathers had prospered during seven hundred years.
>
> The retrospect became melancholy, and we began to be extremely chilly; sitting out of doors was too severe a test for this July day, and we made towards the house again. (pp. 78–9)

The Biblical high mountain from which all the kingdoms of the world were revealed by Satan is not dissimilar to Mary Martin's soaring mountain. Everything that could be seen belonged to her. If the allusion is present, she is both an ideal figure (the tragic queen of Connemara whose family gave its all for the dying poor in the famine) and a ruler whose power (for good) is associated with the powers of darkness. There is a suspensive ambiguity, as if between two worlds. Somerville writes that Mary was (perhaps) possessed by a dying vision. This vision was (literally) a prospect of her imagination (her kingdom seen from the other side of the Atlantic), but her visionary kingdom also represented the ineluctable termination of seven hundred years of history by the famine. The Martins sought to alleviate it, but the Martins' wealth was also, paradoxically, its cause.

Violet Martin, sitting in Mary's seat, is by blood and breeding part of that same historical process, and like her predecessor she is an impoverished power. She is a (spiritual) refugee in her own kingdom. Mary Martin's prospect of her kingdom cannot now be seen (except in the imagination) as a 'cloud of mist' has descended upon the scene, and although it is still the height of summer there is a *frisson* in the air (a seasonal suggestion that Elizabeth Bowen was to take up later in the motif of 'the last September'). Martin and Somerville, struck by the melancholy nature of the obscured 'retrospect' (not prospect), accordingly make for the comfort of (deserted) Ballinahinch 'again'. The house metaphorically represents both historical continuity (the seven hundred years during which the Martins held power in this place) and familial connection, a sign of the communal tie of kinship to which they return. But it is also deserted. Despite this there is nowhere else for Martin and Somerville to go (except to continue their unhoused journey in the 'governess' cart).

Modernity and tragic retrospect are, accordingly, both present at Ballinahinch, and the 'vision' here involves the juxtaposition of past and present in unsettling and unsettled proximity. It is thus thematically at one with the meditation on Aran that set the ancient Dun Aengus against the intrusive presence of the resident magistrate, and in 'Cheops in Connemara' the iconological juxtaposition of the National School with the primeval chaos of the limitless bog. What connects these disparate elements (and it is the only connection) is the transhistorical intelligence of the writer, who is herself ineluctably involved in the processes of history. The writer's problem, and it is a problem that becomes increasingly acute under the pressure of the political events that dismembered the United Kingdom, is to find a way to structure by words what is resistant to order. How can one unite things that are falling apart? The theme of the fictions of Martin and Somerville, which grow from and in relation to the essays of the 1890s, is the Forsterian theme 'only connect', and the failure to connect – the breakdown of Union in Ireland – is their tragic conclusion.

The tragic country house fictions are *An Irish Cousin* (1889), *The Real Charlotte* (1894), *Mount Music* (1919), *An Enthusiast* (1921) and *The Big*

House of Inver (1925). Although Martin died in 1915, parts of the subsequent novels were rooted in their collaboration, and Martin's imaginative influence was overwhelmingly present for Somerville, as the late collections of reminiscences and essays eloquently testify. Like the country house fictions of Lever and Trollope, these works cover a broad period of Irish history, more or less taking up where Lever and Trollope left off and moving from the Parnellite era to the civil war that was initiated by the events of 1916. The other major affinity in Irish fiction is with Edgeworth, and like Edgeworth, Somerville was eventually to turn in disgust from what she called the 'lunatic asylum' of contemporary politics. Whereas Edgeworth merely moved her country house setting elsewhere in the United Kingdom, Somerville returned to her youth and to the time when she first met Martin. *French Leave* (1928) leaves Ireland for the happier territory of the Parisian art world Somerville had known as a young woman, and the late essays and reminiscences were informed by the deep passion and idealisation of her love for Martin.

But there were wider affinities. The Forsterian theme, 'only connect', has already been suggested. The other contemporary with whom Martin and Somerville shared common preoccupations was Henry James. In *An Irish Cousin*, for instance, they employed the familiar Jamesian device of the transatlantic visitant, *The Real Charlotte* is an Irish variant of *A Portrait of a Lady*, and there are thematic affinities between *The Spoils of Poynton* and *The Big House of Inver*, and between *The Princess Casamassima* and *Mount Music*. Which is merely to reiterate the fundamental argument that the country house as a symbol of civilisation was a transnational subject, and Ireland was a place where the meaning of civilisation was acutely questioned.

The allegory in *An Irish Cousin* is transparent but complex. Martin and Somerville called the fiction their 'shocker'. The (characteristically) comic designation contains, however, two intertextual references, for the word alludes specifically to Dion Boucicault's 'national' melodrama, *The Shaughraun*, and more generally to the tradition of the Gothic novel.[9] Accordingly Durrus House, the location of the fiction, is invested with a sinister secret: the familiar 'mad woman in the attic', Moll Hourihane, whose nocturnal perambulations alarm our heroine, Miss Sarsfield. The name Hourihane suggests a variant of (Cathleen ni) Houlihan, and Moll, according to the usual conventions of Gothic allegory, represents the *unheimlich* return of the repressed, the excluded Irish people. Rats stir 'behind the arras' in Durrus House, and it is no surprise to the reader of Gothic shockers that the dark figure of Uncle

Dominick is haunted by evil secrets. He has no legal claim to the house, and Moll Hourihane is his illegitimate daughter. Little ingenuity would be required to turn this example of 'Irish Gothic' into a confession of postcolonial guilt, with Durrus House representing the dark side of the Somervilles' Drishane, upon which it is modelled. If further confirmation were required, one might evoke the attics of the Irish R. M.'s Shreelane (ten years later), which are full of the unseen (but overheard) presence of the clan McCarthy.

The Gothic melds with Edgeworthian techniques. Miss Sarsfield marries a hero called Nugent (the son of the great house of O'Neill). Both names (like Edgeworth's Ormond and Grace Nugent) are invested with substantial, although indeterminate, historical and literary allusion. Our heroine, however, although historically rooted by name to the expatriate nationalist hero Patrick Sarsfield, is historically liberated by transatlantic culture. She is portrayed not as a nationalist type but as that familiar figure in Irish fiction: the visitor from outside Ireland. But she is here given unfamiliar treatment, because the outsider, rather than reading Ireland wrongly (the common convention), is gifted with superior insight and intelligence. She is specifically welcomed at Durrus House as one who will 'civilise' the place, and like the conventional heroine of female romance she is given a choice of two suitors: Nugent and the son of the house, Willy. The problem with Willy is that he is a representative of the great house gone 'native' (as Major Yeates might put it, camped in the 'laager' of Shreelane). He is redolent of the stables and the folk. The most prominent book in the library at Durrus is a volume of *The Turf, the Chase, and the Road*. The (allegorical) resolution of Willy's descent into 'Irishness' is his sexual liaison with (and compelled marriage to) the daughter of Moll Hourihane. It is an incestuous introversion, and it has its symbolic correlative in the suicide of Uncle Dominick in the bog-hole of Poula-na-coppal (over which mad Moll raises the Irish keen). Miscegenation is a union with the dark side of the self, an *amour de la boue* that is regressively destructive. Historically, therefore, the long cultural roots of the novel reach down to the intentions of the Statute of Kilkenny to draw a frontier between 'English' and 'Irish'.

The attraction of Nugent, on the other hand, is his very Englishness. The son of an ancient house, he has been educated at Harrow and Oxford and his culture is European. He would therefore have been at home in the enlightened world of writers, philosophers and politicians in which Edgeworth moved. Symbolically the affinity between Miss Sarsfield and Nugent is represented by their common taste in music.

She plays the pianoforte, he the violin, and they share a love of Corelli and Brahms. (European music also united Martin and Somerville). At the climax of the novel Nugent begs Miss Sarsfield to 'come away from this – you mustn't stay here' (p. 284).[10] What she must come away from is the Ireland represented by the dilapidated world of Durrus House and, on a more symbolic level, by Poula-na-coppal, a bog-hole that, Uncle Dominick cries, can never run dry and that for him represents 'the end of the world' (p. 280). If the 'union' of marriage stands for the choice for 'Ireland' (the Edgeworthian theme) then the Irish cousin is offered either regression into an apocalyptic dark place that can never be reclaimed for the civilised world, or movement into a wider, more enlightened world, where the harmony of art signifies the progressive culture of a cosmopolitan and European tradition, available through England.

Much the same allegorical and symbolic devices are used in the far more complex and darker fiction of *The Real Charlotte*. Here the name of the 'heroine' of the story, Francie Fitzpatrick, suggests an allegorical (and a national) signification in her role. Once again, long historical roots and a European connection are implied. As Charlotte Mullen claims, the Fitzpatricks have Butler blood, from somewhere back in time. It is the declared intention of Charles Dysart of Bruff House to civilise Francie, whose family, as it were, has gone native. It is 'his missionary resolve to let the light of culture illuminate her darkness' (p. 276).[11] That enlightenment is expressed by Dysart in his introduction of Francie to the poetry of Dante Gabriel Rossetti (a poet who links English culture to Italian origins), and Dysart's pre-Raphaelite taste, which is deeply implicated with his hesitant sexuality, leads him to idealise Francie's physical beauty in much the same way as pre-Raphaelitism idealised the artist's model. In this context the nomination Dysart/'dies art' may not be coincidental. His mother is more down to earth, for she is horrified by the possible misalliance, which she expresses in an image of miscegenation (and thus regression to Irish savagery): 'of all the man-eaters I have ever seen, she [Francie] is the most cannibalistic' (p. 239). This is a mere wit-play with words, but it is rooted in a traditional dichotomy in which Francie, the 'cannibal' who is to be illuminated by 'culture', is cast by Lady Dysart in the role of a Caliban. Symbolically, Francie is seen by Martin and Somerville as a force of nature: 'as a sea-weed stretches vague arms up towards the light through the conflict of the tides, her pliant soul rose through its inherited vulgarities, and gained some vision of higher things' (pp. 315–16). The great questions asked by the novel are what might that 'light' be, and what are those 'higher things'? They are, in Francie, both unknowable and unreachable. She is possessed by a hunger of the imagination that cannot draw real aliment from things as they are. Christopher Dysart, for instance, is seen by her as 'unparalleled' as a person, 'unknown as a type' and 'infinitely remote'. For the reader of the fiction, however, the inadequacies of Dysart as a man and the limitations of his culture are manifest. Like Gustave Flaubert's Emma Bovary and Henry James' Isabel Archer, Francie's hunger of imagination cannot be satisfied.

Our concern, however, is with the signification of place and not the intricacies of character. Francie's 'native' element is petit-bourgeois Dublin but her aspiration carries her towards an alliance with Bruff House. After her marriage to a mere land agent (thus between two worlds) residual aspiration propels the honeymoon couple to see the monumental splendours of Paris and Versailles before returning to their home called Rosemount (paradise lost in a land agent's garden).

The position of the Fitzpatrick family itself (Francie's point of entry into the 'civilised' world) is represented by their rental (it is not an inherited possession) of Albatross Villa:

> The house that the Fitzpatricks had taken in Bray for the winter was not situated in what is known as the fashionable part of the town. It commanded no view either of the Esplanade or of Bray Head; it had, in fact, little view of any kind except the backs of other people's houses, and an oblique glimpse of a railway bridge at the end of the road. It was just saved from the artisan level by a tiny bow window on either side of the hall door, and the name, Albatross Villa, painted on the gate posts; and its crowning claim to distinction was the fact that by standing just outside the gate it was possible to descry, under the railway bridge, a small square of esplanade and sea that was Mrs. Fitzpatrick's justification when she said gallantly to her Dublin friends that she'd never have come to Bray for the winter only for being able to look out at the waves all day long. (p. 356)

The nomination of this backstreet dwelling as a 'Villa' links the pretension of the Fitzpatricks to the classic tradition of villa culture and the Roman world. They are (unknowingly) the late heirs of Cicero and Pliny, or the Italian *villeggiatura* removed now to the winter seaside. Or to come closer to their own culture, this is the Fitzpatrick's 'Tusculum', their attempt to follow the fashionable world of Maria Edgeworth's 'Tales of Fashionable Life'. It is just possible to discern a small square of 'esplanade' (a French term formerly of military art), which stands for that world of fashion. They have 'a room without a view' (to play with the Forsterian phrase).

Thus the Fitzpatricks have inherited, as it were, the form of country house culture without the substance. Accordingly when Francie walks out with Roddy Lambert (the land agent) they take themselves to the public park in Bray, because suburbia has inherited a taste for landscape improvement and landscape gardening. They stop from time to time 'to look down at the river, or up at the wooded height opposite, with conventional expressions of admiration' (p. 376). At the end of another walk, and not being of the class to enter St George's Yacht Club, Roddy takes Francie to a hotel for afternoon tea ('the nicest thing I've done to-day' she says). The service provided by the hotel, the comfortable lounge and the sense of class distinction all mirror the conventions of country house living. Roddy's courtship recalls for Francie the known world of Bruff House and the world of 'higher things'. One might compare, from another country house novel, Jane Austen's Fanny Price at Portsmouth, and the way in which her experiences there recall Mansfield Park.

But why 'Albatross' Villa, and why the (oblique) outlook on the winter sea? Perhaps one should not seek to allegorise symbolic language that arises from the indeterminable depths of the writer's imagination. But the image of Francie as a seaweed instinctively reaching towards the light suggests a train of association of ideas, ambiguous perhaps, in which the great solitary bird represents the individual freedom to soar above the sea (which Francie can never achieve) or, with ironic ambiguity, that her aspiration is an albatross hung about her neck and the sea is an indeterminable void. Insofar as her room has a view, the view is merely of something without shape or limit.

The honeymoon episode at Versailles acutely poses the cultural question. Roddy and Francie feel that Paris is the right kind of place to visit (as did Edgeworth, and Somerville herself), and Versailles above all must be visited. Versailles is the greatest expression in architectural form and landscape art of civilised power in Europe. As Yeatsian adulation perceived it, Versailles is symptomatic of that form of society which aristocracies create for some brief moment of time, and Martin and Somerville seem to top even Yeats: 'the supreme expression of art in nature ... stretched out before them [Francie and Roddy] in mirrors of Triton and dolphin-guarded water and ordered masses of woodland'. But Roddy and Francie can neither literally nor metaphorically speak the language; the 'gilded ceilings and battle pictures' of the rooms of state merely jade the perfunctory and uncomprehending eye, and both hungry and exhausted they abandon 'the stately splendours of the terraces' for 'the simplicities of a path leading into a grove of trees'. They come to a *locus amoenus* in the grove:

> An enclosed green space in the wood, a daisy-starred oval of grass, holding the spring sunshine in serene remoteness from all the outer world of terraces and gardens, and made mysterious and poetical as the vale in Ida by the strange pale presences that peopled every nook of an ivy-grown crag at its further side. A clear pool reflected them, but waveringly, because of the ripples caused by a light drip from the overhanging rock; the trees towered on the encircling high ground and made a wall of silence round the intenser silences of the statues as they leaned and postured in a trance of suspended activity; the only sound was the monotone of the falling water, dropping with a cloistered gravity in the melodious hollow of the cave.
>
> 'I'm not going to walk another foot,' said Francie, sitting down on the grass by the water's edge; 'here, give me the oranges, Roddy, no one'll catch us eating them here, and we can peg the skins at that old thing with its clothes dropping off and the harp in its hand.' (pp. 409–10)

Obviously there is no connection between Francie and the statue of Apollo, the 'old thing' at which she will throw her orange peel. Francie's vulgarity is indicative of the (inevitable?) failure of Dysart's missionary endeavour to raise her into the 'light'. Conversely Francie's bored contempt might be interpreted as historically justified. Versailles is itself no more than the husk of an ancient regime, the plumage (to use Thomas Paine's word) of a degenerate culture overthrown by revolution, and thus not worth even the perfunctory admiration of the jaded sightseer. Be that as it may, the crux here is not so much Francie's position but that of the mediating writer, and our own position of seeing Francie seeing.

With the *locus amoenus*, Martin and Somerville return to one of the fundamental poetic myths of European civilisation. The orange that Francie holds in her hand is (for the classically educated reader) the golden apple of the Trojan story – *detur pulchriori* – for this 'green space' is nominated as 'a vale in Ida' and Francie's beauty is the disruptive force that sows disastrous discord in her own society. The paradox is that only a reader capable of interpreting the sign system of a garden such as that at Versailles is capable of picking up the writers' allusion. But these (static, learned) images of beauty formalise latent force. These highest manifestations of civilisation contain the savage. This is most obvious in the 'battle pictures' that decorate the gilded ceilings of the palace, from which epic world Roddy and Francie have just emerged, but even in the *locus amoenus* force is implicit in the 'dolphin-guarded water' and the 'ordered masses' of trees. Art transforms the real application of military control and political regimentation into the emblematical forms of garden architecture. But the Vale of Ida itself was the source of the most savage war recorded by the Apollonine muse of classical antiquity.

This allegorisation of the episode fails, however, to reveal the most extraordinary quality of the writing: its mystic quality. This place is invested with a profound stillness, upon which Francie and Roddy trespass and yet which survives their interruption: 'the trees towered on the encircling high ground and made a wall of silence round the intenser silences of the statues as they leaned and postured in a trance of suspended activity'. Within this 'trance' (and the use of the word suggests Yeats) a series of multiple mirrors is created; the human visitors perceive the scene, but the trees and statues seem to look upon them, and we perceive the perceivers. Martin and Somerville return here to one of the fundamental images of classical art, that of the mirror, for that is the function of the reflective pool. But the writers disturb that classical image by adding that it reflects 'but waveringly, because of the ripples caused by a light drip from the overhanging rock'. Classical culture cannot quite resolve things into the perfection of static form. Instead, between classical stasis and modern intrusion there is a strange remoteness, as if the 'cloistered gravity' of art removes it to the contemplation of something other than the everyday people who are, it seems, trespassing on sacred ground. Martin and Somerville continue their description by adding that, even as Francie speaks, the Apollo with his lyre is 'regarding them from the opposite rock with classic preoccupation'. That Apollonine gaze is both remote and incomprehensible, inalienably other, but it is also another manifestation of the gaze both of the writers and of us as readers seeking to connect and comprehend the interrelationship of these disparate things.

The affinity between this fiction and the work of E. M. Forster and Henry James has already been suggested. But, as a meditation on 'art in nature', the affinities of Martin and Somerville here are with John Keats, Walter Pater and W. B. Yeats. Art has an aesthetic quality that through the working of the imagination transcends nature, and an iconological function by which it gives perfect form to the highest aspirations of that civilisation from which it originates. Yet it is never out of nature, and therefore art is subject to those temporal processes of social and ideological change (let us call them 'history') in which meanings are shaped, changed and lost. The infinite plurality of individual point of view disturbs the Platonic perfection of ideal beauty and unchanging form. The self-contemplation of the Apollonine ideal, the 'sun king' whose will shaped this garden, the interpretative imagination of the writers' (and readers') gaze, and the intercalation of Francie (as a Helen of the suburbs) are connected here (but only in their disconnection) by the power of fiction.

As far as (mere) storyline is concerned, the failure to connect Helen of the suburbs to elite culture needs no elaboration. The misalliance between Albatross Villa and Bruff House is self-evident and skilfully dramatised in the acute embarrassment of Francie in the cold social vacuum of the country-house party at Bruff. Equally self-evident is the cultural sterility of the countryhouse ideal in current practice. The symbolism is perhaps too overt: Lord Dysart trundling through his landscaped gardens in his bathchair; Lady Dysart, whose cleverness is reduced to solving 'the acrostics in her society paper' and whose scholarship is directed to resolving 'the prophetic meaning of the Pyramids' (p. 73); Christopher, whose all too acute sense of his own inadequacy as an aesthete and artist has reduced him to provincial pottering at mere photography. Yeats might have had *The Real Charlotte* in mind when he wrote that 'an empty shell' was now an appropriate image for 'the inherited glory of the rich', and that the modern keeper of a great 'ancestral house' was now no more than a 'mouse'.

Martin and Somerville prefer a different series of images. When Christopher seeks to escape the marginality of Ireland (what he describes as 'Lismoyle form') it is to enter the greater world as an 'unpaid *attaché* to old Lord Castlemore at Copenhagen' (p. 375). It is an 'attachment' to something to which he does not belong, and he quits in disgust, for the qualities the post demands 'would grace the discharge of a doctor's butler'. The dismissive word 'butler' reduces one of the great families of Ireland (to which Francie was related, so it was claimed) to their original servile office. All a butler carries to his office now is the 'grace' that was once (consider Spenser) a sign both of divine election and of the perfection of courtly art. His diplomatic career joins his other abandoned career as a writer, 'like the skeletons that mark the desert course of a caravan' (p. 429).

The imagery of death suggested by the skeleton in the desert has its correlative in the story when Francie is killed when in pursuit of the romantic ideal represented by her love for a British soldier, Hawkins, her Sydney and her perfect man. As she rides apace in pursuit of this (false) ideal she comes upon an Irish funeral, 'with its barbarous and yet fitting crudity' (p. 507). As the coffin draws abreast of her, one of 'the savage classes' (Norry the Boat) rises 'like a great vulture opening its wings for flight' and emits 'the Irish Cry' (p. 509). Francie's horse panics, and Francie is thrown headfirst on to the road. On a purely realist reading, this termination of the fiction may appear abrupt and melodramatic. But the story is allegorical and symbolic. In Ireland the savage still retains the power to destroy. The civilised merely leave skeletons in the desert.

This is a deeply pessimistic, even nihilistic conclusion. And yet within the fiction there exists, and persists, a passionate desire to preserve and revitalise whatever it is that is represented by the 'former civilisation' (p. 58) of the ancient country house and demesne. Francie's desire for the 'light' is passionate and real. Its significance is emphasised by reduplication. The eponymous protagonist of the fiction is Charlotte Mullen, and the driving force of Charlotte, her obsession, is to obtain and re-establish the former gentry estate of Gurthnamuckla. She will make the house again a gentleman's seat and, by marriage to the land agent, Roddy Lambert, found a new dynasty. Had she succeeded the novel might be fitted into a conventional social history in which the emergent middle classes in Ireland replace the old aristocracy (witness Jason Quirk in Edgeworth's *Castle Rackrent*). Instead Charlotte acquires the estate but fails to restore the former civilisation or establish her line. It is as if *Castle Rackrent* had been told from Jason's (not Thady's) viewpoint, and Jason had found his new property merely an empty chalice. Charlotte acquires the substance but not the real presence, and condemned to a sterile old age she is left with an inheritance but no inheritor.

But the paradox remains. There is an aspiration after something represented by the civilisation of the country house, not realisable and yet deeply inherent, both socially and psychologically. That desire to repossess and recreate is the *leitmotif* of *The Big House of Inver*.[12] Here the house as locus becomes, as it were, the major character of the fiction, and also the signifier of the entire history of Ireland represented through the history of the Prendevilles' estate (Plate 8). As a sign of the original wars of conquest and settlement there is at Inver an ancient tower, the dwelling of the senile owner of the present great house, 'the Captain' (old Jas). The estate itself has been sold, and the new social order is settled at Demesne Lodge, the seat of 'the land grabber' John Weldon, former steward of the estate (an Edgeworthian theme).

Between the tower and Demesne Lodge, high on a promontory, over-looking the sea and symbolically as well as geographically separate from the mainland, is the splendour and the shell of the great Palladian house of Inver itself. The purpose of both the families in the fiction, the ancient Prendevilles and the new Weldons, is to reconnect the lands of the estate to the house, and accordingly to restore the house. The connection will be made by an act of union: it is the 'savage' (p. 83) will and desire of the bastard daughter of the Prendevilles, Shibby Prindy, that Peggy Weldon should marry the 'beautiful' young Kit Prendeville. Ignorant in her taste but passionate and 'elemental' (p. 140) in desire, Shibby, with whatever money she can raise, is seeking to refurnish the house with the detritus of local auctions. Peggy's father, however, has plans for his daughter to marry a rich Englishman – one of the 'cognosenties', whose wealth (secured by industrial capital) will purchase and restore the ancient house. Peggy's heart is given to Kit, but from the beginning the Prendevilles have been associated with 'the wild Irish' (p. 8) and Kit is no different. His affair with the insane daughter of a low publican ruins his relationship with Peggy, who chooses security without love by marriage to an Englishman. He buys the house and Shibby's pathetic furnishings are auctioned (although she retains the family portraits), but the house (seemingly spontan-eously) burns to the ground. The 'Gothic' suggestion is that the ghost of the ancient chatelaine, Lady Isabella (Shibby's namesake), has burnt it to prevent it falling into unworthy hands; the more literally minded might blame the pipe of old Jas.

Mere summary may indicate the allegorical bones of the subject – the desire to connect and its failure – but the symbolic penumbra is both vaguer and more luminescent. What is it about the house that drives Shibby (with an all-consuming passion), the phlegmatic English connoisseur (with canny financial judgement) and the Weldons them-selves, who, at least in the person of Peggy, aspire beyond merely the grabbing of land? The description of Inver House resists an easy answer:

> Inver House embodied one of those large gestures of the minds of the earlier Irish architects, some of which still stand to justify Ireland's claim to be considered a civilised country. It was a big, solemn, square house of three stories, built of cut stone, grandly planned, facing west in two immense sweeping curves, with a high pillared portico between them and stone balustrades round the roof, and enormous carved stone urns wherever such could suitably be placed ... A flight of limestone steps led to the hall-door, and under

the balustrades on either side of them Robert had inset the 'marriage-stones' that he had taken from the elder house among the Demesne trees, big blocks of limestone, carved with the names, very arbitrarily spelt, and the coats-of-arms, of his ancestors and their wives, and over the door he had built in a grey slab, with the family crest, a mailed hand, and the family motto, '*Je Prends*,' carved on it. (pp. 8–9)

Perhaps part of the passion that Inver generates lies outside the text, for it is a bigger and much grander version of the real Ross House, which Martin herself laboured to preserve, restore and save, with calloused hands scything the thistles from the drive, papering, plastering, carpentering within, a real-life Shibby Pindy. Perhaps also, at least for the learned reader, any classic example of English Palladianism is invested with something of the ideological significations of villa culture. This is implicit in what the authors call 'those large gestures of the minds of the earlier Irish architects'. These architects at least had some conception of the appropriate material signs of 'a civilised country', and Robert Prendeville, we are told elsewhere, 'gave his architect a free hand'. It is clear, however, that there is a gap between the civilised gesture that the architecture represents and the Prendevilles themselves. The mailed hand and the family motto, 'I take' (but cannot hold, Martin and Somerville will comment), are obvious enough, as is the unlettered culture of the family, as signified by the uncertain spelling of the marriage stones, which testify to the dynastic affiliations by which the military caste expanded their power. In *Ancestral Houses* Yeats wrote of the violent men in Ireland who called in artist and architect to provide that sweetness their own lives lacked, and Martin and Somerville, in their juxtaposition of the civilised with the savage, are very close to Yeatsian paradox here.

The bald description does not aestheticise the house in the manner, say, of *The Spoils of Poynton*, nor sentimentalise place as deep-rootedness, as in Forster's *Howards End*. The isolation and precariousness of Inver House is intrinsic to its place and history, but it is the very vulnerability of the house as monument that attracts the preserver or restorer. There is a desire in the English and Irish, old family or new, to unify the house on the promontory with the mainland, a desire proleptically denied by the significations of the architecture itself. The stone urns incorporated into the original design of the house suggest, even from the inception, a *memento mori*. Nothing lasts, even monuments raised in stone. Except of course, as classical culture suggested, the volatile words of the writer: *exegi monumentum*[13] (Plate 9).

At the heart of the novel, and its symbolic *leitmotif*, is the ironic interplay established by Martin and Somerville between high art and the mundane present. It is a more extended treatment of the Versailles episode in *The Real Charlotte*. For instance Italian architects have made, in Lady Isabell Prendeville's room, a work of beauty and magnificence that tells of the 'happy conjunction of art and wealth', and a 'generous taste' which could make the best of both. But the present wreck of the room acts now as 'the sign manual of brutalised human creatures, a deliberate destruction that transcends all other forces'. The iconological sign of that confrontation between the high art of a Renaissance tradition and the present world is the signification given to the portraits of Lady Isabella herself and her Prendeville husband, 'Beauty Kit'. These icons of high culture are reflected in the modern presence of their living simulacra, ignorant and illegitimate Shibby Pindy and her half brother Kit. It is ancestral 'beauty' (a reiterated word) that Kit has inherited and that makes Peggy Weldon love him. Their love is mutually recognised when, in a crucial episode, they visit the house together and see the ancient portraits:

> In the drawing-room of the Big House Kit and Peggy were sitting, hand in hand, on that central jewel of Miss Pindy's achievements, the atrophied Chesterfield sofa. They were looking at the portraits of Beauty Kit, and of his wife, the Lady Isabella.
>
> 'He's supposed to be like me,' said Kit, looking approvingly at his namesake, 'what do you think?'
>
> He put a possessive arm round her, and took her chin in his hand, turning her face so that she must look at him. Kit was as much in love [with her] as it was in his power to be, and looked deep into her eyes and laughed, out of sheer delight in her. (p. 215)

This lacks the poetic richness of the Versailles episode in *The Real Charlotte* (the dead Violet Martin is only a ghostly presence), but the juxtaposition between Kit and the portrait works in the same way as that between Francie and Apollo. The *ancien régime* ambience is established by the iconological use of the 'old Chesterfield sofa' (a pathetic sign of Shibby's purchases). The decadence of the old order is implicit in the allusion, via 'Chesterfield', to the notorious letters of the fourth Earl, which glamorised 'the morals of a whore, and the manners of a dancing master' (in Johnson's words).[14] So Kit, who is related to this world, has only a modicum of genuine love to give Peggy Weldon. And yet the beauty of the artefacts, the images of the original Christopher and Isabella, are countervailing presences. The moral and the aesthetic are brought together in confrontation. But rather than the 'Apollonine' remaining a static presence, as in the Versailles episode, here the artwork itself becomes a kind of living presence. The Gothic mode melded into this story reasserts the return of the repressed as the ghost of Lady Isabella walks Inver House, mocking the attempts of the present generation to restore the mansion. It is suggested that it is she who eventually destroys the house when it is about to go out of the family.

The presence of the ghost of Lady Isabella fundamentally reverses one of the commonest motifs in nationalist/postcolonialist interpretations of fiction in Ireland. It is not the dispossessed *Volk* who haunt the place from which they have been evicted by a sadistic invader. Rather what has been evicted is the sense of 'beauty', of high taste and culture, which has been brutalised by the new powers who now hold all the land of Ireland, except the ruin of Inver House, high on its promontory. Of course the civilisation the historical Lady Isabella embodied is itself subject to criticism, but what is beyond criticism is the beauty of the portraits, which preserve an icon of perfection across the ravages of time and circumstance, and which heart-wrenching beauty is separable from both person and circumstance. Thus 'Beauty Kit' died ravaged by smallpox, but the portrait has not been subject to such decay. This is a familiar aesthetic motif in the works of Horace and Ovid, in Shakespeare's sonnets, and in the writings of Keats and Yeats. But perhaps the closest analogy is Oscar Wilde's *The Picture of Dorian Grey*. The portrait of Lady Isabella is the *genius loci*. But that genius will not let itself be vulgarised, nor repossessed by the adoring savage, by the acquisitive middle classes nor by modern connoisseurship. It is not transferable between consumers as a property, but possesses an unavailable integrity.

Kit and Peggy fulfill different functions, in relation to this icon. The Prendeville son merely follows the degenerate tradition of his family (and of early Irish history) by 'going native' and immersing himself among 'the Wild Irish'. But Peggy has a special relation to the newly emergent middle class ('middle' because midway between the savage and the civilised). She is the daughter of the local 'land grabbers', the Weldons, but her mother is English and she has been educated in Paris. She is bilingual in French and English (not Gaelic and English), and although her father has no real understanding of her taste in literature and music (so much embroidery with which women amuse themselves) her taste is genuine. Thus when she first visits the house, the like of which she has never seen before, she is fascinated by it, and her love of beauty is vivified by the real presence of her lover, Kit. There is an aspiration to high culture in Peggy, like that of Francie Fitzpatrick in *The Real Charlotte* but better grounded and more likely to succeed. It had been only vaguely present in her grandfather, who had made of Demesne Lodge a parody of a country house (feeling himself to be 'a patron of Art for Art's sake as Pope Julius might have felt' – p. 68). But Peggy has moved closer to the world of knowledge and feeling that Martin and Somerville themselves know and embody, and in the fiction she has much the same function as Margaret Schlegel in Forster's *Howards End*. She is thus the antithesis of the familiar icon of Cathleen ni Houlihan (of the *Volk*, Gaelic speaking, Catholic and colonially oppressed). If Peggy were to marry a Prendeville the union of demesne with house, of middle class with aristocracy, would betoken a healing of the disunion in Ireland, preservation of the intrinsic aesthetic beauty of the old house (freed from the dark side of its history – *je prends*) and reincorporation of the culture of Ireland into the wider world signified by Peggy's English mother and Parisian education. Only connect . . .

This is a connection denied by the tragic conclusion of the fiction. Ireland denies such fortunate unions. The self-generated fire at Inver might be construed as an evasion by Somerville of the causes of those other socially generated fires that were to destroy great houses in the 1920s. This fiction obviously resists incorporation into the immediate issues of the civil conflict in Ireland. But Somerville's two previous country house novels, *Mount Music* (1919) and *An Enthusiast* (1921), were both political. That specific politicisation is not our subject here except insofar as the century of terrorism provoked by the Easter Rising in 1916 may stand as an obvious example of the original 'savagery' in Ireland that seven centuries of 'civilisation' had failed to obliterate.

An Enthusiast requires little attention, for it is a simple, allegorical novella about a descent into anarchy. The protagonist of that fiction, Dan Palliser of Monalour House, has dedicated himself to the enlightened (Edgeworthian) ideals of improved (cooperative) agriculture and non-sectarian education. These ideals are rejected by his community. He rents out his ancestral home (Monalour) to an Englishman, the former colonial administrator Lord Ducarrig; but he is drawn back to his house by his love for Ducarrig's wife. What unites the (unavailable) Englishwoman and the idealistic Irishman is their common love of music, and especially that German music which expresses their love: *Du meine Seele, du mein Herz.* (p. 243) Spiritually, they are both members of a wider European culture. The country house where their loving spirits meet is a place in which, thematically, the combination of stern yet decorative architecture, the 'symbols of civilisation and affluence',

(p. 100), represent the unity of man and woman. But there is no escape from the violence of the times. Republican gunmen attack the house, and when Palliser drives them away, wielding only the sword his unionist father carried in the Crimean War, he is shot by Lord Ducarrig in the confused crossfire. The allegory requires no comment. Monalour is now a place where ignorant armies clash by night.

Mount Music is less pessimistic, but only because the youthful aristocratic protagonists survive to carry forward their love and culture. The fiction achieves something of the political complexity of Lever's fictions, perhaps because it is suffused with the disappointed idealism of Somerville's own Home Rule ideals. She came, bitterly, to acknowledge the warnings given her by (unionist) Martin. As in *An Enthusiast* the basic allegory is simple. The theme, yet again, is 'only connect'. There are two demesnes in the fiction, that of the Protestant unionist Talbot-Lowrys of Mount Music ('pterodactyls' who can no longer survive) and the Roman Catholic Coppingers of Coppinger's Court. Will marriage unite young Christian of Mount Music with her lover, Larry, across the religious divide? A bridge across the local river (with a Protestant church on one side and a Roman Catholic church on the other) provides an obvious symbol of connection. Larry sees himself as a Catholic Parnell who will provide the political focus needed to bring all sides together, and he is drawn deep into nationalist affiliations. His ideals are in vain, and he is outflanked from a less liberal, more sectarian position. He finds that in Ireland people 'hate one another for the love of God' (p. 265). At the end of the novel Somerville uses a symbolic device (familiar from George Eliot and D. H. Lawrence), and a destructive inundation of the river brings catastrophe. Only then – in the deserted shell of Mount Music, in the presence of death and destruction – are Christian and Larry united.

This political allegory is enthused and vivified with a deep passion that arguably arises in part from Somerville's own love for her home, Drishane (which is written into *Mount Music* in the same way as Ross is implicit in *The Big House of Inver*). Another strand of passion seems to derive (it cannot be proven) from Somerville's equally deep love for the dead Violet Martin. As Larry to Christian, so Edith to Violet. Separation and displacement are familiar themes in Irish literature, and are often associated with eviction from home and diaspora. That theme relates as much to exile from a great country house as from a cottage, and seems here to be inextricably linked to Somerville's inner experience of past and forthcoming loss. 'This place is turned into a wilderness' (p. 165).

Mount Music, as locus, is a symbol both of harmonious civilisation (as the allegorical name indicates) and of that familial and familiar jumble which is indicative of home for generations of people. The ideal here is imbricated with the quotidian. In this fiction this sense of belonging is not the idealisation of Yeats' 'ancestral houses', but is lovingly created by the detail in which we come to know the house and the everyday life of the family in its fullest range, from the library (where the turf fire is never extinguished), with its dusty squirrel-hoards of objects that defy classification, and redolent with the smell of old books, tobacco smoke and hounds (p. 89); right through to the descent via the back stairs to the realm of armies of cockroaches and marauding rats (p. 167). There is, in particular, an elaborate description of the 'long and lofty drawing-room', founded on the taste of the great-grandmother of the family, a gallery of (indifferent) family portraits and fading land-scape paintings, rich with ottomans and Italian marble, Georgian glass and Chinese porcelain:

> There were long and implacable sofas, each with its conventional sofa-table in front of it; Empire *consoles*, with pieces of china incredibly diverse in style, beauty, and value, jostling each other on the marble slabs; woolwork screens, worked by forgotten aunts and grand-mothers, chairs of every known breed, and tables, tables everywhere, and not a corner on one of them on which anything more could be deposited. The claims of literature were acknowledged, but without enthusiasm. A tall, glass-fronted cupboard, inaccessibly placed behind the elongated tail of an early grand piano, was filled with ornate miniature editions of the classics, that would have denied an effort – had such ever been made – to remove them from their shelves, whereon they had apparently been embedded in cement, like mosaic. It was a room ... with rubbish contending successfully with museum pieces, with the past and present struggling in their eternal rivalry; yet, a human place, a place full of the magnetism that is born of past happiness, a place to which all its successive gener-ations of sons and daughters looked back with that softening of the heart that comes, when in, perhaps, a far-away country, memories of youth return, and with them the thought of home. (p. 142)

To explicate fully the cultural history this room contains would involve writing the history of the fundamental relationship of dynastic property (expressed in the iconography of family portrait and idealised land-scape) to imperial expansion and trade (signified by Chinese porcelain and 'ottoman' sofa). The taproots of this history would lead via Renaissance Italy (the Italian marble of the fireplace) to the ancient world, embedded now (like some mosaic from a ruined Roman villa) in the unread but culturally correct classics (English, French, Italian, Latin and Greek?) in the library cupboard. The current social functions of the (with)drawing room are indicated by the plethora of tables and chairs, which speak of the incessant demand made upon the house as the locale of that system of dynastic (and political) networking known as 'the house party'. More minutely, the gender divisions of male and female are apparent in the distinction between this withdrawing room (for women) and the masculine world of the Mount Music (working) library. The products of female leisure are represented in the withdrawing room by firescreens, watercolours and pencil drawings. Of particular significance for this story is the presence of a grand piano, because (once again) taste in music is an indication both of common spirituality and of social division. Christian associates the music of Mendelssohn with her love for Larry; his involvement in the 'jungle' of nationalism outside the country house is signified by his participation in consciousness-raising sessions of national airs in town.

There is a sense that this is a civilisation that is being buried under the accumulation of its own material inheritance: there is no room for 'anything more [to] be deposited'. Ancient works of incredible beauty and diversity are becoming museum pieces, solidifying, as it were, into a mosaic (a Yeatsian image), or into a literary inheritance that is 'bedded in cement' and thus inaccessible, although still there. Yet at the same time there is in the writer an abiding attachment to this place because it is 'a human place' where men and women across the generations have been happy together, so the derivative artefacts from high classical culture, the amateur watercolours, the woolwork screens 'worked by forgotten aunts' and the unheard melody of family music around the piano will continue in the hearts of 'successive generations of sons and daughters'. The 'far-away country' of which Somerville writes is far more than the imperial domain of the United Kingdom (that wider world outside Ireland that generations of her family have served loyally and with distinction). These are the 'blue remembered hills' of A. E. Housman's lament, those 'memories of youth' which are part of our common humanity. Here they are associated with Edith's love for the lost Violet and her recognition that the sense of 'home' (the world of Drishane and Ross) will be lost in an Ireland where the aim of the armies of ignorance (like mad dogs fighting, she writes) is merely 'to have your desire of your enemy' (p. 266).

The spirit of the place is Christian. I have no doubt (but no proof) that Christian is Violet Martin transfigured through the imagination of the artist. Somerville herself, like Larry Coppinger, Christian's fictional lover, is a painter and writer. Larry's love for Christian compels him (it becomes 'the most important thing in the world') to idealise her by portraiture, a motif familiar from *The Real Charlotte* and *The Big House of Inver*, but different here because original and artefact are one. There is no ironising disjunction. How could there be if Christian is the idea of Violet Martin? Although Larry is a mere amateur, in this portrait he achieves his masterwork, combining something of the idealism of pre-Raphaelitism with the fluid brilliance of Sargent. If there is irony in the depiction of the portrait it comes from the incomprehension of Larry's own social circle, who find his style beyond their comprehension. Perhaps, too, the modern reader may find something in Somerville's account outside current experience, for what inspires Larry is more than Christian's intelligence and beauty. For him the transformatory moment of vision comes when her horse is spiked on the hunting field (by a nationalist Catholic farmer) and she goes to fetch a gun to destroy the crippled animal:

> Her courage, oh God! her courage! How she had ridden that little mad devil of a mare! There wasn't a man out who would have got over that big country as she had! And then, when the cur had done his dirty work and bolted, was there a whimper or a cry from her? She had faced the music; she had started off to get the gun herself. (p. 182)

Christian embodies (and it is in the body of a woman) the old aristocratic virtues of courage, control and stoicism, and they are shown in horsemanship. '"Noble horsemanship," Shakespeare called it, recognising in it some fine output of soul.'[15] The hunting field had always been the place of display for the warlike skills of the aristocracy. Therefore, it was also the place where the power of chivalric civilisation ritualised savagery in symbolic killing (compare the 'cur' who, like a terrorist, kills and runs away). Here the necessary act of killing is that inflicted by Christian on her fatally wounded 'devil of a mare'. It is, symbolically, a samurai-like act of suicide.

At the end of the novel both great families, the Talbot-Lowrys and the Coppingers, have committed another act of suicide by selling their estates. But what is newly established is the union of Larry and Christian, the artist who has created the icon of Christian, and the aristocrat whose great courage and intelligence has inspired the artist (the old classic theme). For the rest, there is only remembrance of things past: '"I have nothing left now," she said to herself, "but memories, hungering memories"' (p. 284), but those memories are the potential source both of a harmony no longer possible in the contemporary world and of hope for a better future. This hope finds expression in a mystic moment on Cnochan an Ceoil Sidhe (the Hill of Fairy Music) when Christian and Larry recognise their love:

> The mist, golden and green, that comes with an autumn sunset, half hid, half transfigured the wide distances of the valley of the Broad-water; the darkness of the woods, blended from this aspect into one, of Mount Music and Coppinger's Court, was softened by its veils; the far hills were transparent, as if the light had fused them to clearest brown, and topaz, and opal glass. The hill side, above and beneath them, glowed and smouldered with the ruby-purple of heather.... The sunset
>
> > 'bloomed and withered on the hill
> > Like any hill-flower';
>
> but long those two stood by the Druid stone, knowing, perhaps, the best moment that life could give them, facing the dying radiance with hearts that were full of sunrise. (pp. 204–5)

For some readers this may seem overly sentimental, but iconographically this epiphany for Larry and Christian is an idealisation of the relationship between Edith and Violet. That is the source of the sentiment, but the autobiographical element is not our concern. The epiphany is especially associated with the sense of place, a religious location at which two houses, Mount Music and the Court (Drishane and Ross?), are united by two lovers even at an historical moment of decline and fall, that 'dying radiance' which for them will also be the threshold of a new dawn. After Martin's death, Somerville, in her late autobiographical writings (as in *Mount Music*), sought to record the depth of her love for Martin, and this is inextricably tied into her accounts of the soon-to-be-obliterated traces of the lost civilisation they have known in their familial homes, Drishane and Ross (Plates 10 and 11). So intense is the relationship of person to place that Somerville still names 'Ross' as her coauthor, thus identifying Martin with the physical body of her house. In *Irish Memories* Somerville describes that association with the house as an act of 'love', an image that Molly Keane later picked up when she wrote of these writers' 'sexual love for the house and its demesnes'. In Martin's own words, Ross is a 'Sleeping Beauty', one which she will reawaken with a kiss.[16]

Martin's account of her attempt to reawaken Ross, preserved in her letters to Somerville, is an extraordinary social record. It places the reader at a moment of transformation in history when the vestiges of what Shakespeare called the 'bond' that held together the feudal community are being broken apart by what in more modern terms might be called the development of individualism and acquisitive capitalism. Now, to use Martin's words, 'no one cares a button for anything but their own gain.'[17] But our main concern is with the intrinsic bond that unites writer to house, so that 'Ross' stands for person and place, and, iconologically, both stand for the civilisation they embody.

It is a long association, for the Martins have been established in their homeland for seven hundred years; their marriages recorded in marriage stones (as at Inver); survivors, like the present house, so Martin writes, of many Atlantic storms; rooted, in traditional iconography, like the trees of the demesne to which she tends with assiduous dedication. The house was once a fortified tower, hence, perhaps, Somerville's description of it as a 'sentinel'. But subsequently the house acquired the external signifiers of enlightened neoclassical civilisation: an elementary portico for a doorway rising over a former moat, a Venetian window, binding neoclassicism to the quasi-Roman virtues of the Venetian republic and empire, and a series of urns that decorate the roof (as at Inver), characteristic *memento mori* that recall ancestral greatness and remind that all power is transitory and all civilisations decline and fall. This is a commonplace iconography, but nonetheless unusual because of the location of the house on the frontier of Connemara. 'Civilisation in Siberia could not be more surprising', writes Martin. But even at Castletownshend, where 'the high level of civilisation' is represented by the close proximity of several 'quality' houses, Somerville writes of the 'isolation' of the demesnes as apostles of 'an alien civilisation' and (in an image also used in *The Real Charlotte*) as the homes of the first missionaries 'at the Court of the King of the Cannibal Islands'.[18]

The missionaries are from the original European *imperium*. In Somerville's words, country house culture was built 'upon the rock of the classics' (alluding to St Peter). Hence it comes naturally to Somerville to write that 'Martin should have sacrificed herself to the Lares and Penates of Ross – Ross, the love of which was rooted in her from her cradle'. Somerville unites classical religion to Christian, and although the phrase 'Lares and Penates' is merely conventional, the implicit conventions are, as Somerville suggests, inherent. 'Gentry houses', she continues, 'were once disseminators of light, of the humanities; centres of civilisation; places to which the poor people rushed, in any trouble, as to Cities of Refuge.' St Augustine may be in her mind here, for the house has acquired something of the aura of the *Civitatis Dei*.[19]

There follows Somerville's panegyric of Martin as the embodiment of all that was best in 'Ross':

> She had a gift for doing, happily and beautifully, always the right thing, at no matter at what cost to herself.... One remembers the Arab steed, who dies at a gallop. It was not only that she was faithful and unselfish, but she so allied her intellect to obliterating all traces of her fidelity and her unselfishness, that their object strode, unconscious, into the soft place that she had prepared and realised nothing of the self-sacrifice that had gone to its making. With her, it was impossible to say which was the most beautiful, the gentleness of heart, or the brilliance of intellect. I have heard that among the poor people they called her The Gentle Lady; in such a matter, the poor people are the best judges.

In this tribute, Martin, joins the 'Olympians' (to use a Yeatsian word). Of course this is Platonic idealisation no longer reflected in the mirror of this world: 'Ross' is dead. It is also self-evidently aristocratic, thus its use of the image of the Arab steed 'dying at a gallop' as an icon of the gentry, and the evocation of the gentle lady as the friend of the poor (always, symbiotically, at the gate of the city of refuge). But the 'gentleness of heart' (no mean quality in a time of war) and 'brilliance of intellect' have a wider sphere. They are associated (and in conjunction with Somerville) with works of art. Both gentle intellects share a love of painting and music (Schumann, Schubert and Bach, which fell on deaf ears even at Drishane), and above all both Martin and Somerville are readers and makers of works of literature. They belong to the transnational and transhistorical world of those who 'read books, and had travelled beyond Galway town.'[20] Participation in that wider sphere is an escape from the 'nets' (to use Joyce's word) of Irish provinciality and savagery, which ultimately turned on the very 'sentinels' of civilisation.

In Ireland toleration, Somerville writes in *Wheel-Tracks*, is not regarded as 'an inevitable feature of civilization' and the hatred directed at country house culture during the time of civil war causes her to lament what she believes fell with that culture: 'the ruined homes have passed, and cannot return. So also have passed, and are still passing, the prosperity and civilization that only wealth and culture have it in their power to give to a country which has never had a superfluity of either of these.'[21] This is an apologia that neither nationalist nor postcolonial history has accepted. Somerville records that she was called a 'bloodsucker' (the familiar vampire image) and a 'carrion crow' by the forces of the intolerant. Castletownshend was a plum target for republican insurgents: rich in country houses, too remote for military protection. It is part of the dark irony of things that the Somervilles' home, Drishane, was protected (at the request of the Free State government to the truncated United Kingdom) by the presence of a warship which at night shone a searchlight upon the house as a deterrent. But not all in Castletownshend were so protected. Somerville's brother, Boyle, by politics a Home Ruler, was later shot six times at the door of his house, and his genitals blown away. This remains a not unfamiliar occurrence. The traitorous act for which the old man was summarily executed was that he had written references for young men in Castletownshend wishing to join the British navy. The patriots who carried out this act of war modestly declined to reveal their names. Hence they cannot be commemorated as they deserve.[22]

It is difficult for writers to 'place' themselves in such circumstances when the very place to which they belong is the target of civil war. 'The Jungle was creeping in...the wild triumphed...' Ireland is a lunatic asylum where the insane lead their keepers. (These are the images even of the *Irish R. M.* stories.)[23] But for Somerville there at least remains her love for a sacred place. Ross becomes an empty shell once Martin is dead, but it continues to be a symbol of enduring beauty married to the landscape (Plate 12):

> The beauty of Ross is past praising. I think of it as I saw it first, on a pensive evening of early spring, still and grey, with a yellow spearhead of light low in the west. Still and grey was the lake, too, with the brown mountain, Croagh-Keenan, and the grey sky, with that spear-thrust of yellow light in it, lying deep in the wide, quiet water, that, was furrowed now and then by the flapping rush of a coot, or streaked with the meditative drift of a wild duck; farther back came the tall battalions of reeds, thronging in pale multitudes back to the shadowy woods; and for foreground, the beautiful, broken line of the shore, with huge boulders of limestone scattered on it, making black blots in the pearlgrey of the shadows.

This is from the inception of the chapter devoted to Martin in *Irish Memories*, and simply labelled 'Herself'. It is one of the few passages in Irish country house fiction where the house is naturalised in the countryside itself (in English fashion) rather than within the demesne as a region separate from circumambient nature. 'Ross, and its lake and its woods, is Galway', writes Somerville, and Ross is also Martin herself. In the reiterated emphasis on the beauty of the still scene the literary tradition of Keats meets Yeats. The only visual imperfections in the scene, the 'blots' made by the limestone rocks, are shortly changed to 'a collar of gems, that respond to the suggestions of the sky', a qualification that suggests Somerville was consciously idealising and regretted the intrusion of the earlier hint of disjunction in the scene touched (even in spring) by elegiac memory. It is elegiac because Martin is dead and Ross is yielding to the 'pensive evening' as Martin has become one of the 'pale multitudes' that belong in the shadow of the woods. This memory, like Keats' grecian urn and Yeats' golden bird, is removed from the troubled temporal world, preserved in its perfect stillness as an icon of beauty by the writer, and preserved by the writing for all readers.

Except even here the savage still (subliminally) intrudes. The yellow light in the west is described first as a spear-head and then as a spear thrust. If this is the penetrative pain of memory, the 'tall battalions' of reeds suggest the continuing, natural presence of some unpersonified but militant force that even here, in this place and with this subject, cannot be written out of Ireland.

6
'The Duchess Too is Dead': Bowen and Gregory

Elizabeth Bowen's *Bowen's Court* (1942) and Lady Augusta Gregory's *Coole* (1931) conclude this enquiry.[1] Both works were written after the dissolution of the political Union, and thus chronological limitation is violated. But both writers were born into the old country house order and the actual houses iconised by Bowen and Gregory belonged to that other union, the imaginary European civilisation (rather than the separatist nation) from which the architectural form of the houses and their literary idealisation derive. The history of the houses is a kind of 'time trope'. Both writers desired (in vain) to preserve the fabric of court and park. Bowen and Gregory were chatelaines, one by inheritance the other by marriage, but their houses now exist only in what Bowen called 'thought-form'.[2] The causes of the loss were mundane: exigent market forces. That in itself had an iconographic function: it separated the loss of these houses from the demonology of Irish history: the republican *auto-da-fé* in which 'the garrisons' were burnt out.

That Irish history was grimly intrusive, but it is not the subject here. The concern here is neither Bowen's historical position as the writer of an astringent valediction on the death of the Protestant Ascendancy in Ireland, nor Gregory's role as the creator of an Anglo-Irish literary renaissance.[3] *Bowen's Court* and *Coole* belong (in the present argument) in a wider context: that extraordinary, transnational, efflorescence of literature in English that marks the historical decline and fall of the country house order and in the process, idealises the house *per se* as an icon of transhistorical value. More specifically, Bowen's and Gregory's texts are closely related to Edith Somerville's autobiographical writings, and also belong with works such as Vita Sackville-West's *Knole of the Sackvilles* (1922) and the Duchess of Devonshire's *The House: Living at Chatsworth* (1982), and even William Howard Adams' *Jefferson at Monticello*

(1983) – for the phenomenon involves the entire English-speaking world. In memorialising their houses as icons, Bowen and Gregory occupy an intermediate historical position between the actual decline and fall (in which court and park were lost) and the resurrection of the house as the cultural idea that underlies what is now called 'the heritage industry'. Indeed, Coole Park has become part of that industry. Ireland wants tourists, and tourists want country houses. Each summer there are queues at Kilkenny Castle, the notorious statute of separation yielding to a wider union.

To tell that wider story in its entirety is beyond the scope of this book, so *Bowen's Court* and *Coole* have been chosen as typical texts. They form a complementary pairing: one is a nostalgic apologia (thus looking back to Somerville) for country house civilisation, the other is a celebration of an attempted revival founded on the learning and patronage of a great house. Coole Park is not just an Irish heritage site, it is a European marker.

The date 5 August 1914 is crucial to Bowen's account of the decline and fall of her civilisation, and the crucial locus is Mitchelstown, the great house to which Bowen's Court was locally related. Since Young's visit to Mitchelstown formed part of the prolegomenon to the present book, it is appropriate for the same place to mark its conclusion. Mitchelstown was rebuilt in the early nineteenth century as an Irish 'Windsor Castle', more locally unionist and less a sign of the international enlightenment than the house Young had known. One thing did not change, however, between Young's visit and the twentieth century. The house remained a remote marker of civilisation. Even in August 1914, Bowen records, mention of the word 'war' did not seem to have reached the locality, and on the day that Britain declared War on Germany 'the newspaper did not come'. Mechanically following the old social routine of the country house order, a garden party had assembled at Mitchelstown. The host received the guests 'at the far end of Big George's gallery' since a 'chill wind' blew from the Galtee mountains. That chill wind, of course, was that of change, about to blow away the old world of Mitchelstown and Bowen's Court. The choice of location to receive the guests is also loaded with signification. The name 'George' unites the former owner of the castle with the patron saint of England, and beyond that, in European tradition, with imperial Roman *georgic* (the farmer as virtuous colonist). But the particular 'big' George of Mitchelstown was the notorious, mad, impoverished former owner whom Alexis de Tocqueville had once used as a dark example of the condition of Ireland, but whom, in Bowen's sympathetic, symbolic, reordering of history, went mad because 'democracy' had broken the feudal bond by which he held his tenants (the 'King Lear' syndrome). It was this breaking of the bond that provoked the agrarian riots that are marked, so the Irish Tourist Board account of Mitchelstown records, in the martyrs' memorial in the town square (discussed in the prolegomenon to this enquiry).[4]

Had the garden party passage in *Bowen's Court* (p. 434 f.) been from a fiction like *The Last September*, Bowen's depiction might be read as a consistent part of the sad, astringent satire of decline and fall. 'Tell me,' demands one of the characters in that fiction, 'what do you mean by...civilisation?', and expects no very favourable answer.[5] This civil society in Mitchelstown, cocooned by space from time, carries out the effete and snobbish rituals of a perpetual 'Sunday Afternoon' (to weave in another Bowen title) only remotely aware of the savage at the gates (having emerged from the Galtee mountains). One might also observe that this passage, like *The Last September*, carries a frisson of excitement that comes from the temporal proximity of violence. But here the excitement generated by 'the tremendous news' as it breaks is used by Bowen to express a sense of potential class regeneration through participation in war:

> Almost every one said they wondered if they really ought to have come, but they *had* come – rightly: this was a time to gather....The tension of months, of years – outlying tension of Europe, inner tension of Ireland – broke in a spate of words. Braced against the gale from the mountains, licking dust from their lips, these were the unmartialled loyalists of the South. Not a family had not put out, like Bowen's Court, its generations of military brothers – tablets in Protestant churches recorded deaths in remote battles; swords hung in halls. If the Anglo-Irish live on and for a myth, for that myth they constantly shed their blood. So, on this August 1914 day of grandeur and gravity, the Ascendancy rallied, renewed itself.

This is an atavistic passage, self-consciously and strategically so, and in its sectarianism and racialism ostensibly Irish. For the first time the words 'Ascendancy' and 'Anglo-Irish' (rejected in this enquiry) retrospectively emerge. But there is a wider context. The 'outlying tension' is European. The 'grandeur and gravity' of this day are bound up with the rediscovery by an officer class of its ancient historical role in Europe. Or at least this is what a woman of that class claims, just as Mary Martin identified herself with the exploits of the armies of Napoleon. So Lady

Gregory bred for the war of 1914 that Major Robert whom Yeats mythologised. One might also set this passage from Bowen transhistorically and transnationally against the call to arms of the menfolk of another country house order, that depicted in Margaret Mitchell's *Gone With the Wind* (consider the resonance of Bowen's words 'the South' translated to Tara). Or to move forward to the Second World War, one could place the Mitchelstown party in relation to Virginia Woolf's gathering at Poyntz Hall in *Between the Acts*, with the Battle of Britain raging remotely in the skies while the Dyces of Denton and the Wickhams of Owlswick come together: '*Adsum*, I'm here, in place of my grandfather or great grandfather...'[6] In *Bowen's Court* the locus of the gathering is the terrace of the house that Bowen calls the Irish Windsor Castle. That locus places the gathering on the historical cusp between that point in the progress of civilisation when castles were turned into country houses, and the atavistic renaissance of the violence from which crown and state had evolved, and to which it now returns. 'War...hasn't started anything that wasn't there already' – so Stella Rodney was later to claim in Bowen's *The Heat of the Day*.[7] The savage is always residual in the civil order. The martial rededication that Bowen evokes is something she both recognises within her historical tradition and is repelled by its consequences. The sequence is not celebratory. On the contrary it bemoans the collapse of the old order in Europe and the consequential destruction of the very place of the gathering:

> It was an afternoon when the simplest person begins to anticipate memory – this Mitchelstown garden party, it was agreed, would remain in every one's memory as historic. It was, also, a more final scene than we knew. Ten years hence, it was all to seem like a dream – and the Castle itself would be a few bleached stumps on the plateau. To-day, the terraces are obliterated, and grass grows where the saloons were. Many of these guests, those vehement talkers, would be scattered, houseless, sonless, or themselves dead. That war – or call it now that first phase of war – was to go far before it had done with us...

She runs together in her retrospection both the events of the First World War and the by-blow of those events in Ireland in 1916, and the inescapable progression towards the renewal of war in 1939, which was at its height when *Bowen's Court* was written (in the *blitzkrieg* of the 1940s). She was writing 'during a time when all homes were threatened and hundreds of thousands of them were being wiped out' (p. 454).

Thus the destruction of Mitchelstown, the bombs that were even then falling on England (p. 418) and the entire dislocation of European culture that began in August 1914 were all part of the same process, what she calls 'the savage and austere light of a burning world' (p. 454). That process she relates to the failure of what she had thought of as 'a lasting order': 'And to what did our fine feelings, our regard for the arts, our intimacies, our inspiring conversations, our wish to be clear of the bonds of sex and class and nationality, our wish to try to be fair to everyone bring us? To 1939.' (p. 125) The 'fine feelings' she describes are those of liberal sensibility, intricately related to the taste for high culture and an aspirational self-liberation. Like James Joyce's 'young artist', she too had sought to escape from the 'nets' of social restraint. Although she substitutes 'sex and class' for Joyce's concern with religion (for the humanism of the enlightenment which is the 'order' to which she belongs is not preoccupied with sectarian issues) yet she is at one with Joyce in rejecting 'nationality' as a categorical restraint. In this respect, her liberal sensitivity as a writer separates her from those very militant and patriotic attitudes she described in the garden party at Mitchelstown in August 1914. She is, as it were, the finer consciousness and conscience which arises above the tradition of her class, but it is an aspiration which has failed. What will replace the garden party on the terrace of vanished Mitchelstown (no more than a dream now) are other significant *loci*, places such as the Somme, Stalingrad, Belsen, Hiroshima.[8]

To set the country house as a civilised ideal against a century and a world at war is like trying to place straws against the 'wind'. There is in all Bowen's writing always the suspicion that the civilised subject is something which isn't there – that never was there (to draw upon the pessimism of *The Last September*).[9] There is a butterfly's wing fragility about the subtle social sensitivities of many of her fictional characters and a Jamesian concern for 'things' which Bowen called, in 'Sunday Afternoon', the 'aesthetic of living' which is a form of separation from life itself. The dying rose petals falling on the papers on an escritoire in *The Heat of the Day* in war-bombed London may serve as a icon and, at Danielstown (in *The Last September*) the 'immutable' portraits of the ancestors look down remotely on a family fiddling while Rome burns. (A Somervillean icon, witness *The Big House of Inver*.)

Yet there remains the idea of Bowen's Court itself as something, somehow, better even than its owners (a place which Bowen writes 'made all the succeeding Bowens' – p. 32) and which, at least as she wrote as the bombs obliterated 'hundreds of thousands of homes', still stood as a sign of the continuity of an ideal order. One might make to this the same objection as Paine made to Burke, this is to concern oneself with the plumage and to forget the dying bird. Nonetheless, *Bowen's Court* is concerned with a substantial social and cultural phenomenon. The house was built to fulfil both an historical need (the requirement of imperial government) and to express the higher aspirations of the governing class. The thing itself, and the ideology of the thing, have a major historical presence. What else does the present ever have of the past except a detritus of artefacts, or how do we (whoever 'we' are) define present identity except by the construction of our historical memory? Preserved objects are the *aide memoire* of our selfhood. That is the autobiographical argument of *Bowen's Court*. Conversely, what 'we' choose to destroy of the past are representations of those things in our inheritance we wish to reject or forget. The reason for writing *Bowen's Court* was that this locus had not been negligible and should not be forgotten. To be rooted in the past is to be at home in some form of symbolic order, and the bombs that were destroying the homes of Europe were deracinating all people. Without a home we are all cultural refugees.

At least something like that identification of self with home and historical continuity might be teased out from what McCormack (1993) has characterised as the numinous opacity of Bowen's prose, which sets up only to back off and to qualify in eddies of uncertainty and suggestivity. But some fundamental *topoi* are clearly enunciated in her writing. There is, for instance, the 'Tudor' imperative to order the disordered. Bowen claims that the historical movement that took her family to Ireland 'imposed one kind of mould of civilization – fruitful land, busy ports, thriving strong little cities, foundries, markets, bridges, and roads'.[10] Hence the establishment of country houses. This is an argument familiar from Spenser and Davies, although the stadial progression is now qualified by the postnationalist phrase, 'one kind...of civilization'. The ideal *raison d'être* for the expression of that civilisation in architectural form was that the builders began 'to feel, and exert, the European idea – to seek what was humanistic, classic and disciplined'.[11] Accordingly Bowen's account of the country house draws upon the usual vocabulary of that humanist ideal. She writes of the social 'politeness' of the order, of the demesne as a centre of 'the good life', and even of the 'grace' with which country house living was invested, although these words float in her prose without the kind of resonance that Spenser, Pope or Austen might have given them, more securely anchored in tradition. (Another phrase, 'good behaviour' has been made notorious by Molly Keane, nibbling at the crumbs of the tradition.) The ideal and the mundane never coincide of course, but at least while the country house stood it possessed a Platonic function: 'Classic and bare and strong, the house embodied that perfect idea of being that, in actual living, cannot realize itself'[12] (the particular example is burnt Moore Hall). Mere 'dreams' Yeats called this idealism, a word Bowen herself uses, or turns characteristically to the ghost story to express the nature of a past apprehended only by the sensitive imagination of Bowen's Court itself. She writes:

> What runs on most through a family living in one place is a continuous, semi-physical dream. Above this dream-level successive lives show their tips, their little conscious formations of will and thought. With the end of each generation, the lives that submerged here were absorbed again. With each death, the air of the place had thickened: it had been added to. The dead do not need to visit Bowen's Court rooms...we had no ghosts in that house...because they already permeated them. Their extinct senses were present in lights and forms. (p. 451)

We have no ghosts because the dead are always present. What is living in the present is the past. That is what is left of 'civilisation' in 1942.

The civilisation at Bowen's Court originated in the European Enlightenment. The foundation stone of the house is dated 1775. Henry III (as he is called), the maker of the house, 'was a man of his century, esteeming reason, order and light.... He honoured life as he saw it, honoured life's inherent future' (p. 31). He thought of the 'elevation' of his family, expressed in the perpendicular height of his home, and of uniting that family 'as closely as possible to society'. But he also thought of establishing an ideal form of living. 'His sense of what was august in humanity made him make his house an ideal mould for life. He was more than building a home, he was setting a pattern' (p. 169). Implicit in Bowen's vocabulary (and it may be no more than the subliminal connotations of the English language) are two fundamental European iconographic ideas. One is the 'universal man', the ideal masculine form (inscribed within both circle and square) that is the sign of the Vitruvian/Palladian tradition of humanistic architecture, which measures the modular order of the universe from the divine order of the male body and thus makes of the country house an 'ideal mould' to express its owner. Today the Jefferson Memorial in Washington, DC, is perhaps the best known, and last, expression of that tradition, where the giant form of a great founding father of the American *imperium* and union stands centrally under a great dome that expresses the order and mathematics of the universe. (Both the memorial and *Bowen's Court* date from the 1940s, and thus both, with deliberate archaism, express allegiance to the same ideal of civilisation in a time of cataclysmic war.)

The other subliminal idea is expressed by the word 'august', for this too, like the Vitruvian/Palladian icon, unites the Enlightenment to Rome, and in its Augustanism ties Bowen's Court both to the idea of the 'golden age' of the arts with which Augustanism was associated, and to the *pax Romana*, the imperial system of law that ended the chaos of the Roman civil wars. (Hence, by deliberate allusion, the name given to Lady Gregory of Coole Park – Augusta.) The Renaissance *Romanitas* of the house runs through Bowen's description, with references to Venetian window, Pompeian decoration, Palladian forms and 'pillared temples' (p. 23), and the general invocation: 'with its parapet cut out against a bright blue sky this might almost be a building in Italy' (p. 22). The imperialism implicit in this enlightened culture is unapologetic in the builders. Ultimately the origin of the august 'pattern' of the founding father of Bowen's Court is *Genesis* (where this enquiry began). Reason, order and light – 'let there be light' – express themselves through the operation of imperial power.

In the circumambient landscape at Bowen's Court the ruins of earlier social orders – the remains of Spenser's Kilcolman Castle, for instance – indicate the passing of earlier power. Retrospectively, Bowen's 'liberal' conscience (or postcolonial guilt if one will) causes her to apologise for the 'inherent wrong' of such impositions. But the house itself ineluctably expresses, through the generations it has shaped, its shaping ideal:

This is Bowen's Court as the past has left it – an isolated, partly unfinished house, grandly conceived and plainly and strongly built. Near the foot of mountains, it has little between it and the bare fields that run up the mountainside. Larger in manner than in actual size, it stands up in Roman urbane strongness in a land on which the Romans never set foot. It is the negation of mystical Ireland: its bald walls rebut the surrounding, disturbing light. Imposed on seized land, built in the rulers' ruling tradition, the house is, all the same, of the local rock, and sheds the same grey gleam you see over the countryside. So far, it has withstood burnings and wars. (p. 31)

Isolation, separation, imposition, foundational Europeanisation, all these elements in the description are traditional elements of the locus.

Bowen's Court strives to be 'urbane', which English word suggests affiliations both to the ideal of polite and civil society, and, by derivation, to the *urbs* of which Rome was the historical prototype. The claim *civis Romanus sum* was not confined merely to the city within the walls. At this late stage in the present book much of this often quoted passage requires little comment. But there are subliminal changes to a familiar iconography. Although the 'local rock' is a material fact, as an iconographic sign it carries a signification that is utterly different from the icon of 'the bog' that is so prevalent in this tradition (the illimitable, unreclaimable, unmapped wilderness that is the sign of 'Ireland'). There is fixity here, not unrelated to the survival by the house of 'burnings and wars', and the word 'local' suggests an integration between house and place, which emerges (later in *Bowen's Court*) in the writer's appeal for reconciliation in Ireland. This is now, by long presence, as much a part of the locus ('local') as the very rock itself. And in this hard land there is also a local illumination. That 'disturbing light' which falls across the 'Roman urbane strongness' in Ireland is a different kind of illumination from the 'reason, order and light' of Henry III, but the implication is that this too might be a form of enlightenment, changed by place and time. This allusion, if such it is, may be the slightest of concessions to the idea of 'the two civilisations' in Ireland. Or is it a return to the foundational idea of Ireland as a frontier, a new world and newfoundland that 'disturbs' the culture of Europe by questioning its foundational assumptions?

If this is so, the 'unfinished' nature of the house (which is a material fact spelled out in detail elsewhere in Bowen's description) is also an iconographic statement. What Henry III was about was not completable. This is another commonplace topos in the present enquiry (witness Edgeworth's *The Absentee*), but subject to subtle renegotiation in Bowen's account. The most significant room in the main structure of Bowen's Court to express that unfinished state is the Long Room, the highest chamber of state within the elevation. The Italian decorators brought in to embellish the house were paid off before they reached its top, the fireplaces in the room remained (in the main) unlit, and the society balls for which the Long Room was designed could never take place there as the floor would not carry them. Yet, 'though right at the top, and empty, it remains the core of the house; when one returns to Bowen's Court after an absence one never feels one has really come home again until one has been up to the Long Room' (p. 25). At the top, and yet empty; without social function, yet a place essential to visit: the paradoxes are made by Bowen for the room, and express the essence of the house. One may compare the Long Room to Bowen's (often quoted and Flaubertian) characterisation of the 'ideal book': 'a hermetic world ... about nothing, stayed itself on itself by its inner force'.[13] Or since Jefferson's Monticello has been introduced as another icon of the Enlightenment, the empty dome room there, a form without a function, is, like the Long Room, expressive of uncompletable idealism, although at Monticello the ideal is of the wholeness of an ordered culture, rather than, as at Bowen's Court, an unobtainable harmony patterned into the social dance.

But by the time that Bowen is writing, presence (return to the empty space of the Long Room) and departure are the very nature of her life. The social reality is one of retreat within and from the house. The drawing room is already empty, except for a grand piano (the signifier of that desired harmony Somerville evoked in *Mount Music*), and the dining room has become crowded with things and bereft of people. Family portraits replace the family, the pictures on the wall 'exude ... dusk' and time passes to the 'halting tick' of a grandfather clock. For dinner the family (still following the ritual of evening dress) gather in the hall, the site of 'hospitable' reception (to return to a *topos* from the ultimate paragraph of Bowen's *The Last September*).

Unlike Danielstown, which was 'executed' in fiction, Bowen's Court has survived, temporarily. In the meantime it is the library that is the locus for everyday living, and has even been adapted to 'the modern pattern of living'. The last retreat for the family as their space shrinks is the traditional location of culture (where Maria Edgeworth had centred herself a century before). That culture is still represented by the 'dry calf bindings' of old books. The 'afterglow' of the evening lingers here, but the dual aspect of the room ensures that it receives the morning sun, which is 'often still misty' (p. 27). Perhaps that misty morning light may be a symbol of potential renewal, if only because the 'thought-form' of the house and the library itself are residual presences. The books of the house and the book of the house remain.

The tenacity of that presence is the elaborated subject of *The Heat of the Day*, which was published seven years after *Bowen's Court* and gives an ultimate resonance to the valedictory theme. That text, rather than the earlier *Last September*, will be read here as a gloss upon Bowen's history of the lost demesne. In *The Heat of the Day*, set mainly in 1942, Ireland has returned to its original position beyond the frontiers of Europe. That is the symbolic signification of the 'real world' neutrality of Eire. But Europe, rather than being the centre of civilisation, is now the site of savagery – the war, catalogued by the names of battles abroad. But at home 'the garrison' (p. 95) in England has been betrayed even by its own, decadent, 'armed property', a crippled former soldier, Robert Kelway of the (satirised) villa ironically called Holme Dene. This is no 'home' for it is permanently for sale by owners who are unable to move but are always ready to 'shift'. Even the oak beams of the house (signifiers of both permanence and England) are 'imitations'. 'Reassemble it anywhere; you get the same illusion' (p. 121). This is a Forsterian theme, with roots in Edgeworth's *The Absentee* and beyond.

In contradistinction stands the Irish country house, Mount Morris, the inheritance of the owner's English cousin, Roderick. His legacy is to 'care' for 'the old tradition' the house represents; or is it to use the old tradition in any way he cares? Bowen's text is loaded with explicit irony. The novel's centre of consciousness is Roderick's mother, Stella – and what literary resonances, Renaissance and Irish, gather round her name. She herself (a divorcee) belongs nowhere, living as she does in a rented flat, among other people's furniture, in war-torn London. But by crossing the frontier from the war to Mount Morris, by paradoxical reversal of the usual dichotomy of civilisation and savagery, she enters the preserved locus of a former civilisation (and of inherited order) that is now the Irish country house.

Everywhere is the clutter and the everyday instructions of the former owner (buried without 'sociable' ceremony in England – p. 67). It is as if there were another act to Chekhov's *The Cherry Orchard* and one returned to find the estate ownerless but intact, waiting for 'better times' (p. 315). The isolation of Ireland has placed Mount Morris 'outside time', or alternatively in 'another time, rather than another country' (p. 163). The imaginative consciousness comes to the house without light, except that of the fading western evening, which lingers longer in Ireland than in England, Stella recalls. That image needs no explication. As she explores the inner spaces of Mount Morris she comes to the library, dimly lit by the remaining 'particles' of sunset and exuding an 'ancient smell' that 'reached the senses from the [indifferent] books cased back into the walls'. The other 'focus of darkness' in the library is an oil painting of 'horsemen grouped apprehensively at midnight'. The culture of the past is, as it were, a subliminal presence, uneasy, uncommunicative, and yet suspended out of time in this place. On the staircase a Venetian window still shows a 'glimmer' (of enlightenment?), 'ever wholly extinguished only by blackest night' (p. 166). But as the sun finally sets and blackest night establishes itself, Stella (starlight) continues her exploration by lamplight. Ultimately she finds herself gazing at the light of her lamp reflected back on itself in a mirror. Stella then distinguishes her own features and becomes 'for the moment immortal as a portrait' (p. 173). It is in this dark situation of suspended animation that Stella's heart cries out 'Oh to stay here for ever, playing this ghostly part!' One feels that one puff of the cold wind from the Galtees might extinguish this one remaining lamp and 'universal darkness' will bury all.

It is an extraordinary image of the fragility of the old order, preserved only by a solitary, exploratory consciousness. Yet the house still stands, and will remain for occupation by her son to make of the tradition what he will. Although this is only a fiction, the idealisation is given a kind of permanent body by the written word. That peculiar, indeterminate state is fixed by an historic icon. On the wall of the drawing room there is an image of the sinking Titanic. Perplexingly Bowen writes that the 'significance' of this image 'would never be known'. Her comment is a warning to the hasty iconographer who would dispose of the country house in the bonfire of *The Last September*, and thus would read the image of the Titanic as a sign of the sinking of the old order of things. But in the image the ship is suspended half below, half above the water, and thus will always remain partly in the dark and partly in a blaze of light (with the famous band still playing – as it played on the terrace of Mitchelstown). Art preserves, and as Roderick states to his mother, after the hurt of history it is 'the only thing that can go on mattering' (p. 300).[14]

It is twenty-one years since Stella was last here, and it was here that Roderick was conceived, destined to care for the estate in whatever future there may be. Since the fiction is set in the year of the battles of El Alamein and Stalingrad, that twenty-one years takes us back to 1921. Stella's earlier memories of Mount Morris belong to the period that marked the separation of Ireland from the United Kingdom, and thus the creation of the fissure between a world at war and the continuity and permanence that Mount Morris in 'Ireland' still embodies, at least to the receptive imagination that cares for 'the old tradition', if only in anyway it cares. 'Only connect' again.

Which may explain the conclusion of the fiction. At the end another mother, who has given birth to an illegitimate son, symbolically called Victor, has herself gone home, albeit to a far meaner place. As she walks by the English seashore the 'homecoming bombers' pass invisibly overhead, to be succeeded by what at first is only a sound. She knows the sound and holds up her child in the hope that he might remember this moment. 'Three swans were flying a straight flight. They passed overhead, disappearing in the direction of the west.' If this is an Irish fiction, and one of reconnection, then that westward world to which the swans fly is Ireland, as reconstituted by Bowen. We know that this is their destination, for Stella has seen swans settled on the river at Mount Morris. Beyond that imaginatively preserved locus there is a real country house. Those flying swans are taken from the the work of the last great country house poet writing in English, born into the Union and conscious of his place in Renaissance tradition. The swans, of course, are an allusion to Yeats and are headed for the lake at Coole Park.[15]

Coole Park belongs to the the last generation of symbolic country houses in the European tradition. Yeats linked it, by his idealisation of Major Robert Gregory as the Irish Sidney, to Penshurst in England, and beyond that with Urbino and the civilisation of the Renaissance in Italy. Lady Augusta Gregory's elaborated idealisation of the house in *Coole* is not dissimilar to Alexander Pope's 'Augustan' use of Twickenham as a cultural icon and a form of self-expression (with himself as Horace). Perhaps closest to Coole in this wide-ranging tradition is Thomas Jefferson's Monticello, a model of high culture for national imitation. Jefferson's use of his library as the basis for the Library of Congress is equivalent in intention to Lady Gregory's centring of the 'literary Renaissance' in Ireland at Coole and her campaign (*in memoriam* Hugh Lane) to obtain a great collection of European paintings for Dublin. A great house is an instrument of national education.

Coole was also, in a straightforward historical way, an imperial power house and an instrument of territorial control. The public career of Sir William Gregory of Coole was in keeping with his status. In his proconsular role in Ceylon (to adopt a Roman analogy) he developed his territory as if it were his own estate by public works (and just administration) for which he was monumentally commemorated. 'These are imperial works and worthy kings' Pope wrote in the *Epistle to Lord Burlington*. In the United Kingdom, as a convert to the Liberal Party he was concerned with agrarian reform, he chaired the Commons committee of enquiry into accommodation for the British Museum, he became a trustee of the National Gallery, and he was made an Irish privy councillor. The marriage of Sir William to Augusta Persse of Roxborough was a dynastic settlement uniting adjacent properties. If the Persses had also united with the Martin dynasty (as was possible) huge tracts of the west coast would have been consolidated by kinship (and entail).

Sir William was 'the last of the Romans'. Lady Gregory was aware, after her husband's death, that the territorial base of familial influence was unsustainable. But her personal influence, through her network of friends and acquaintances, remained immense. From the beginning that potency had expressed itself in iconographic (even iconological) form. There were the famous 'signature fans', which expressed her role as a great society hostess. Gladstone, Browning, Trevelyan, Randolph Churchill, Henry James, Theodore Roosevelt and Ellen Terry serve as representative examples, uniting the great world of politics with that of literature and the arts. This was, at the century's end, the same kind of social matrix as the one in which Maria Edgeworth had moved, although now extending beyond the United Kingdom and Europe to embrace North America and the outposts of the great empire that the Gregorys served. It was still the world of an 'enlightened' culture and still observing the mores of the *ancien régime*. The famous signature tree at Coole (upon which visitors inscribed their names) had the same iconic function as the fan, but extended from the woman's world to the demesne itself (Plate 13). Throughout the country house tradition, the trees of the great estates were emblems of continuity and investment (familial and material) in a long future. The seven woods of Coole were one of the notable features mythologised by Yeats, and Lady Gregory was deeply and emotionally committed to planting and maintaining the woods (thus following the example of Sir William). Fan and tree iconologically united Lady Gregory's role in the dynastic marriage market and her function as chatelaine of her home. Particular emphasis is placed on that home as the rendezvous of the great writers who formed her circle and in some cases (notably Yeats) were recipients of her patronage. The civilisation of the country house was preserved by acts of writing.

She also hoped to preserve the material form of the house for her son Robert, being well aware, as her autobiography indicates, that the house and land were detaching (the real life equivalent of the fate of the big house at Inver). The house, removed from its function as the centre of an estate and a system of administration, increasingly had no other function than as a place of the heart's affections. But after the heroic death of Robert (like six of the Persses) fighting for the United Kingdom in the First World War (he seems to have gloried in the man-to-man combat of aerial warfare) his wife – Margaret, née Parry – had no desire to remain at Coole. Lady Gregory's journal entry for 17 May 1921 indicates why:

England. This morning [George Bernard Shaw] said, 'There is bad news in the papers, but Margaret is not hurt,' and told me of the shooting of Captain Blake and his wife and the two officers, and then I saw a telegram for me from Margaret, 'sole survivor of five murdered in ambushed motor.' It was a bad shock, the thought of the possibilities...and then though she is safe, thank God, it is impossible to know how it will affect her outlook and the life of the children and, through them, mine.

Margaret had been returning from a tennis party. The patriotic insurgents who had stopped the car had ordered the women to separate themselves from the men, but one, who was pregnant, had refused to leave her husband. She had therefore been killed with him *pour encourager les autres*. The journals also graphically describe the counterterrorist terrorism of the Black and Tans, atrocity met by atrocity. One might substitute 1798 for the 1920s.

Coole, no longer a power house or a dynastic home, was left with one function only: to serve as an embodiment of deeprooted civilised values that, although shaken, as the great trees of the estate had been by the Atlantic storm of 1903, might stand and survive to better times. The house came to represent a stemma not just of a family, but of a tradition – 'my Athenaeum', which 'gave my mind its ancestry', as Lady Gregory wrote of the real Athenaeum in London and the classic roots of European civilisation.[16] So in describing the building itself the old traditions automatically reasserted themselves:

> The house, which was built when Robert Gregory, the Nabob, purchased the estate, was...very typically Irish, a simple three-storeyed cube of six bays on the east front, having a central therme window surmounting a tripartite Palladian window above a square porch. In its setting of parkland without ha-ha, Coole did not give the feeling of having been built for defence as do many Irish eighteenth century houses, but rather as a dwelling where all were welcome. (p. 8)

What is typically Irish is to be typically Palladian. We return, by way of the Whig republic of Great Britain and Ireland, to the Venetian republic and beyond that to Augusta's Augustan Rome. This was a house not won by conquest (nor in need of the signifiers of defence) but secured by legal purchase (just as the liberal administration of the United Kingdom secured, by subsequent Land Acts, new laws of tenure). Within the shelter of the law, the classical house was at peace. Thus it was a 'dwelling where all were welcome', which was Lady Gregory's reworking of the fundamental motif of Jonson's seventeenth-century celebration of Penshurst Place: 'all come in'. The house unified the community. This was a motif that Lady Gregory's contemporary,

William Morris, repeated in the idealisation of Kelmscott in the socialist Utopia of *News from Nowhere* (1890/1).

Traditionally there were no exclusions in that community. King and peasant were equally welcome at Penshurst, and if clear hierarchies of power and dependency remained in place, then in Morris's future vision at Kelmscott all distinctions of class disappeared. In Ireland the poetic equivalent to Jonson's poem was Yeats' 'Coole Park'. But in Yeats' celebration of Coole, 7 September, 1929, the inclusive community was narrowed. He praised the house as a place where 'traveller, scholar, poet take their stand'. He knew Coole through its role as a pantheon of culture, and his insistence that this was a place where one should take a stand reintroduces into the imagery an element of history that Lady Gregory had been at pains to write out: the defensive nature of the country house. What was to be defended, however, was not so much the (indefensible) physical place, but a culture; and the location of culture at Coole was ultimately (and traditionally) the library, among the 'Beloved books that famous hands have bound,/Old marble heads, old pictures everywhere.'[17] When Yeats conjured in his mind's eye an image of Lady Gregory, it was as a writer seated before her great ormolu table.

It is in keeping with this idealisation that it is in the library that the 'tour' of the house begins in Lady Gregory's *Coole*. But the Yeatsian celebration of 'books and the woman' (to parody Pope) is imprecise. Merely to commend books for their fine bindings, and busts and pictures for their antiquity, might suggest an aestheticism that is dangerously moribund. Compare with Yeats, for instance, Timon's not dissimilar library in Pope's *Epistle to Burlington*. Although a great library may serve as the genetic code by which one generation becomes renascent in the next, it may also become the sepulchre of learning that is never read. This is an issue directly raised in *Coole*. There is a subtle and vital gradation in Lady Gregory's account of the accumulation of culture in the library, for many of the books, she states explicitly, are 'dumb' to her. The foundational collection by the builder Robert Gregory was once 'prized by some whose love of literature may have sent an ancestral pulse to the mind of later children of the house' (p. 19), but for her they were no more than the archaeological remains of the past. The same is true of the majority of the Greek and Roman texts that were the inspiration of her husband: 'For eye may not profit by the meaning nor ear by the mighty sound now shut up within their covers. I use no symbolism in using the old saying "They are Greek to me"' (pp. 20–1). But she uses a telling symbolism when she acknowledges that much of the great collection is 'on the shelf'. This is 'the epithet used of men who have gone out of office or grown old' (p. 17).

In the still living culture of the house, the place where one might 'take a stand', only a handful of books from the 'beloved' collection are the furniture of the mind of their owner. Lady Gregory selects those 'great books' which she would not willingly let die: Johnson's *Dictionary of the English Language*, Clarendon's *History*, Evelyn's *Sylva*, North's translation of *Plutarch*, Froissart, Malory, Bunyan's *The Pilgrim's Progress* and Cervantes' *Don Quixote*. To which she adds, by rote, Shakespeare and the King James Bible. With the exception of Johnson's dictionary none of these texts was written later than the seventeenth century, and even the dictionary was a retrospective endeavour grounded in the 'classics' of the English tongue. The view of history incorporated in these books involves the history of great men, great wars and empires. (One recollects that Lady Gregory celebrated her lover, Wilfrid Scawen Blunt, as 'one of Plutarch's men'.)[18] Three of the texts are rooted in the idealism of feudal chivalry, seen, as in Cervantes, from a perspective that is retrospective but sympathetic. Clarendon was one of the great conservative historians of English tradition, and presumably Shakespeare, in this company, was interpreted as a conservative (and deeply patriotic) dramatist. *Silva* was chosen because of the fundamental signification of the planting of trees in the establishment *in saecula saeculorum* of the great country house. *The Pilgrim's Progress* is a classic of the Protestant spirit, valiant against all disaster.

The literary canon these texts construct is rooted in the *litterae humaniores* of classical antiquity united with the chivalric idealism of Gothic culture. It is an aristocratic tradition and one that sees the English language as reaching its apogee in the sixteenth and seventeenth centuries. We know that Malory was the inspiration for Lady Gregory's charming bowdlerisations of the Gaelic epic, and if the concern here was 'mere Irish' one might specifically link Lady Gregory to Sir Samuel Ferguson and Standish O'Grady in her attitude towards Gaelic culture and note the irony of her identification with the Tudor epic as a model for the civilisation of Ireland. But that would be to reduce literature to politics and to judge all literature in Ireland by where it stands on the sectarian divide. This is a reduction that Lady Gregory repeatedly denies. It is the purpose of the 'great masters' of literature to 'free' the 'intellect' and to establish (and this is a remarkably idealistic phrase) a 'radiant sanity of vision' so much wanting 'in poor Ireland'. As she wrote of Hugh Lane, so might it be said of great books: what is 'fine' ennobles by its 'beauty'. Her imagery ultimately becomes religious (drawing upon Yeats): 'Literature is the forgiveness of sins.'[19]

Such (might one call it Arnoldian?) idealism is anathema to political historicism, but our concern is with the fictions of civilisation. This is where Lady Gregory takes her stand. Burn this (and the republicans came knocking on her door at Coole, and burnt Roxborough – and its library – the place of her nativity) and you burn the *logos* of European culture, as expressed in the English language. This is the idealist position. But it is not exactly the everyday one, for if the library is the repository of the great tradition of the inherited past, it is not the quotidian living space of this woman at this time. Coole expresses a personality and a life as well as a tradition, and in the dynamic interrelation of symbolic spaces the books that inhabit Lady Gregory's own living space are of a different order from those which still possess residual vitality in the library: Susan Ferrier, Frances Burney, George Eliot, Mrs Gaskell, Jane Austen and the Brontës, to which add 'some novels written in Ireland, most of them by my friends' – Emily Lawless, Somerville and Ross and (an odd man out) James Stephens. These comprise one element of the (imported) culture of the living space of the Coole drawing room. We have moved to a far more familiar culture than that of the library: the kind of reading in (predominantly female) novelistic fiction that is now the territory of university English Literature, weighted towards a predominantly female readership, popular and post-Renaissance and thus freed from the difficulties that, for instance, kept even Lady Gregory from the furniture of Sir William's mind. It is, of course, the territory occupied by this present text. The popular novel and the English Literature degree are the (increasingly tenuous) links that join those texts which are actually read with those texts which reside only in scholarly libraries.

One link between 'the great tradition' and this emergent new tradition is provided by the words 'my friends'. In isolation this may seem merely biographical. The living house symbolises the life of its (last) chatelaine. But if one places Coole in the tradition of Pope's Twickenham and, beyond Twickenham, the tradition of the classic villa, one of the essential idealisations of the 'good life' was its dedication *libertatae et amicitiae*: to freedom and friendship. Those admitted to the companionship of the house are chosen not for their wealth or for their utility in the *cursus honorum* and its servility to the way of the world. They are present because of their intrinsic worth, which worth reflects the integrity of the owner of the house. 'Friendship is all the house I have', Lady Gregory wrote to Yeats.[20]

Hence the worth of the chatelaine is determined by those whom she and the family have known and valued. These connections are established both by symbolic presence, most obviously that of portraiture, and by the symbolism of gift culture and preserved mementos. The accumulation is immense and *Coole* is a long, symbolic inventory of the generational contents of a large house, listed not as a bill of sale but as a memento of a civilisation for which the act of writing is a last act of union, of holding together, before the 'spoils' (to use the word with a Jamesian connotation) are dispersed (and the house lost), for with the dispersal is lost the interconnectedness of the symbolic order and thus its meaning. Only in the 'letter' can the 'spirit' still give life.

John Quinn's celebration of the house, quoted by Lady Gregory in her autobiography, serves both as a summary of the country house tradition at that point in history and as a testimony to its power of transmission:

> From this old house, the house in which were stored up so many memories of statesmen, soldiers, authors, artists, and other distinguished people, with its great library, its pictures, statues, and souvenirs gathered from many lands, nestling in the soft climate of the west of Ireland under the grey skies and surrounded by the brilliant greens and rich browns of west Ireland landscape, or bathed in the purple glow of the air as the sun declined, I carried away two vivid impressions: first, the realization of a unique literary friendship between the chatelaine and the poet Yeats; and, second, of the gentleness and energy of this woman ... who has, at the cost of infinite time and pains, proved herself to be, with Yeats, the directing genius of the new Irish Drama. (p. 380)

An old house, filled with old books gathered from many lands that have found their home ('nestling') in the Irish landscape – thus Quinn places Coole somewhat in the Epicurean tradition of Sir William Temple in the seventeenth century (he loved old books to read, old friends to converse with and old wood to burn). But Quinn also writes in a late Romantic elegaic manner. There is an imperial purple in the air, but it is that of a declining sun. But as with Somerville's similar celebration of Ross, the house is integrated with the land. It is not a demesne planted in a 'pale' (civilisation separated from savagery) but is the source of 'friendship', which is civilising because literary, expressed both in the bond between Lady Gregory and Yeats (who found the 'leisure' – *otium* – to write at Coole) and in the chatelaine's creation of the 'new' (and hence vital for the future) Irish Drama (capital D, for this is high art).

The prosaic nature of Quinn's account gives it authority. It might seem churlish to press behind the text to look for something other. But our subject, the dichotomy (yet symbiosis) between civilisation and savagery, cannot conclude by reading the iconology of Coole merely in terms of its own idealisation, where all savagery has vanished in the embrace of art and artefacts. Let us come a little closer to the things themselves within the house absorbed, in Quinn's account, by generalisations.

In Lady Gregory's text the artefacts in Coole are lovingly detailed as family and personal records. So detailed is the symbolic inventory that one might use almost any object to establish the long taproots of European civilisation, its particular historical point of origin and *raison d'être*. One can choose typical examples of how these things also reveal the contradictory pressures within that civilisation. For instance run an eye along the books designated by Quinn as the 'library'. On the same shelves as Lady Gregory has placed her copy of 'Martin Ross' she keeps John Mitchel's *Jail Journal* – 'more powerful than all the rest' (p. 29). She makes no comment, but Violet Martin and John Mitchel cannot be placed together merely as cultural artefacts. It was Mitchel who promulgated what could be viewed as the greatest obscene racial assertion in the history even of Ireland: that the famine was an act of genocide perpetrated by the colonial oppressor upon the Irish people. On the other hand Martin was united by blood and literary symbolism to that colonial dynasty which (as they told their story) had sacrificed both the riches of their estates and even their lives to save whomever they could from the natural disaster of the potato blight. The Martins were bound by 'chivalry' (so Somerville wrote) to 'close intimacy with the people'. 'No adequate tribute has ever been paid to those Irish landlords – and they were men of every party and creed – who perished martyrs to duty, in that awful time.' So Somerville claimed.[21] What iconographic strategy, or what amnesia, is operative in Lady Gregory that she should place a Martin and a Mitchel cheek by jowl?

To take another instance, more than two pages of *Coole* are devoted to a description of the contents of 'an ivory casket, the Jewel box of the last Queen of Candy' (p. 44f.) The queen was opposed to the incorporation of her lands into the imperial settlement of Ceylon, but her lady-in-waiting, 'a good honest rebel in heart', was won over to 'fidelity' to the British *imperium* by Sir William when he gave to her 'a brooch representing the Tudor Rose'. That in itself is remarkable for its historical implications in Ireland, for Sir William's choice of a Tudor rose was no accident. In this very box Lady Gregory kept precious childhood relics of her son, Robert,[22] and also a collection of 'little song books' of Lord

Edward Fitzgerald. Robert, who was a unionist by political persuasion, died fighting against the forces of imperial Germany. Lord Edward was a rebel of 1798 who would have called the armies of France into Ireland in the romantic belief that the French revolutionaries were disinterested liberators of Europe. Just as the library shelves incorporated incompatible interpretations of Irish history (Mitchel and Martin) so the casket contained two lives of aristocratic fighting men who supported radically opposed causes. Was this also amnesia or a conscious awareness that only within an artefact can utterly opposing forces, and forces of violence, be formally contained?

And what of the very literature that Coole itself produced as a centre of patronage? Throughout this enquiry literature has been taken by the writers in question as a self-evident sign of civilisation, but is that idea only 'safe' when it is, as it were, 'cemented' (to use Somerville's term) on library shelves? Yeats asked, 'did that play of mine send out the men the English shot?' (a loaded political statement). The play to which he referred was *Cathleen ni Houlihan* (1902), jointly written with Lady Gregory. It is a celebration of the rising of 1798 and a call to Irishmen to shed blood again. Had the writers forgotten Scullabogue? Was this desire to play with fire (and Roxborough was burnt when the events of 1798 were re-enacted) symptomatic of what Synge called (in relation to his *The Playboy of the Western World*) the 'psychic state' of Ireland, a place intoxicated by tales of violence? When the call to pursue politics by bloodshed was answered in 1916, Gregory's first reaction was shock at the actions of those she called murderers and terrorists (she later changed her mind). Perhaps she still recalled the warning given to Sir William when seeking to drain the Kiltartan boglands: '*Manam an diabhal*, your blood on your own head'. But her own writing and patronage called for that very blood.[23]

Or consider Lady Gregory's epic translation: *Cuchulain of Muirthemne* (1902). Her protagonist was to assume a special place in the subsequent idealisation of Easter 1916. A statue of Cuchulain stands outside the post office at which the Irish republic was proclaimed. A representative quotation serves to illustrate what is celebrated by the high aesthetic of Coole. It is chosen from the ideological selection of the *Field Day Anthology of Irish Writing* (Deane, 1991) under the heading 'cultural nationalism':

And he bid the men of Ireland to give out shouts, and Cuchulain came against them in his chariot, doing his three thunder feats, and he used his spear and his sword in such a way, that their heads, and their hands, and their feet, and their bones, were scattered through the plain of Muirthemne, like the sands on the shore, like the stars in the sky, like the dew in May, like snow-flakes and hailstones, like leaves of the trees, like buttercups in a meadow, like grass under the feet of cattle on a fine summer day. It was red that plain was with the slaughter Cuchulain made when he came crashing over it. [24]

The relationship between this 'cultural nationalism' and the killing fields at the post office deeply troubled Yeats (witness *The Death of Cuchulain*, 1939). Gregory's text is innocent of that self-questioning. The above passage romanticises slaughter by naturalising it as part of the natural beauty of nature itself or, the imagery suggests, the beauty of a well-tilled estate, rich with trees, and with buttercups in the meadows, upon which the cattle feed on fine summer days. Somehow art can do this by removing the text both from the circumstances of origin and from the consequences of ideology (like the portrait of Lady Isabella in Somerville's *The Big House of Inver*). At least that is what the Field Day term 'cultural nationalism' implies, separating 'culture' from the actual business of killing in the same way as the community in Synge's *The Playboy* isolates the story of murder from killing itself. This is intrinsic to the Homeric tradition from which this text, in Lady Gregory's translation, ultimately derives. The 'world's greatest war story', as she calls it (p. 35) is one of the foundational texts of the great library at Coole (foundational also in European civilisation), available for Lady Gregory in the translation of the 'scholar-Governor of India, J. G. Cordery'. She writes: 'The copy of the red-bound Iliad in my white bookcase is enriched for me, as his work was made happier to him, by the many pencilled corrections or suggestions on its margins made by my husband when he was our guest here for a while.' Killing in war is now only the subject of learned annotation; the text itself has become an object of value, beautifully bound and set within the library. Or to put it another way, Homer's Achilles and Cuchulain, the Irish Achilles, have been raised to the status of 'beautiful, lofty things' (to borrow Yeats' phrase). Lady Gregory at work at her ormolu table at Coole Park, as Yeats iconised her, performs an idealising function as a transmitter of the artefacts that constitute a civilisation somehow separable from the 'fury and the mire of human veins'. Yet self-evidently it is not separable. Cuchulain did indeed inspire those men the English shot, and who shot both English and Irish (and in their thousands).

One last example, directly from the text of *Coole*, will close the argument. It concerns Gregory's place in the great tradition of country house patronage, and the roots of that tradition in European civilisation. The country house historian Edward Malins, in his introductory essay to the Dolmen edition of *Coole*, brings the story of the house to a conclusion by uniting Gregory to the most famous patron of the arts in classical antiquity, the Augustan Maecenas. Malins' elegaic (and ironic) purpose is to lament the fall of high culture. (A Dolmen is the commorative stone which marks the site of a tomb.) He is able to unite Gregory with Maecenas because the Roman was iconised at Coole by a bust first set within the house, and then moved to serve as an emblem in the garden, where it stood facing the signature tree (Plate 14). Lady Gregory writes of the icon:

> A... sunny resting place is under that bust of Maecenas that is itself sheltered overhead by a great mass of green ivy boughs, for in the afternoon the sun before vanishing westward sends its heat into the heavy iron bench and into the very bones of whoever rests there.
>
> So that the oldest of my father's sons... would in his later days come from his home some seven miles to east, the home of my childhood, to bask for an afternoon hour: would be content there even alone, it may be his mind going back on autumn days to that Crimean September when he was one of those Royal Fusiliers who, as Kinglake tells, driving back a Russian column from the heights of the Alma 'bought their triumph with blood.' In my childhood we were told he had shot seven Russians.... I never heard him talk of those days, but one evening is clear in the eyes of memory when a young brother, learning the piano, played with his little fingers 'Partant pour la Syrie' the air composed by Hortense Napoleon's mother and used by the French army of those days as its battle anthem. (pp. 103–4)

If the argument of this enquiry has carried conviction, the implications of this last quotation will require little comment. The bust of the great patron is naturalised among the trees of a country house demesne. The light that falls upon the scene is that of a declining western sun. This is the place where ancient bones have been brought to rest, and where one celebrates the (far-removed) glories of warfare (fought heroically hand to hand in the past). Now, in the country house, that ancient savagery is harmonised by the art of music and by the writer's art, which will preserve this icon for posterity. Those who have eyes to see, let them see. This is the civilisation of Europe.

Notes

1 Introduction

1. Leerssen (1995).
2. *Notes on the State of Virginia*, Query XIX (1781–4) *The Portable Thomas Jefferson* (1975) ed. Merril D. Peterson, New York: Penguin Books.
3. *An Essay Concerning Civil Government* (1690) (John Locke, *Social Contract*, World's Classics edn, n.d., p. 49).
4. For the iconography of these foundational architectural forms see (initially) Fryd (1992) and Scott (1995); for Monticello see Kelsall (1999) and for the university see Wilson (1995).
5. *Topographica Hibernica*, III, p. 10; *Expugnatio Hibernica*, II, p. 35.
6. Quoted in Bradshaw *et al.* (1993), p. 8. A useful survey of primary material is provided in Hadfield *et al.* (1994).
7. Milton, *Observations of the Articles of Peace*, II, 181.
8. Bradshaw *et al.* (1993), pp. 215, 210.
9. Hyde (1967), p. 132.
10. Ni Chuilleanáin. (1996) p. 248.
11. For the 'two civilisations' debate see Foster (1995): 'History and the Irish Question' and 'Varieties of Irishness: Cultures and Anarchy in Ireland'; Leerssen (1995, Leerson *et al.* (1996a, 1996b); Lyons (1973): 'The battle of the two civilisations'; Lyons (1979); Deane in *Ireland's Field Day* (1985): 'Civilians and Barbarians'; and more generally Deane (1997).
12. Girouard (1981).
13. A. W. Hutton (ed.), *Arthur Young's Tour in Ireland (1776–1779)* (2 vols, London: George Bell & Sons, 1892).
14. Ibid., vol. I, p. 463
15. See pp. 167–75.
16. See Daniel Augustus Beaufort, *Memoir of a map of Ireland...* (1792), who extracts for 'particular notice' among 'the happy consequences that flow from the settlement of the country, the progress of civilization, and the improvement of the arts, manufactures and commerce' (p. xiv) 'the elegance and regularity' of the urban planning of Mitchelstown, and especially 'a college, founded a few years ago by the late lord Kingston' (p. 97). Beaufort was a recommended text by Edgeworth, see p. 51. On the ideological significations of maps see Barnes *et al.* (1992). For recent accounts of the architecture of Mitchelstown see Craig (1982) and Breffny (1975). For the history of the Mitchelstown demesne see Bence-Jones (1988, 1996).
17. Ackerman (1990). For an introduction to the English literary tradition see Kelsall (1993), and more specifically Gill (1972), McClung (1977) and Kenny (1984).
18. Palladio, *Four Books of Architecture* (1570), II, 12.
19. Morgan, *Patriotic Sketches of Ireland, Written in Connaught* (1809), pp. 219–20.
20. For Swift and the Irish country house see Fabricant (1982).

21. See Bradshaw *et al.* (1993), Canny (1983), Coughlan (1989), Murphy (1999), Steevens (1995) and the special issue of Irish University Review (1996) on Spenser and Ireland. More generally see Dudley and Novaks (1972), Honour (1975) ch. 3, 'True Men' and White (1978), pp. 150–82.
22. Morley (1890), pp. 290–1.
23. Moryson, *An history of Ireland from the year 1599 to 1603* (1735), vol. II, pp. 377–8.
24. Spenser, *A View of the State of Ireland* (1605) in Morley (1890), p. 105.
25. Morley (1890), pp. 272–3.
26. Froude (1881), p. 6.
27. Morley (1890), pp. 270, 193.
28. Hume and Voltaire quoted in O'Brien (1997), pp. 89, 46.
29. McCormack (1985). See also McCormack (1993).
30. Edgeworth (1867), vol. III, p. 244.
31. For instance Cairns and Richards (1988), Kiberd (1995), Deane (1991) and, specifically to the present enquiry, Dunne (1984).
32. Howe, *Ireland and Empire* (Oxford University Press, 2000). See also Bolton (1983), pp. 239–57.
33. Lloyd's position is an extreme example of a tendency manifest, for instance, in Eagleton (1995, 1998) and Gibbons (1992). Heathcliff in Eagleton and the Whiteboys in Gibbons are Irish archetypes and thus the 'savage' is privileged against the 'civilised'. See also Lloyd (1993); Foley and Ryder (1998) and *Nationalism, Colonialism and Literature* (Minneapolis: University of Minnesota Press, 1990).

2 Edgeworthstown 'Rebuilding'

1. Maxwell (1887), p. 123.
2. Lucretius, *De rerum naturae*, I, 101: such are the evils to which religion can sway men.
3. For a review of the debate on the 'simianization' of the Irish by English Victorian caricature see Foster (1995), pp. 171–94.
4. Edgeworth's account and the quotations below are contained in *Memoirs of Richard Lovell Edgeworth* . . . (2 vols, 1820), vol. II, 205 f.
5. H. J. Butler and H. E. Butler (eds), *The Black Book of Edgeworthstown and other Edgeworth Memories, 1585–1817* (London: Faber and Gwyer, 1927). The greater part of the 'Black Book' (not reprinted) consists of 'Letters Patent, Title Deeds, Deeds of Settlement' that express 'a clear and honest title' to the lands (ibid., p. 6). For the Edgeworth family history see Butler (1972) and Hurst (1969).
6. See Kelsall (1993) on the celebration of Appleton House in the time of civil war. The *sponte sua* motif is the golden age myth that in the beginning the earth brought forth its fruits without the labour of man.
7. Hall (n.d.), vol. III, p. 276 f. The Latin tag is from Horace, *Odes*, XXX, 1 where he claims that he is writing a monument more lasting than brass.
8. Onians (1988).
9. I am highly indebted to the editorial matter of the 'Pickering' edition of *The Novels and Selected Works of Maria Edgeworth* (London: Pickering and Chatto, 1999) and to the editions of the Irish fiction by McCormack and Walker (1972), Butler (1992), Connolly (2000) and Thomson and Walker (2000). Since Ritchie is a key point of reference, her text of *The Absentee* has been

used, and, accordingly, the parallel Macmillan editions of *Helen* and *Belinda*. All other Edgeworth texts are from the *textus receptus* of the same period: the J. M. Dent, Aldine editions. An essential statement of the Edgeworths' enlightened unionist position is their review of John Carr's *The Stranger in Ireland* in the *Edinburgh Review*, 10 (April 1807), pp. 40–60, which accepts the Spenser/Davies account of the 'civilisation' (a reiterated word) of Ireland and rejects the designation 'Protestant Ascendancy'. The secondary literature is substantial, and documented in the modern editions. In addition to the works cited there I have used Butler (2000), Cary (1991), Corbett (1994), Dunne (1991), Hollingworth (1997), McCormack (1973, 1990) and Tracy (1985). I note my minority position in reading *Castle Rackrent* as a retrospective fiction (and thus marginal to this enquiry). See for instance Julian Moynahan who claims that this work is a 'prophecy' of the future state of 'the big house'. *Anglo-Irish: The Literary Imagination in a Hyphenated Culture* (Princeton University Press, 1994), p. 23. There is general agreement, however, that Edgeworth's Irish fictions are open-ended allegories (see the example given in note 14 below).

10. vol. I, p. 389.
11. p. 110.
12. See for instance '[A] Poem occasioned by a view of Powers-Court House' (1741), which combines Pope's panegyric of the Man of Ross with that of Bathurst and Burlington, but omits Pope's satirical contrast between an ideal order and its perversion in figures like Sir Balaam and Timon. 'Sketch'd in your House the candid Heart we view,/Its Grace, Strength, Order, all reflecting you.' (158–9).
13. *Satire.* VI, 292–3.
14. The name is a typical example of Edgeworth's open-ended allegory. 'Of the mother' may be a classical allusion to Virgil's idealisation of ancient 'mother' Italy. Alternatively the 'mere' has been read as a lake and the allusion to 'O'Donoghue' as implying the return of the Irish Arthur. Either way, in the letter of the text she is a chatelaine.
15. McCormack and Walker (1972).
16. Mr Burke forbids even that symbolic act and Larry burns Old Nick's 'duty turf' instead. For a radically different reading of Catholic resistance at this time see Whelan (1996), and for a review of the issues see Foster (2001), pp. 211–34.
17. See Tobin (1988).
18. Juvenal, *Satire* III, 183: either 'everything at Rome is expensive', or (in Sir Robert Walpole's sense of 'price') 'you can buy anything at Rome at a price'.
19. Letter to Mrs Ruxton, 5 February 1817 (Pickering, edn of *Ormond*, p. xii).
20. Letter to Michael Pakenham Edgeworth, 14 February 1834 (Butler, 1972, *Maria Edgeworth*, pp. 452–3).
21. Mary Martin's father died of famine fever, contracted when succouring his tenants (this sacrifice is transferred to her in the myth), and she was unable to maintain the encumbered estate, which was sold. She became a novelist and died in the United States. She was related both to Violet Martin (see pp. 138–42 below) and to Edward Martin of Tillyra Castle, and was cofounder, with Lady Gregory and others, of the Abbey Theatre. The house survived, becoming the seat of the Maharaja Jam Sahib of Nawagar

('Ranji' the cricketer), a popular figure who landscaped the demesne. It is now an excellent (and hospitable) sporting and tourist hotel.

22. For the symbolic significations of bogs see Trumpener (1997), ch. 1.
23. Ibid., p. 62. For the interrelationship between Scott and Edgeworth see Cahalan (1983). Cahalan places 'civilisation' and 'anarchy' as alternative poles in Scott's topography. See also Snell (1998).

3   Edgeworth's Heir: Charles Lever

1. Serious interest in Lever has only recently revived. See Bareham (1991), Jeffares (1996), Kreilkamp (1998) and Haddelsey (2000). I have also drawn on O'Keefe (1977), Morash (1992), Moynahan (1994) and Rix (1982). *Luttrell of Arran* is discussed in my essay in G. Carruthers and A. Rawes (eds), *English Romanticism and the Celtic World* (Cambridge: Cambridge University Press, forthcoming).
2. Text from the Chapman and Hall edn (1872).
3. Benvenuto Cellini, *Autobiography* (London: Phaidon Press, 1949), pp. 485–6.
4. Kelsall (1993), p. 124 f.
5. Text from Smith Elder edn (1872), p. 70.
6. Text from Chapman and Hall edn (1872), p. 597.
7. Castlereagh, although the holder of Irish estates, acted on behalf of Pitt's English administration.
8. Text from Routledge edn (n.d.), p. 458.
9. Jonathan Swift, 'The Blunders, Deficiencies, Distresses, and Misfortunes of Quilca'. As the servants 'fall into the manners and thieveries of the natives', Swift finds himself 'in danger' of sinking into Irish 'barbarity'.
10. See also the 'state of Ireland' analysis in chapter 82 of *Tom Burke of Ours*: 'the social state of the people was rotten to the very core. Their highest qualities, degraded by the continual force of poverty, misrule, and superstition, had become sources of crime and misery.' They expected some quasi-Messianic, violent and sudden solution to their ills.
11. Text from Macmillan edn (1906).

4   Trollope as Mr Kurtz

1. Text from Tracy (1989). All quotations from Trollope's Irish novels are from the World's Classics Reprints except *The Landleaguers* (Stroud: Allan Sutton, 1991). See Hamer (1989) and McCormack (1982). I am highly indebted to Tracy, and also Asmundsson (1971), Bareham (1986), Cronin (1980), Donovan (1956), Gilead (1986), Hennedy (1972), Hynes (1986), Kelleher (1995), Maxwell (1955), Overton (1982), Polhemus (1968), Pollard (1978), Sadleir (1927), Tracy (1982), Terry (1977, 1999) and Wittig (1974).
2. Virgil, *Georgics*, II, 458: 'O blest farming folk, too blessed if only they knew their own blessedness.'

5   Only Connect: Violet Martin and Edith Somerville

1. Froude (1881), vol. III, pp. 558, 584.
2. Horace, *Epistles*, I, ii, 27: fit for nothing but to be consumers of the fruits of the earth.
3. Biographical information from Collis (1968), Lewis (1989a, 1989b).

4. All quotations from ch. 2 ('The Big House') from Corkery (1924). The Martins of Ballynahinch (*sic*) are one of Corkery's major examples.
5. Ibid., p. 25.
6. In this chapter I have made particular use of Cronin (1972, 1985), Flanagan (1966), Kennedy (1989), Martin (1982), O'Brien (1965), Power (1964), Robinson (1980), and *Somerville and Ross: A Symposium* (1968) and MacDonagh (1970).
7. Text from Longmans, Green and Co. edn (1933).
8. Text from Virago edn (1990).
9. See Moynahan 'The Politics of Anglo-Irish Gothic: "The Return of the Repressed"' in Kosok (1982), pp. 43–53.
10. Text from Thomas Nelson edn (n.d.).
11. Text from Zodiac Press edn (1972).
12. Text from William Heinemann edn (1927).
13. See chapter 2, note 7.
14. Boswell (1754) *Life*, vol. I, p. 266. There is possibly an allusion to Chesterfield's role as Lord Lieutenant of Ireland, and thus as a signifier of departed aristocratical rule.
15. *Dan Russell the Fox* (1911), p. 182.
16. *Irish Memories* Longmans Green and Co. edn, (1933), p. 8; *Letters*, (Lewis, 1989b), xviii, p. 78.
17. *Letters* (Lewis 1989b), p. 98.
18. For Ross see *Irish Memories* (1933), p. 6 f., and for Castletownshend see ibid., p. 66. See also *Letters* (Lewis, 1989b), p. 98 on civilisation in Siberia.
19. *Irish Memories*, p. 210, 157.
20. *Stray-aways*, p. 5.
21. *Wheel-Tracks*, pp. 22, 213.
22. See O'Neill (2000).
23. 'The Finger of Mrs. Knox', 'When I First Met Dr Hickey'.

6 'The Duchess Too is Dead': Bowen and Gregory

1. Texts: *Bowen's Court & Seven Winters* (London: Virago Press, 1984) and C. Smythe (ed.) *Coole* (Dolmen edn, 1971).
2. 'The Back Drawing Room' in *The Collected Stories of Elizabeth Bowen* (New York: Vintage Books, 1982), p. 202.
3. From a substantial bibliography I am particularly indebted to G. Cronin (1965), Davenport (1974), Glendenning (1977), Johnson (1987), Jordan (1992), Lee (1999), Leray (1994), Madden-Simpson (1987), McCormack (1993), Miller (1999) and Tracy (1998). For Gregory see Kohfeldt (1985) and Smythe (1995). My marginalisation of *The Last September* excludes a substantial body of writing on Bowen and the country house. As with Edgeworth's *Castle Rackrent* I find this satirical text neither normative nor proleptic.
4. Myer (ed.), *Alexis de Tocqueville: Journeys to England and Ireland* (New York: Anchor Books, 1968), p. 152 f., recording a visit of 27 July 1835. The estate still boasted 'fine crops' and 'clean and convenient cottages', in contrast to the wretched poverty beyond. According to de Tocqueville, Big George 'went off his head' because he was £400 000 in debt to 'Catholic merchants in Cork'. Bowen's interpretation, however, is still the view of Bence-Jones

(1996), p. 187. Although the Land League disorders were some forty years later, they derived from Catholic emancipation.

5. Penguin edn, p. 92.
6. See Kelsall (1993.).
7. Penguin edn, p. 33.
8. McCormack (1993), p. 216. The idea of the 'savage' within 'civilisation' is symbolically explored in the Lawrentian country house story 'Summer Night'. See G. Cronin (1985).
9. p. 82.
10. Hermoine Lee (ed.), *The Mulberry Tree: Writings of Elizabeth Bowen* (San Diego, etc.: Harcourt Brace Jovanovitch, 1986), p. 175.
11. 'The Big House' in *The Mulberry Tree*, p. 25 f.
12. Review of *The Moores of Moore Hall* in *The Mulberry Tree*, p. 150.
13. Bowen, *The Heat of the Day*, p. 90. See also *The Shelbourne* (1951), where the hotel is a signifier of enduring style and order, especially during civil conflict, serving afternoon tea while gunfights rage on Stephen's Green outside.
14. Tracy (1998) notes the parallel between the imaginary *civitas* of 'Mysterious Kôr': 'By the time we've come to the end, Kôr may be the one city left: the abiding city'. It abides because it is imaginary. *Collected Stories* p. 730. See also the argument in 'The Bend Back' that 'we will the past from fiction rather than history', *The Mulberry Tree*, p. 57. Deirdre Laigle analyses the self-reflexive nature of Bowen's argument in 'The Image of the Big House', in Elizabeth Bowen: *'The Last September'*, *Cahiers du Centre d'Etudes Irlandaises* 9 (1984), pp. 61–80.
15. The Yeatsian symbolism is contextualised in Jordan (1992), p. 168.
16. Colin Smythe (ed.), *Seventy Years: Being the Autobiography of Lady Gregory* (Gerrards Cross: Colin Smythe, 1974), p. 131.
17. W. B. Yeats, 'Coole Park and Ballylee' (1931).
18. In the introduction to his *Diaries* (*Coole*, p. 32).
19. *Seventy Years*, pp. 445, 297, 179, 351.
20. See Kohfeldt (1985), p. 280. See also Lady Gregory's lament on the ruins of Roxborough, where she feels herself to be the last of her generation of aristocrats (the last of the Mohicans) *Seventy Years*, p. 294.
21. *Irish Memories* (1933), pp. 11, 18.
22. The school reports of Robert's son Richard (now nominally the heir to the estate) were kept in the box.
23. *Seventy Years*, p. 212.
24. *Cuchulain of Muirthemne* (London: John Murray, 1902), pp. 336–7.

Bibliography

Ackerman, James S. (1990) *The Villa: Form and Ideology of Country Houses* (London: Thames & Hudson).

Allingham, William (1999) *Laurence Bloomfield in Ireland* (1864) (Poole: Woodstock Books).

Asmundsson, Doris (1971) 'Trollope's First Novel: a Re-examination', *Eire-Ireland*, 6, pp. 83–91.

Avery, Bruce (1990) 'Mapping the Irish Other: Spenser's *A View of the Present State of Ireland*', *English Literary History*, 57, pp. 263–79.

Banim, John (1997) *The Anglo-Irish of the Nineteenth Century* (1828) (Poole: Woodstock Books).

Bareham, Tony (ed.) (1980) *Anthony Trollope* (London: Vision Press).

Bareham, Tony (1986) '"First and Last": Some Notes Towards a Re-appraisal of Trollope's *The Macdermots of Ballycloran* and *The Landleaguers*', *Durham University Journal*, 78 pp. 311–17.

Bareham, Tony (ed.) (1991) *Charles Lever: New Evaluations* (Gerrards Cross: Colin Smythe).

Barnes, Trevor J. and James S. Duncan (eds) (1992) *Writing Worlds: Discourse, text and metaphor in the representation of landscape* (London and New York: Routledge).

Beaufort, Daniel Augustus (1792) *Memoir of a map of Ireland: illustrating the topography of that kingdom, and containing a short account of the present state, civil and ecclesiastical; with a complete index to the map.* (London: W. Faden, J. Debrett, and James Edwards).

Beckett, J. V. (1986) *The Aristocracy in England 1660–1914* (Oxford: Blackwell).

Belanger, Jacqueline (1998) 'Educating the Reading Public: British Critical Reception of Maria Edgeworth's Early Irish Writing', *Irish University Review*, 28, pp. 240–55.

Bellamy, Liz (1998) 'Regionalism and nationalism. Maria Edgeworth, Walter Scott and the definition of Britishness', in K. D. M. Snell (ed.), *The Regional Novel in Britain and Ireland, 1800–1990* (Cambridge: Cambridge University Press), pp. 54–77.

Bence-Jones, Mark (1987) *Twilight of the Ascendancy* (London: Constable).

Bence-Jones, Mark (1988) *A Guide to Irish Country Houses* (London: Constable).

Bence-Jones, Mark (1996) *Life in an Irish Country House* (London: Constable).

Bew, Paul (1978) *Land and the National Question in Ireland* (Dublin: Gill & Macmillan).

Bhabha, Homi K. (1994) *The Location of Culture* (London and New York: Routledge).

Bolton, G. C. (1983) 'The Anglo-Irish and the Historians', in Oliver Macdonagh, W. F. Mandle and Pauric Travers (eds), *Irish Culture and Nationalism, 1750–1950* (London: Macmillan), pp. 239–57.

Bradshaw, Brendan, Andrew Hadfield and Willey Maley (eds) (1993) *Representing Ireland: Literature and the origins of conflict, 1534–1660* (Cambridge: Cambridge University Press).

Breffny, Brian de and Rosemary ffolliott (1975) *The Houses of Ireland* (London: Thames and Hudson).

Brownell, Morris R. (1980) *Alexander Pope's Villa* (London: Greater London Council).

Butler, Harriet Jessie and Harold Edgeworth Butler (eds) (1927) *The Black Book of Edgeworthstown and other Edgeworth Memories, 1585–1817* (London: Faber & Gwyer).

Butler, Marilyn (1972) *Maria Edgeworth: A Literary Biography* (Oxford: Clarendon Press).

Butler, Marilyn (ed.) (1992) *Castle Rackrent and Ennui* (London: Penguin).

Butler, Marilyn (2000) 'Irish Culture and Scottish Enlightenment: Maria Edgeworth's Histories of the Future', in Stefan Collini, Richard Whatmore and Brian Young, *Economy, Polity and Society: British Intellectual History 1750–1950* (Cambridge: Cambridge University Press), pp. 158–80.

Byrne, Richard J. (1983) 'Moore Hall, 1952. An Introduction to George Moore on the 100th Anniversary of His Birth', in Janet Egleson Dunleavy (ed.), *George Moore in Perspective* (Gerrards Cross: Colin Smythe), pp. 25–38.

Cahalan, James (1983) *Great Hatred, Little Room: The Irish Historical Novel* (Syracuse, NY: Syracuse University Press).

Cairns, David and Shaun Richards (1988) *Writing Ireland: Colonialism, nationalism and culture* (Manchester: Manchester University Press).

Cannadine, David (1990) *The Decline and Fall of the British Aristocracy* (New Haven, CT, and London: Yale University Press).

Canny, N. (1983) 'Edmund Spenser and the development of an Anglo-Irish identity', *Yearbook of English Studies*, 13, pp. 1–19.

Cary, Meredith (1991) 'Privileged Assimiliation: Maria Edgeworth's Hope for the Ascendancy', *Eire-Ireland*, 26, pp. 29–37.

Castell, Robert (1728) *The Villas of the Ancients Illustrated* (London: printed for the author).

Chuilleanáin, Eiléan Ni (1996) 'Forged and Fabulous Chronicles: Reading Spenser as an Irish Writer', *Irish University Review*, 26, pp. 237–51.

Collingwood, R. C. (1992) *The New Leviathan or Man, Society, Civilization and Barbarism*, ed. David Boucher (Oxford: Clarendon Press).

Collini, Stefan, Richard Whatmore and Brian Young (2000) *Economy, Polity and Society: British Intellectual History 1750–1950* (Cambridge: Cambridge University Press).

Collis, Maurice (1968) *Somerville and Ross: A Biography* (London: Faber & Faber).

Connolly, Claire (ed.) (2000) *Ormond* (London: Penguin).

Connolly, P. (ed.) (1982) *Literature and the Changing Ireland* (Gerrards Cross: Colin Smythe).

Corbett, Mary Jean (1994) 'Public Affections and Familial Politics: Burke, Edgeworth and the "Common Naturalization" of Great Britain', *English Literary History*, 61, pp. 877–97.

Corkery, Daniel (n.d.) *The Hidden Ireland: A Study of Gaelic Munster in the Eighteenth Century* (Dublin: Gill and Macmillan, reprint of 1924 edn).

Cosgrove, Denis and Stephen Daniels (eds) (1988) *The Iconography of Landscape* (Cambridge: Cambridge University Press).

Coughlan, Patricia (ed.) (1989) *Spenser and Ireland: An Interdisciplinary Perspective* (Cork: Cork University Press).

Craig, Maurice (1976) *Classic Irish Houses of the Middle Size* (London: Architectural Press).

Craig, Maurice (1982) *The Architecture of Ireland from the Earliest Times to 1880* (London: Batsford).

Cronin, Geárád (1985) 'Interior and Exterior: The Big House and the Irish Landscape in the Work of Elizabeth Bowen', *Gaeliana*, 7, pp. 57–76.

Cronin, John (1972) *Somerville and Ross* (Lewisburg: Bucknell University Press).

Cronin, John (1980a) *The Anglo-Irish Novel. The Nineteenth Century*, vol. 1 (Totowa, NJ: Barnes and Noble).

Cronin, John (1980b) 'Trollope and the Matter of Ireland', in Tony Bareham (ed.), *Anthony Trollope* (London: Vision Press), pp. 13–35.

Cronin, John (1985) '"An Ideal of Art": The Assertion of Realities in the Fiction of Somerville and Ross', *Canadian Journal of Irish Studies*, 11, pp. 57–78.

Davenport, Gary T. (1974) 'Elizabeth Bowen and the Big House', *Studies in the History of Romanticism*, 8, pp. 27–34.

Davies, Sir John (1612) *A Discovery of the True Causes Why Ireland Was Never Entirely Subdued* (see Morley, 1890).

Deane, Seamus (ed.) (1991) *The Field Day Anthology of Irish Writing*, 3 vols (Derry and London, Field Day and Faber).

Deane, Seamus (1997) *Strange Country: Modernity and Nationhood in Irish Writing since 1790* (Oxford: Clarendon Press).

De Vere, Aubrey (1848) *English Misrule and Irish Misdeeds: Four Letters from Ireland Addressed to an English Member of Parliament* (Port Washington, New York and London: Kennikat Press, 1970) reprint of the edn of 1848.

Donovan, Robert A. (1956) 'Trollope's Prentice Work', *Modern Philology*, 53, pp. 179–86.

Dooley, Terence (2001) *The Decline of the Big House in Ireland* (Dublin: Wolfhound Press).

Downey, Edmund (1906) *Charles Lever, his life in his letters*, 2 vols (Edinburgh and London, William Blackwood and Sons).

Duckworth, Alistair M. (1981) 'Fiction and some uses of the country house setting from Richardson to Scott', in David C. Streatfield and Alistair Duckworth (eds), *Landscape in the Gardens and the Literature of Eighteenth-Century England* (Los Angeles: William Andrews Clark Memorial Library), pp. 91–128.

Dudley, E. and Maximilian E. Novaks (eds) (1972) *The Wild Man Within: An Image in Western Thought from the Renaissance to Romanticism* (Pittsburgh, PA: University of Pittsburgh Press).

Dunne, Tom (1984) *Maria Edgeworth and the Colonial Mind* (Cork: National University of Ireland).

Dunne, Tom (1987) *The Writer as Witness: Literature as Historical Evidence* (Cork: Cork University Press).

Dunne, Tom (1988) 'Haunted by history: Irish romantic writing, 1800–1850', in Roy Porter and Mikulás Teich (eds), *Romanticism in National Context* (Cambridge: Cambridge University Press), pp. 68–91.

Dunne, Tom (1991) '"A gentleman's estate should be a moral school": Edgeworthstown in Fact and Fiction, 1760–1840', in Raymond Gillespie and Gerard Moran (eds), *Longford: Essays in County History* (Dublin: Lilliput), pp. 95–121.

Eagleton, Terry (1995) *Heathcliff and the Great Hunger: Studies in Irish Culture* (London and New York: Verso).

Eagleton, Terry (1998) *Crazy John and the Bishop and Other Essays on Irish Culture* (Cork: Cork University Press).

Edgeworth, Maria (1867) *A Memoir of Maria Edgeworth with a selection of her letters* (privately published).

Edgeworth, Maria (1950) *A Tour in Connemara and The Martins of Ballinahinch*, ed. H. E. Butler (London: Constable).

Edgeworth, Richard Lovell (1820) *Memoirs of Richard Lovell Edgeworth, Esq. Begun By Himself and Concluded By His Daughter, Maria Edgeworth*, 2 vols (London: R. Hunter and Baldwin, Cradock and Joy).

Edwards, Owen Dudley (1983–4) 'Anthony Trollope: The Irish Writer', *Nineteenth Century Fiction*, 38, pp. 1–42.

Fabricant, Carole (1982) *Swift's Landscape* (Baltimore, MD: Johns Hopkins University Press).

Flanagan, Thomas (1959) *The Irish Novelists, 1800–1850* (New York: Columbia University Press).

Flanagan, Thomas (1966) 'The Big House of Ross-Drishane', *The Kenyon Review*, 28, pp. 54–78.

Foley, Tadgh and Seán Ryder (1998) *Ideology and Ireland in the Nineteenth Century* (Dublin: Four Courts Press).

Foster, R. F. (ed.) (1992) *The Oxford History of Ireland* (Oxford: Oxford University Press).

Foster, R. F. (1995) *Paddy and Mr Punch* (London: Penguin).

Foster, R. F. (2001) *The Irish Story: Telling Tales and Making it up in Ireland* (London: Allen Lane).

Froude, James Anthony (1881) *The English in Ireland in the Eighteenth Century* (London: Longman Green).

Fryd, V. G. (1992) *Art and Empire: The Politics of Ethnicity in The U.S. Capital, 1815–1860* (New Haven, CT: Yale University Press).

Genet, Jacqueline (ed.) (1991) *The Big House in Ireland: Reality and Representation* (Dingle: Brandon Books).

Gibbons, Luke (1992) 'Identity Without a Centre: Allegory, History and Irish Nationalities', *Cultural Studies*, 6, pp. 358–75.

Gibbons, Luke (1996) *Transformations in Irish Culture* (Cork: Cork University Press).

Gilead, Sarah (1986) 'Trollope's Ground of Meaning: *The Macdermots of Ballycloran*', *Victorian Newsletter*, 69, pp. 23–9.

Gill, Richard (1972) *Happy Rural Seat: The English Country House and the Literary Imagination* (New Haven, CT, and London: Yale University Press).

Giraldus Cambrensis (1863) *The Topography of Ireland and the History of the Conquest of Ireland, translated by Thomas Forester*, ed. Thomas Wright (London: H. G. Bohn).

Girouard, Mark (1981) *The Return to Camelot: Chivalry and the English Gentleman* (New Haven, CT: Yale University Press).

Glendenning, Victoria (1977) *Elizabeth Bowen: Portrait of a Writer* (London: Weidenfeld & Nicolson).

Grant, Elizabeth (1991) *The Highland Lady in Ireland: Journals 1840–50* (Edinburgh: Canongate Classics).

Guiness, Desmond and William Ryan (1971) *Irish Houses and Castles* (London: Thames & Hudson).

Haddelsey, Stephen (2000) *Charles Lever: The Lost Victorian* (Gerrards Cross: Colin Smythe).

Hadfield, Andrew and John McVeagh (eds) (1994) *Strangers to That Land: British Perceptions of Ireland from the Reformation to the Famine* (Gerrards Cross: Colin Smythe).

Hall, Mr and Mrs S. C. (n.d.) *Ireland: Its Scenery, Character, &c.*, 3 vols (London: Virtue).

Hall, Wayne E. (1980) *Shadowy Heroes: Irish Literature of the 1890s* (Syracuse, NY: Syracuse University Press).

Hamer, Mary (ed.) (1989) *Castle Richmond* (Oxford: World's Classics).

Harden, O. E. M. (1971) *Maria Edgeworth's Art of Prose Fiction* (The Hague: Mouton).

Hare, Augustus J. C. (1894) *The Life and Letters of Maria Edgeworth*, 2 vols (London: Edward Arnold).

Henn, Thomas Rice (1976) 'The Big House', in *Last Essays* (Gerrards Cross: Colin Smythe), pp. 207–20.

Hennedy, Hugh L. (1972) 'Love and Famine, Family and Country in Trollope's *Castle Richmond*', *Eire-Ireland*, 7, pp. 48–66.

Hollingworth, Brian (1993) 'Completing the Union: Edgeworth's *The Absentee* and Scott the Novelist', in J. H. Alexander and David Hewitt (eds), *Scott in Carnival* (Aberdeen: Association for Scottish Literary Studies), pp. 502–11.

Hollingworth, Brian (1997) *Maria Edgeworth's Irish Writing: Language, History, Politics* (Basingstoke: Macmillan).

Hone, Joseph (1939) *The Moores of Moore Hall* (London: Jonathan Cape).

Honour, Hugh (1975) *The New Golden Land: European Images of America from the Discoveries to the Present Time* (New York: Random House).

Howe, Stephen (2000) *Ireland and Empire* (Oxford: Oxford University Press).

Hurst, Michael (1969) *Maria Edgeworth and the Public Scene: Intellect, Fine Feeling and Landlordism in the Age of Reform* (London: Macmillan).

Hutton, A. W. (ed.) (1892) *Arthur Young's Tour in Ireland (1776–1779)*, 2 vols (London: George Bell & Sons).

Hyde, Douglas (1967) *A Literary History of Ireland* (1899) (London: Ernest Benn).

Hynes, John (1986) 'Anthony Trollope's "Creative Shock": Banagher, 1841', *Eire-Ireland*, 21, pp. 124–31.

Ireland's Field Day (1985) (London: Hutchinson).

Jameson, Frederic (1981) *The Political Unconscious* (Ithaca: NY: Cornell University Press).

Jameson, Frederic (1990) *Nationalism, Colonialism and Literature* (Minneapolis: University of Minnesota Press).

Jeffares, A. Norman (1996) *Images of Invention: Esays on Irish Writing* (Gerrards Cross: Colin Smythe).

Johnson, Toni O'Brien (1987) 'Light and Enlightenment in Elizabeth Bowen's Irish Novels', *Ariel*, 18, pp. 47–62.

Jordan, Heather Bryant (1992) *How Will the Heart Endure: Elizabeth Bowen and the Landscape of War* (Ann Arbor: University of Michigan Press).

Kelleher, Margaret (1995) 'Anthony Trollope's *Castle Richmond*: Famine Narrative and "Horrid Novel"?', *Irish University Review*, 25, pp. 242–63.

Kelsall, Malcolm (1993) *The Great Good Place: The Country House and English Literature* (Hemel Hempstead: Harvester Wheatsheaf).

Kelsall, Malcolm (1999) *Jefferson and the Iconography of Romanticism: Folk, Land, Culture and the Romantic Nation* (Basingstoke: Macmillan).

Kennedy, Dorothy A. (1989) 'The Big House in Irish Literature: A Study of Somerville & Ross, W. B. Yeats, and Sean O'Casey', *Bulletin of the Irish Georgian Society*, 32, pp. 6–30.

Kenny, V. C. (1984) *The Country House Ethos in English Literature* (Hemel Hempstead: Harvester Wheatsheaf).

Kiberd, Declan (1995) *Inventing Ireland* (London: Jonathan Cape).

Kohfeldt, Mary Lou (1985) *Lady Gregory: The Woman Behind the Irish Renaissance* (London: André Deutsch).

Kosok, Heinz (1982) *Studies in Anglo-Irish Literature* (Bonn: Bouvier Verlag Herbert Grundmann).

Kreilkamp, Vera (1998) *The Anglo-Irish Novel and the Big House* (Syracuse, NY: Syracuse University Press).

Laigle, Deidre (1984) 'Images of the Big House in Elizabeth Bowen: *The Last September*', *Cahiers du Centre d'Etudes Irlandaises*, 9, pp. 61–80.

Lansbury, Carol (1981) *The Reasonable Man: Trollope's Legal Fiction* (Princeton, NJ: Princeton University Press).

Lecky, W. E. H. (1892–6) *A History of Ireland in the Eighteenth Century*, 5 vols.

Lee, Hermoine (ed.) (1986) *The Mulberry Tree: Writings of Elizabeth Bowen* (San Diego, CA: Harcourt Brace Jovanovitch).

Lee, Hermoine (1999) *Elizabeth Bowen* (London: Vintage).

Leerssen, Joep (1995) 'Wildness, wilderness, and Ireland: Medieval and early-modern patterns in the demarcation of civility', *Journal of the History of Ideas*, 56, pp. 25–39.

Leerssen, Joep, A. H. van der Well and Bart Westerweel (eds) (1995) *Forging in the Smithy: National Identity and Representation in Anglo-Irish Literary History* (Amsterdam and Atlanta: Rodopi).

Leerssen, Joep, A. H. van der Well and Bart Westerweel (1996a) *Rembrance and Imagination: Patterns in the Historical and Literary Representation of Ireland in the Nineteenth Century* (Cork: Cork University Press).

Leerssen, Joep, A. H. van der Well and Bart Westerweel (1996b) *Mere Irish and Fíor-Ghael: Studies in the Idea of Nationality, its Development and Literary Expression prior to the Nineteenth Century* (Cork: Cork University Press).

Leray, Josette (1994) 'The Big House and the Second World War in Elizabeth Bowen's *The Heat of the Day*', *Eire-Ireland*, 19, pp. 33–40.

Lewis, Gifford (1989a) *Somerville and Ross: The World of the Irish R. M.* (Harmondsworth: Penguin).

Lewis, Gifford (1989b) *The Selected Letters of Somerville and Ross* (London and Boston: Faber & Faber).

Lloyd, David (1987) *Nationalism and Minor Literature: James Clarence Mangan and the Emergence of Irish Cultural Nationalism* (Berkeley, CA: University of California Press).

Lloyd, David (1993) *Anomalous States: Irish Writing and the Post-colonial Moment* (Dublin: Lilliput Press).

Lloyd, David (1999) *Ireland after History* (Cork: Cork University Press).

Lyons, F. S. L. (1970) 'The Twilight of the Big House', *Ariel*, 1, pp. 110–22.

Lyons, F. S. L. (1973) *Ireland Since the Famine* (London: Fontana).

Lyons, F. S. L. (1979) *Culture and Anarchy in Ireland 1890–1939* (Oxford: Clarendon Press).

Macdonagh, Oliver (1970) *The Nineteenth-Century Novel and Irish Social History: Some Aspects* (National University of Ireland).

Macdonagh, Oliver, *et al.* (eds) (1983a) *Irish Culture and Nationalism 1750–1950* (London and Basingstoke: Macmillan).

Macdonagh, Oliver (1983b) *States of Mind: A Study of Anglo-Irish Conflict 1780–1980* (London: Allen and Unwin).

Madden-Simpson, Janet (1987) 'Haunted Houses: The Image of the Anglo-Irish in Anglo-Irish Literature', in Wolfgang Zach and Heinz Kosok (eds), *Literary Interrelationships: Studies in Irish and Comparative Literature* (Tübingen: Gunter Narr Verlag), pp. 41–6.

Mandler, Peter (1997) *The Fall and Rise of the Stately Home* (New Haven, CT, and London: Yale University Press).

Mark, Gordon St. George (1976) 'Tyrone House, Co. Galway', *Quarterly Bulletin of the Irish Georgian Society*, 19, pp. 22–69.

Martin, David (1982) 'The "Castle Rackrent" of Somerville and Ross', *Études-Irlandaises*, 7, pp. 43–53.

Martineau, Harriet (1852) *Letters from Ireland* (London: John Chapman).

Maxwell, Constantia (1955) 'Anthony Trollope and Ireland', *Dublin Magazine* (Oct.–Dec.), pp. 6–16.

Maxwell, W. H. (1887) *History of the Irish Rebellion in 1798* (London: George Bell & Sons).

McClung, William Alexander (1977) *The Country House in English Renaissance Poetry* (Berkeley, CA: University of California Press).

McConville, Michael (1986) *Ascendancy to Oblivion. The Story of the Anglo-Irish* (London: Quartet Books).

McCormack, W. J. (1973) '*The Absentee* and Maria Edgeworth's notion of didactic fiction', *Atlantis*, 5, pp. 123–35.

McCormack, W. J. (ed.) (1982) *The Kellys and the O'Kellys* (Oxford: World's Classics).

McCormack, W. J. (1985) *Ascendancy and Tradition in Anglo-Irish Literary History from 1789 to 1939* (Oxford: Clarendon Press).

McCormack, W. J. (1990) 'French Revolution ... Anglo-Irish Literature ... Beginnings? The Case of Maria Edgeworth', in Hugh Gough and David Dickson (eds), *Ireland and the French Revolution* (Dublin: Irish Academic Press), pp. 229–43.

McCormack, W. J. (1993) *Dissolute Characters: Irish Literary History through Balzac, Sheridan Le Fanu, Yeats and Bowen* (Manchester: Manchester University Press).

McCormack, W. J. (1994) *From Burke to Beckett: Ascendancy, Tradition and Betrayal in Literary History* (Cork: Cork University Press).

McCormack, W. J. and Kim Walker (eds) (1972) *The Absentee* (Oxford: World's Classics).

McMahon, Sean (1968) 'John Bull's Other Ireland: A Consideration of *The Real Charlotte* by Somerville and Ross', *Eire-Ireland*, 3, pp. 119–35.

McMaster, Juliet (1982) 'Trollope's Country Estates', in *Trollope Centenary Essays*, ed. John Halperin (London: Macmillan), pp. 70–85.

Middleton, Conyers (1810) *The Life of Marcus Tullius Cicero*, 3 vols (London).

Miller, Kristine A. (1999) '"Even a Shelter's Not Safe": The Blitz on Homes in Elizabeth Bowen's Wartime Writing', *Twentieth Century Writing*, 45, pp. 138–58.

Mingay, G. E. (1976) *The Gentry: The Rise and Fall of a Ruling Class* (London: Longman).

Montgomery-Massingberd, Hugh and Christopher Simon Sykes (1999) *Great Houses of Ireland* (London: Laurence King).

Morash, C. (1992) 'Reflecting Absent Interiors: The Big House Novels of Charles Lever', in Otto Rauchbauer, *Ancestral Voices: The Big House in Anglo-Irish Literature* (Hildesheim: Georg Olms Verlag), pp. 61–76.

Morgan, Lady: Sydney Owenson (1809) *Patriotic sketches of Ireland, written in Connaught* 2 vols (London: Phillips, 1807) ed.cit., Baltimore, 1809.

Morgan, Lady: Sydney Owenson (1825) *Absenteeism* (London: Henry Colburn).

Morley, Henry (ed.) (1890) *Ireland under Elizabeth and James the First* (London: George Routledge & Sons).

Moryson, Fynes (1735) *An history of Ireland, from the year 1599, to 1603. With a short narrative of the state of the kingdom from the year 1169. To which is added, a description of Ireland*, 2 vols (Dublin: S. Powell for George Ewing).

Moynahan, Julian (1994) *Anglo-Irish: The Literary Imagination in a Hyphenated Culture* (Princeton, NJ: Princeton University Press).

Murphy, Andrew (1999) *But the Irish Sea Betwixt Us: Ireland, Colonialism, and Renaissance Literature* (Lexington: University Press of Kentucky).

Myer, J. P. (ed.) (1968) *Alexis de Toqueville: Journeys to England and Ireland* (New York: Anchor Books).

Myers, James P. (1983) *Elizabethan Ireland: A Selection of Writings by Elizabethan Writers on Ireland* (Hamden, Conn.: Archon Books).

Nationalism, Colonialism, and Literature (1990) (Minneapolis: University of Minnesota Press).

O'Brien, Conor Cruise (1965) *Writers and Politics* (London: Chatto & Windus).

O'Brien, Karen (1997) *Narratives of Enlightenment: Cosmopolitan History from Voltaire to Gibbon* (Cambridge: Cambridge University Press).

O'Keefe, Thomas (1977) 'Maria Edgeworth and Charles Lever: The Big House and the Garrison', *Eire*, 19, pp. 81–92.

O'Neill, Joseph (2000) *Blood-Dark Track* (London: Granta).

Onians, J. (1988) *Bearers of Meaning: The Classical Orders in Antiquity, the Middle Ages, and the Renaissance* (Princeton, NJ: Princeton University Press).

Overton, Bill (1982) *The Unofficial Trollope* (Brighton: Harvester).

Parsons, Deborah L. (1997) 'Souls Astray: Elizabeth Bowen's Landscape of War', *Women*, 8, pp. 24–32.

Pickering (1999) *The Novels and Selected Works of Maria Edgeworth*, 12 vols (London: Pickering & Chatto).

Polhemus, Robert M. (1968) *The Changing World of Anthony Trollope* (Berkeley and Los Angeles: University of California Press).

Pollard, Arthur (1978) *Anthony Trollope* (London: Routledge & Kegan Paul).

Power, Ann (1964) 'The Big House of Somerville and Ross', *The Dubliner* (1964) pp. 43–53.

Quinn, Antoinette (1982) 'Elizabeth Bowen's Irish Stories – 1939 to 1945', in Heinz Kosok, *Studies in Anglo-Irish Literature* (Bonn: Bouvier Verlag Herbert Grundmann), pp. 314–21.

Rauchbauer, Otto (1992) *Ancestral Voices: The Big House in Anglo-Irish Literature* (Hildesheim: Georg Olms Verlag).

Rix, Walter T. (1982) 'Charles James Lever: The Irish Dimension of a Cosmopolitan', in Heinz Kosok, *Studies in Anglo-Irish Literature* (Bonn: Bouvier Verlag Herbert Grundmann), pp. 54–64.

Robinson, Hilary (1980) *Somerville and Ross: A Critical Appreciation* (New York: St Martin's Press).

Robinson, Lennox (1938) *Three Homes* (London: Michael Joseph).

Roestvig, Maren Sofie (1954) *The Happy Man* (Oslo: Akademisk forlag).

Sadleir, Michael (1927) *Trollope: A Commentary* (London: Constable).

Scott, P. (1995) *Temple of Liberty: Building the Capitol for a New Nation* (New York: Oxford University Press).

Sekora, John (1977) *Luxury: The Concept in Western Thought: Eden to Smollett* (Baltimore, MD: Johns Hopkins University Press).

Sloan, Barry (1986) *The Pioneers of Anglo-Irish Fiction 1800–1850* (Gerrards Cross: Colin Smythe).

Smyth, Gerry (1998) *Decolonisation and Criticism: The Construction of Irish Literature* (London: Pluto).

Smythe, Colin (ed.) (1971) *Coole* (Gerrards Cross: Colin Smythe).

Smythe, Colin (ed.) (1974) *Seventy Years: Being the Autobiography of Lady Gregory* (Gerrards Cross: Colin Smythe).

Smythe, Colin (1995) *A Guide to Coole Park* (Gerrards Cross: Colin Smythe).

Snell, K. D. M. (ed.) (1998) *The Regional Novel in Britain and Ireland, 1800–1990* (Cambridge: Cambridge University Press).

Somerville and Ross: A Symposium (1968) (Belfast: Queen's University).

Somerville-Large, Peter (1995) *The Irish Country House: A Social History* (London: Sinclair-Stevenson).

Steevens, P. (1995) 'Spenser and Milton on Ireland: Exclusion and the Politics of Wisdom', *Ariel*, 26, pp. 151–67.

Terry, R. C. (1977) *Anthony Trollope: The Artist in Hiding* (London: Macmillan).

Terry, R. C. (ed.) (1999) *Oxford Reader's Companion to Trollope* (Oxford: Oxford University Press).

Thomson, Heidi and Kim Walker (eds) (2000) *The Absentee* (London: Penguin).

Tobin, Mary-Elizabeth Fowkes (1988) 'The Power of Example: Harry Ormond reads *Tom Jones*', *Reader*, 19, pp. 37–52.

Tocqueville, Alexis de (1968) *Journeys to England and Ireland*, ed. J. P. Myer (New York: Anchor Books).

Topliss, Ian (1986) 'Maria Edgeworth. The Novelist and the Union', in Oliver MacDonagh and W. F. Mandle (eds), *Ireland and Irish-Australia: Studies in Cultural and Political History* (London: Croom Helm), pp. 270–84.

Townsend, Charles (1983) *Political Violence in Ireland: Government and Resistance since 1848* (Oxford: Clarendon Press).

Tracy, Robert (1982) '"The Unnatural Ruin": Trollope and Nineteenth-Century Irish Fiction', *Nineteenth-Century Fiction*, 37, pp. 358–82.

Tracy, Robert (1985) 'Maria Edgeworth and Lady Morgan: Legality Versus Legitimacy', *Nineteenth-Century Fiction*, 40, pp. 1–22.

Tracy, Robert (ed.) (1989) *The Macdermots of Ballycloran* (Oxford: World's Classics).

Tracy, Robert (1998) *The Unappeasable Host: Studies in Irish Identities* (Dublin: University College Dublin Press).

Trumpener, Katie (1997) *Bardic Nationalism: The Romantic Novel and the British Empire* (Princeton, NJ: Princeton University Press).

Vance, Norman (1999) *Irish Literature: A Social History. Tradition, Identity and Difference* (Dublin: Four Courts Press).

Vaughan, W. E. (1989) *Ireland Under the Union, 1801–1870* (Oxford: Oxford University Press).

Vaughan, W. E. (1994) *Landlords and Tenants in Mid-Victorian Ireland* (Oxford: Clarendon Press).

Wayne, Don E. (1984) *Penshurst: The Semiotics of Place and the Poetics of History* (Wisconsin University Press).

Whelan, Kevin (1996) *The Tree of Liberty: Radicalism, Catholicism and the Construction of Irish Identity 1760–1832* (Cork: Cork University Press).

White, Haydn (1978) 'The Forms of Wildness: Archaeology of an Idea', in *Tropics of Discourse: Essays in Cultural Criticism* (Baltimore, MD: Johns Hopkins University Press), pp. 150–82.

Wilson, R. G. (ed.) (1995) *Thomas Jefferson's Academical Village: The Creation of an Architectural Masterpiece* (Charlottesville: University Press of Virginia).

Wittig, E. W. (1974) 'Trollope's Irish Fiction', *Eire-Ireland*, 9, pp. 97–118.

Wohlgemut, Esther (1999) 'Maria Edgeworth and the Question of National Identity', *Studies in English Literature*, 39, pp. 645–58.

Young, Arthur (1892) *Arthur Young's Tour in Ireland (1776–1779)*, ed. Arthur Wollaston Hutton, 2 vols (London: George Bell & Sons).

Zach, Wolfgang and Heinz Kosok (eds) (1987) *Literary Interrelationships: Studies in Irish and Comparative Literature* (Tübingen: Gunter Narr Verlag).

Index

abdication 90–2
Absentee, The (Edgeworth) 42,
  48–58, 134
Ackerman, J. 10
Acropolis 2
Adams, G. 27
Adams, W. H. 166–7
agriculture 11, 83, 106
'Albatross Villa' 146–7
'all welcome' houses 12–13, 180–1
Allingham, W. 130
Allen, Bog of 111–12
anarchy 156–7
ancien régime 42, 63–7, 84–6
anglicisation 14
Apollo, statue of 148, 149
Aran Islands 134–7
Arnold, M. 4
art 148–50
  high art and the mundane
    present 154–6
Atticus 62
auction 92–4
Augustanism 21, 173
Augustine, St 130, 163
Austen, J. 13, 37, 183
  Mansfield Park 44, 95, 147

Bacon, F. 14–15
Ballinahinch 79, 80, 98, 123
  Edgeworth's *Tour in Connemara*
    71, 76–8
  Martin and Somerville 138,
    139–42
barbarian threat 2
barons' wars 14–15, 55
Beaufort, D. A. 51
Belinda (Edgeworth) 41
Benjamin, W. 2
Bible 1–2, 135–6, 173, 182
Big George 167–8, 193
Big House of Inver, The (Somerville
  and Ross) 142–3, 151–6

'Black Islands' 58–9, 66, 67
Black and Tans 180
bog
  Bog of Allen 111–12
  reclamation of 114
Bord Fáilte Éireann 7–9
Borrow, G. 37
Boucicault, D. 143
Bowen, E. 21, 22, 94, 95, 133
  Bowen's Court 7, 21, 25, 166–75
  The Heat of the Day 169, 170, 175–8
  The Last September 13, 170
Bowen's Court (Bowen) 7, 21,
  25, 166–75
Bramleighs of Bishop's Folly, The
  (Lever) 98, 107–9
Brigown Church 7, 8
Browne, H. K. 30, 70, 102
Browning, R. 179
'Bruff House' 145, 146, 150
Bunyan, J. 182
Burke, E. 65, 70, 86
Burney, F. 183
burning of houses 5, 9–10, 29–31,
  132, 156
Butler, T., Earl of Ormond 18, 19, 20
Byron, Lord 44, 80

cabin 119–23
capital investment 13–14, 33,
  83, 97–8, 105, 114, 128–9
Capitol 2, 53
'Carrignacurra Castle' 103, 105–6
Castell, R. 11
'Castello' 98, 107–9
'Castle Hermitage' 58–9, 61, 63
Castle Rackrent (Edgeworth) 10, 100–1
Castle Richmond (Trollope) 115,
  119–21, 123–4
Castlereagh, Lord 99, 101, 192
Castletownshend 137, 162, 164
Cathleen ni Houlihan (Yeats and
  Gregory) 186

Cato 11
Cellini, B. 86, 87–8
Cervantes, M. de 182
charity 65, 66
Charles V 90
Charles IX 88
'Cheops in Connemara' (Martin)
    137–8, 142
Chesterfield, Earl of 154, 193
    Letters 61–2
Chopin, F. 135, 136
Churchill, R. 179
Cicero 11, 53, 62–3
Clarendon, E. H. 182
classical architecture 11–12, 53
    see also villa culture
classical art 148–9
'Clonbrony estate' 52, 56–8
Coliseum 44
colonialism 14, 26
Columella 11
Connemara
    Edgeworth, *Tour in Connemara*
        70–8
    Martin, 'Cheops in
        Connemara' 137–8
    Somerville and Ross, *Through
        Connemara in a Governess
        Cart* 138–42
Coole (Gregory) 21, 25, 133,
    166–7, 178–88
Coole Park 23, 110, 132, 178–80
Cooper, J. Fenimore 42
Corkery, D., *The Hidden Ireland*
    133–4
Cormac mac Art 4
'Corny Castle' 58–9, 65–7
cosmopolitanism 27, 40–1
court 64–7
'Cro'Martin' 79–98
Cromwell, O. 3
cruelty 44
    see also violence
Cruickshank, G. 30, 70, 102
Cuchulain/Cuchulainism 39,
    103, 186–7
Cuchulain of Muirthemne
    (Gregory) 186–7
cultural nationalism 186–7

Davies, Sir J. 3, 15–17, 51, 171
De Vere, A. 130
Deane, S. 186
decline and fall 25, 43–4, 130–2
'Desmond Court' 123
Devonshire, Duchess of 166
Dickens, C. 30, 98, 137
    Bleak House 83
disease 83
displacement 157
Disraeli, B. 80
    Sybil 92–3
dissolution of the monasteries 10
divine providence 115
domestic sphere 95
Domitian 88–9
Drishane 157, 161, 164
Du Maurier, D. 94
Dublin 52, 178
Dun Aengus 134–5, 136
'Durrus House' 143–5

Easter Rising 1916 23, 24, 28, 130,
    156, 186–7
economic analysis 106
Edgeworth, M. 13, 14, 19, 21,
    22, 37, 40–70, 94, 95, 98,
    123, 124, 137, 138–9, 143
    The Absentee 42, 48–58, 134
    Belinda 41
    Castle Rackrent 10, 100–1
    Edgeworthstown 31–6, 38
    Ennui 42–8
    Helen 41
    Ormond 42, 57, 58–70
    Patronage 40–1
    rising of 1798 30–1, 32
    A Tour in Connemara 70–8
Edgeworth, R. L. 13, 24, 31–2,
    33, 39
Edgeworth, T. P. 71
Edgeworthstown 13, 30–40
education 60–2
Eliot, G. 183
Elizabeth of Austria 88
Encumbered Estates Act 25
England 50–1
    Tudor state 14–18
Enlightenment 3, 53

Ennui (Edgeworth) 42–8
Enthusiast, An (Somerville and Ross)
  142, 156–7
European myth, fundamental 1–3
European Union (EU) (formerly
  EEC) 9, 24, 26
Europeanisation 28
Evelyn, J. 182

famine 25, 83, 119–21, 140, 185
Fenians 8, 26, 99, 109, 112, 114
Ferdinand of Austria, Archduke 88
Ferrier, S. 183
Fielding, H. 13, 14
  Tom Jones 60, 61, 131
First World War 7, 167–70
Fitzgerald, Lord E. 185–6
Flaubert, G. 146
Forster, E. M. 132, 133, 149
  Howards End 153, 156
Foster, R. F. 27, 28
fountains 104
France
  ancien régime 42, 63–7, 84–6
  Jacobinism 25, 30, 84
  Paris 68–70, 84
  Versailles 64–7, 146, 147–9
Francis I's saltcellar 88
French Leave (Somerville and Ross) 143
Friel, B. 118
friendship 183
Froissart, J. 182
'frontier' myth 1–2
Froude, J. A. 4, 16, 17, 130

Galt, J. 37
gardens 34, 110, 148–9
Gaskell, Mrs 183
Genesis 1–2, 135–6, 173
Genet, J. 27
'German Britchka' (travelling
  carriage) 72, 73, 74
Giant's Causeway 72
Gibbon, E., *Decline and Fall of the
  Roman Empire* 124–5, 131
Giraldus of Wales 3
Gladstone, W. E. 179
'Glenthorn Castle' 42, 45–7, 48

Gothic architecture 12, 53, 113
Gregory, Lady A. 21, 22, 23,
  82, 110, 133, 168–9
  Cathleen ni Houlihan (with Yeats)
    186
  Coole 21, 25, 133, 166–7, 178–88
  Cuchulain of Muirthemne 186–7
Gregory, M. (née Parry) 24, 179–80
Gregory, Major Robert (son of
  Lady A. Gregory) 23, 169,
    178, 179, 185–6
Gregory, Robert (builder of
  Coole Park) 180, 181
Gregory, Sir W. 178, 185
'Grey Abbey' 124–7

Hall, Mrs S. C. 34–6
Hallam, H. 38–9
'Halloran Castle' 52–3, 55–6
Hardwick Hall 15
Heaney, S., *Beowulf* 21, 22–3
Heat of the Day, The (Bowen) 169,
  170, 175–8
Helen (Edgeworth) 41
Hellas 2, 4
Henry VIII 10
heritage industry 167
high art 154–6
Home Rule 23, 24
Homer 116, 131
  The Iliad 20–1, 187
Horace 11, 129, 131, 155
horsemanship 160
hotel 64–5
Housman, A. E. 159
Howe, S. 26
Hume, D. 17–18
hunger 119–21
hunting 160
Hyde, D. 4

ideal 11–14, 110–11, 132–4
  Bowen's Court 7, 171–3
  Corkery 133–4
  'Cro'Martin' 85–8
  Edgeworthstown 31–4
imperialism 4–5, 26
invasion 135–6
'Inver House' 151–6

IRA 9, 24, 26, 179–80
Irish Cousin, An (Somerville and Ross) 142, 143–5
Irish Memories (Somerville and Ross) 161–3, 164–5
Israel 135–6
ivory casket 185–6

Jacobinism 25, 30, 84
James, H. 89, 111, 132, 133, 143, 146, 149, 179
Jefferson, T. 2, 7, 11, 178
Jefferson Memorial, Washington, DC 172–3
Johnes, T. 13
Johnson, S. 11
  Dictionary of the English Language 182
Jonson, B. 14
  To Penshurst 12–13, 53, 80, 123, 124, 180–1
Joseph 135–6
Joyce, J. 105, 170
Juvenal 11, 43–4

Keane, M. 162
Keating, G. 4
Keats, J. 149, 155, 165
'Kelly's Court' 127–9
Kellys and the O'Kellys, The (Trollope) 124–9, 130–1
Kelmscott 86, 181
Kiberd, D. 28
Kilbeheny 7–8
Kilcolman Castle 18, 20
Kilkenny, Statute of 2, 144, 167
Kilkenny Castle 167
King, Captain 29
King James Bible 182
Kingsborough, Lord 6
Kingston College 9
Knight of Gwynne, The (Lever) 98–102
Kreilkamp, V. 27
Kylemore Abbey 97–8, 100, 113

Land League 7, 130
Landleaguers, The (Trollope) 114
Landseer, E. H. 81

'Land War' 25
Last September, The (Bowen) 13, 170
law 1–2
Lawless, E. 183
lawlessness 67
Leerssen, J. 1
legitimacy 41, 45–6
Lever, C. 21, 22, 79–112, 113, 124
  The Bramleighs of Bishop's Folly 98, 107–9
  The Knight of Gwynne 98–102
  Lord Kilgobbin 98–9, 109–12
  Luttrell of Arran 98
  The Martins of Cro'Martin 71, 79–98, 138
  The O'Donoghue 98, 102–6
library
  Bowen's Court 175
  Coole 181–3
  'Cro'Martin' 81, 85, 86–90
  Edgeworthstown 33–4, 71
Library of Congress 178
licentious terror 101–2
Livy 11
Lloyd, D. 26
Locke, J. 2
'Lodge, The' 98, 103–6
Longford 31
Longleat 15
Lord Kilgobbin (Lever) 98–9, 109–12
loyalty 31–2
luxury 43–4, 88–9

Macdermots of Ballycloran, The (Trollope) 115–19, 121, 122–3
Maecenas 188
Maeve, Queen 81
Malins, E. 188
Malory, Sir T. 182
Marathon 2
Marie Antoinette 65, 66, 84
Markiewicz, C. 82
Marmontel, J. F. 64
Martin, M. 71, 123, 168
  Edgeworth's *Tour of Connemara* 77, 78
  Lever's *Martins of Cro'Martin* 79, 80–2, 94–5

Martin, V.   21, 22, 23, 71, 82, 94, 95,
    130–65, 183, 185
  'Cheops in Connemara'   137–8, 142
  'An Outpost of Ireland'   134–7, 142
  Ross House   12, 25, 153, 161–5
  Somerville and Ross   *see under*
    Somerville, E.
Martins of Cro'Martin, The (Lever)   71,
    79–98, 138
Marvell, A., 'Upon Appleton
    House'   34, 94, 96
Maxwell, W. H.   29–30
Maynooth   37, 97
McCormack, W. J.   52, 171
meadowlands, drained   114
middle classes   92–3
Middleton, C.   11, 62
Milton, J.   3
Mitchel, J.   185
Mitchell, M.   169
Mitchelstown   6–10, 21, 123
  Bord Fáilte Éireann   7–9
  garden party of August 1914 in
    Bowen's Court   7, 167–70
  Young   6–7, 35, 123, 167
mob   29–30, 69–70, 102
monasteries, dissolution of   10
Monticello   2, 7, 10, 107,
    113, 175, 178
Moran, D. P.   4
Morgan, Lady (Sydney Owenson)
    14, 98
Morris, W.   86, 180–1
Moryson, F.   16
Mount Melleray, monks of   10
'Mount Morris'   176–8
Mount Music (Somerville and
    Ross)   142, 143, 156, 157–61
Mount Vernon   10, 11, 113

Narcissus   88
National Trust   93
nationalism   4–5, 23, 83–4
  Bord Fáilte Éireann   7–9
  cultural nationalism   186–7
  Easter Rising 1916   23, 24, 28, 130,
    156, 186–7
  Fenians   8, 26, 99, 109, 112, 114
  IRA   9, 24, 26, 179–80

nocturnes   135, 136
North America   1–2
North, Sir T.   182

O'Donoghue, The (Lever)   98, 102–6
O'Halloran, S.   53
O'Mahony, J.   8
'open door' country houses   12–13,
    180–1
Ordnance survey   33–4
Ormond, Earl of (T. Butler)   18, 19, 20
Ormond (Edgeworth)   42, 57, 58–70
'Ormsby Villa'   47–8
'Outpost of Ireland, An' (Martin)
    134–7, 142
Ovid   155

Paley, W.   137, 138
Palladio, A.   12
Paris   68–70, 84
Parliament Building, Irish   7
partition of 1921   23–4
Pater, W.   89, 149
Patronage (Edgeworth)   40–1
pax Romana   173
Pearse, P.   37
Penshurst Place   12–13, 178, 180–1
Pentateuch   1
Perseus, Cellini's statue of   87–8
Persse, A.   *see* Gregory, Lady A.
plantations   14, 104–5, 134
Pliny the Younger   11
polished blade of Damascus   68
Pope, A.   12, 14, 178, 181
post office   39, 67, 186–7
postcolonial theory   26–7
Pound, E.   123
poverty   66–7, 83, 84, 121
power, shift in   24–5
pre-Raphaelite movement   4–5, 145
'punishment' beating   115–17

Quinn, J.   184–5
Quirinal   87, 88–9

Raleigh, Sir W.   139
Rauchbauer, O.   27
Real Charlotte, The (Somerville and
    Ross)   142, 143, 145–51

Renaissance   104, 178
Renan, E.   4, 106
rentier middlemen   40
Renvyle House   139
republicanism   5, 7–9
resident magistrate's house
    135, 136
revisionism   27
Ribbonism   115–17, 119
Richardson, S.   14
    *The History of Sir Charles
    Grandison*   13, 57, 60–1
Ritchie, A. T.   36–40
Robertson, W.   18
romantic nationalism   7–9
Rome   16–17, 173–4
    empire   43–4
    Quirinal   87, 88–9
    republic   63
Roosevelt, T.   179
Ross House   12, 25, 137,
    153, 161–5
Rossetti, D. G.   145
Royal Irish Constabulary   7, 8
ruins
    cottages   39–40
    country house   122
rural ideal   11
Russian Revolution   25

Sackville-West, V.   166
'safe out'   72, 73–4
Sallust   89
salt-cellar, made by Cellini   88
'salvage man'   67, 104, 114, 127–8
school of Edgeworth   21–4
science   136–7
Scott, Sir W.   24, 36, 38, 42,
    78, 80, 81, 98
Scullabogue massacre   29–30
Second World War   7, 169–70
separation   157
1798 rising   29–31, 42, 44
Shakespeare, W.   2, 60, 114,
    155, 182
    King Lear   15, 16
Shan van Vocht   40, 102
'Sherwood Park'   42–3, 48
Sidney family   12

signature fans   179
signature tree   179
Sinn Fein   23
skeleton in the desert   150–1
Smith, H.   137
socialism   91–2
Somerville, B.   164
Somerville, E.   21, 22, 23, 94,
    95, 130–65, 166, 183, 185
Somerville and Ross: *The Big House
    of Inver*   142–3, 151–6; *An
    Enthusiast*   142, 156–7; *French
    Leave*   143; *An Irish Cousin*   142,
    143–5; *Irish Memories*   161–3,
    164–5; *Mount Music*   142, 143,
    156, 157–61; *The Real Charlotte*
    142, 143, 145–51; *Through
    Connemara in a Governess
    Cart*   138–42; *Wheel-Tracks*
    25, 132, 163–4
Spenser, E.   3, 15–21, 50–1, 60, 78,
    124, 171
    The Faerie Queene   2, 18–21, 63, 115
stable yard   93
'stage' Englishwoman   50
Statute of Kilkenny   2, 144, 167
Stephens, J.   8, 183
subjection   17
swans   177–8
Swift, J.   14, 115
    Gulliver's Travels   78
swinish multitude   69–70
symbiosis   122–4
Synge, J. M.   84, 118, 186, 187

Tacitus   2
Tara   4
taste   86–90
Temple, Sir W.   184
Terry, E.   179
*Through Connemara in a Governess
    Cart* (Somerville and Ross)   138–42
Titanic   177
Tocqueville, A. de   83, 167, 193
tomahawk, culture of the   68
Tone, W.   113
Tour in Connemara, A (Edgeworth)
    70–8
tower   109–11, 112, 113

Trevelyan, Sir G.   179
Trinity College   7, 96–7
Trojan War   148–9
Trollope, A.   21, 22, 98, 113–29
   Castle Richmond   115, 119–21, 123–4
   The Kellys and the O'Kellys   124–9,
     130–1
   The Landleaguers   114
   The Macdermots of Ballycloran
     115–19, 121, 122–3
Tudor state   15–18
Tusculum (Cicero's villa)   11, 62
'Tusculum' (in Edgeworth's
   The Absentee)   52–5
Twickenham   178
Tyrone, Earl of   19
Tyrone House   5

uncompletable idealism   174–5
underclass   51–2
Union   1, 23–6, 28, 38, 99
United States of America   2, 25,
   53, 59, 84, 113
universal man   172–3

Varro   11
Versailles   64–7, 146, 147–9
villa culture   10–12, 107–8, 113
violence   44, 115–18, 136–7
   see also Easter Rising   1916;
     1798 rising
Virgil   2, 11, 20, 21
   The Aeneid   21
Virginia, University of   2, 55
'vulgar', the   95–6

Walker, K.   52
war   15–17, 55–6, 136–7
   barons' wars   14–15, 55
   First World War   7, 167–70
   Second World War   7, 169–70
   Wars of the Roses   19
warlords   15–16
Washington, G.   11
Waugh, E.   111, 132
wealth   89–90
Westminster, Palace of   53
Wheel-Tracks (Somerville and Ross)
   25, 132, 163–4
White House   53, 113
'wild Irish'   75–6
Wilde, O.   155
Windsor Castle   53
Wollstonecraft, M.   91
women, role of   94–6
woods   56, 179
Woolf, V.   37, 132, 169
Wyndham Act   25, 132

Yeats, W. B.   19, 27, 81–2, 86, 97,
   109, 133, 147, 149, 155, 165, 178
   'Among Schoolchildren'   137
   Ancestral Houses   153
   Cathleen ni Houlihan (with
     Gregory)   186
   Coole Park   179, 181, 184, 187
   empty shell   94, 150
   Mary Martin   71
Young, A.   8–9, 10–14, 17,
   18–19, 51, 136
   Mitchelstown   6–7, 35, 123, 167